THE ZAPATISTA EXPERIENCE

JÉRÔME BASCHET

Translated by
Traductores Rebeldes Autónomos Cronopios

The Zapatista Experience

© 2024 Jérôme Baschet
Translation © 2024 Traductores Rebeldes Autónomos Cronopios
This edition © 2024, AK Press
ISBN: 978-1-849-35570-4 (paper)
ISBN: 978-1-849-35571-1 (e-book)
Library of Congress Control Number: 2024939492

AK Press
370 Ryan Ave. #100
Chico, CA 95973
www.akpress.org
akpress@akpress.org

AK Press
33 Tower St.
Edinburgh EH6 7BN
Scotland
www.akuk.com
akuk@akpress.org

The above addresses would be delighted to provide you with the latest AK Press distribution catalog, which features books, pamphlets, zines, and stylish apparel published and/or distributed by AK Press. Alternatively, visit our websites for the complete catalog, latest news, and secure ordering.

Cover design by Herb Thornby
Cover illustration by Dante Aguilera Benitez

Printed in the USA on acid-free paper

Contents

Preface to the English Edition

This book was first published in Mexico in 2018, as the twenty-fifth anniversary of the Zapatista uprising of January 1, 1994, was approaching. Five years later, and a full three decades after the Zapatista rebellion itself, AK Press approached us about publishing this translation, making it accessible to English readers for the first time.[1]

This book was conceived and written during a particularly dynamic stage in the Zapatista struggle, which was marked by numerous national and international initiatives. They were also evaluating their process of building autonomy as seen with the Zapatista Little School. In contrast, the years since 2018 have been extremely difficult ones, and today the air in Chiapas is heavy with uncertainty and danger. I will explain more in the Prologue, but it is important to emphasize from the outset the untrammeled growth of organized crime; the cartels are everywhere. Government programs distribute money in exchange for loyalty to the party, and President Andrés Manuel López Obrador's megaprojects, such as the Mayan Train, advance everywhere.

In this context, Zapatista autonomy had to reorganize itself to confront this adverse situation and strengthen its capacity for self-defense. Between October and December 2023, a long string of communiqués announced important changes, opening a "new stage" in the Zapatista struggle.[2] Notably, they include the reorganization of autonomy, with the disappearance of the Zapatista Rebel Autonomous Municipalities and the Good Government Councils, which had been the pillars of autonomy until now. Another organizational form—based at the local, community level—was simultaneously born. Each will now have a "local autonomous government," and at the regional and zone levels their forms of coordination will now be simpler, as they will no longer include councils of elected authorities.[3]

It is important to emphasize that these decisions do not mean the end of autonomy. The governing bodies have been transformed, but autonomy is still being built in all the areas that are crucial to the life of the communities: education, health, production, collective work, and now—the new modality for using recuperated land—"the common and non-property."[4] Furthermore, the autonomous municipalities and Good Government Councils were not the definitive forms of Zapatista autonomy, nor did they ever claim to be. As this book's first two chapters emphasize, autonomy's organizational forms are fluid. They have continuously transformed from the very beginning, responding to new needs, resolving difficulties, and correcting mistakes. Instead of relying on prior certainties to guide action, the Zapatista principle of "walking by asking questions" (*caminar preguntando*) is a commitment to making the way through practice, prioritizing the *process* of collective creation. "Autonomy has no end," as the teachers at the Zapatista Little School said; it does not aspire to attain a perfect, completed form.

The new stage in the Zapatista struggle has only just begun and so cannot be analyzed. It must test itself through practice, finding its path little by little, before we can describe and reflect upon it. Therefore, this book covers the Zapatista struggle's trajectory and contributions from 1994 until the end of 2023. Although the forms of self-government discussed in chapter 1 no longer exist, they were part of an experience lasting three decades and strengthened by the creation of the Good Government Councils in 2003. For the time being, they are the only experiences that we can know and reflect upon. At the same time, we can't help but wonder about the implications of the internal evaluation that led to their disappearance and what it means for the understanding of the Zapatista experience presented here.

That's difficult to address at the moment. In any case, Subcomandante Moisés's (self)criticism of autonomy, published at the end of 2023, doesn't prevent us from highlighting the experience to now.[5] Even though he argued that a separation had emerged between the authorities and the communities, Moisés also emphasized autonomy's achievements, saying "We learned that, yes, we can govern ourselves."[6] It bears repeating that the autonomy achieved by the Zapatistas is a rare achievement, one of the greatest experiences of rebellious self-government in memory.

In this book, I argue that there are two interrelated reasons why the

Preface to the English Edition

Zapatista experience has become a referent and inspiration for so many struggles around the world. On one hand, they have done much to reformulate an emancipatory perspective that is credible and desirable, one that breaks with previously dominant state-centric, productivist, Eurocentric, modernizing, and patriarchal positions. On the other hand, to build autonomy is to materialize another possible life, making it at least somewhat concrete, despite inevitable limits and difficulties. The Zapatistas have tangibly demonstrated that it is possible to govern collectively from below, to allow self-determined forms of life to flourish.

For these reasons, we must continue learning about the Zapatista experience and sharing its contributions, analyzing them, reflecting on them, and perhaps appropriating them into other struggles across the many corners of the planet. We would be amiss to not gather the many seeds that the Zapatistas have and will continue to sow, in their aspiration to be "good seeds" during dark times.

San Cristóbal de Las Casas
January 2024

Translators' Note

We are a collective of translator-activists inspired by the Zapatista "word"—as they refer to the writings that recount their practice and elaborate their political theory. As Jérôme Baschet explains early in his text, "For the Zapatistas, the word is not simply discourse. It is rooted in practice and implies commitment." He then turns to Subcomandante Marcos, who continues: "We believe that the word leaves traces, the traces chart paths, the paths entail definitions and commitments." Our hope is to make the Zapatistas' word, and thereby its history and constantly inventive trajectory, more widely known to English-speaking activists and theorists. And, most importantly, we hope that all those who share our inspiration will act on it, collectively, from below and to the left.

We first came together as a Zapatista-inspired collective to translate Paulina Fernandez Christlieb's book *Justicia Autónoma Zapatista*, based on her extensive interviews with Zapatista elders and participants in self-government.[1] However, when the Zapatistas decided in the spring of 2021 to undertake the "Journey for Life" to Europe, to "reverse the Conquest," we decided that translating a shorter, more synthetic book with a conceptual overview of the Zapatistas' history and political project would be more immediately useful. Thus, we paused work on *Justicia Autónoma* and turned to one of Jérôme's books. On January 1, 2024, as we were finishing our translation, the Zapatistas celebrated the thirtieth anniversary of their 1994 armed uprising. At a moment when supporters and critics around the world are again asking about the present and future of the Zapatista movement, we think this book—with its updated sections, readings of the most recent Zapatista communiqués, and its copious bibliography of both primary and secondary sources—is timelier than ever. Because, as they turn toward "the common" to survive "the coming storm," the Zapatistas are timelier than ever.

Occasionally, phrases used by the Zapatistas call for inventive translations. Two examples of these are: *caminar preguntando*, which we have translated as "we walk by asking questions"; and *falta lo que falta*, which we translate as "what's missing is yet to come." When such words or phrases have been translated elsewhere in multiple ways, we retain the Spanish in parentheses.

Since 1994 many supporters and enthusiasts have translated EZLN communiques and documents for English-language readers. That effort has been an invaluable resource. We have done our best to cite those translations in the endnotes—though, unconventionally, we have sometimes chosen to use our own translations from the original Spanish for consistency in this volume. This hybrid approach, we think, will reward readers.

Many have participated for shorter or longer periods in this collective. Linda Quiquivix, Paige Andersson, Mitchell Verter, Antonia Carcelen, and Sujani Reddy have all contributed. We are grateful to Zain Salim who tracked down English translations of all of Jérôme's Spanish-language references and did the arduous work of revising the book's extensive footnotes—no mean task. Margaret Cerullo, Anna Rebrii, and Stuart Schussler have been the collective's mainstays. We thank our partners, friends, and children who put up with our interminable meetings.

Introduction

"It doesn't appear in any written texts but rather in the ones
that haven't yet been written and yet have been read for generations, but that's where the Zapatistas have learned that
if you stop scratching at the crack, it closes back up. The
wall heals itself. That's why you must keep at it, not only to
deepen the crack, but above all, so that it doesn't close."

"But if there's no crack, well, we'll make it by scratching, biting,
kicking, hitting with our hands, head, and entire body in order to
make in history what we are: a wound. Then someone will walk
by and see us, sees the Zapatistas hitting ourselves hard against
that wall. Sometimes that passerby is someone who thinks they
know everything. They pause and shake their head in disapproval,
passing judgment and declaring, 'You will never bring down the
wall that way.' But sometimes, every so often, someone else, an
other (*otroa*) will walk by. They pause, look, understand, stare
down at their feet, at their hands, their fists, their shoulders,
and their body and then decide, 'This spot is as good as any.'
We'd be able to hear them as they make a mark on the unmov-
able wall if only their silence was audible. And they go at it."

—*Subcomandante Galeano*
"*The Crack in the Wall,*" Critical Thought in
the Face of the Capitalist Hydra I

The Zapatista Experience

The Zapatista experience is an opening. A break in capitalist domination that has unleashed a terrible and destructive storm across the planet. A crack that allows a glimpse of a tomorrow made of many other worlds, one that is already being built.

This opening is small. For many, it is even imperceptible, non-existent. It is fragile. From its inception and in every moment since, it risks disappearing. Throughout a quarter century of public life, in a feat of everyday heroism, the Zapatistas have put constant and considerable effort into preventing this crack from closing.

And this opening transcends the limits of its size. The Zapatista rupture first took the form of an armed battle cry "¡Ya basta!" (Enough is enough!) on January 1, 1994. *Enough!* to decades of the so-called perfect dictatorship during the PRI's (Revolutionary Institutional Party) one-party state. *Enough!* to five centuries of domination and oppression suffered by Indigenous peoples. A cry of *Enough!* that came like a sudden bolt of lightning to break the dark night of absolute neoliberal rule, which after 1989 celebrated its own immortality as the end of history. The possibility of an alternative to capitalism seemed to have vanished. Hope was in ruins. There seemed to be no choice but to adapt to the world as it is, and that was when the Zapatista *Enough!* arrived to refute the end of history, shaking off the weight of resignation and reopening the future. From then on, despite obstacles and setbacks, the Zapatistas began to chart a new path, reinventing a resonant word-action. Immanuel Wallerstein expressed the planetary impact of the Zapatista opening: "Since 1994, the Zapatista rebellion in Chiapas has been the most important social movement on the planet—the barometer and the igniter of antisystemic movements throughout the world."[1]

The Zapatista opening became more visible and wider starting in 2003, when the Good Government Councils were created. From that moment until now, the Zapatistas have shaped and deepened an experience of self-government in a territory that, although it is fragmented, encompasses more than half of Chiapas. This experience has been built outside of and in a complete break with the Mexican state's institutions, sustaining with daily collective efforts of its own self-governmental bodies, autonomous administration of justice, and health and education systems. This experience is rooted in the Indigenous communities' tradition, while also seeking to invent new forms of life. It opposes and resists the advance of "modernization," which seeks to shape the world according to the needs of the capitalist system. In this sense, Zapatista rebel autonomy has become a concrete and tangible alternative to the dominant logics of capitalism and the state. Today it is one of the most consistent and radical real utopias on a planet devastated by the madness of productivism and economic quantification.

Furthermore, the Zapatista opening not only remains but continues advancing today, a quarter century later. This is no small feat. Out of all the aspects of the Zapatista opening, the one that should astonish us most is its exceptional duration. What has made this capacity to resist and persist possible, especially as they have felt the full weight of the federal army and all manner of counterinsurgency tactics, not to mention the inevitable exhaustion of a struggle that takes place in such a hostile context? And how has it been possible for the Zapatistas to show such capacity for self-transformation throughout their decades of clandestine and public life? Some answers to these questions appear in the following chapters.

Finally, another dimension of the Zapatista opening is that it is not limited to the territorial construction of autonomy, however decisive that may be. Rather, it has always articulated across three scales: one anchored in the forms of life of Indigenous peoples and the particularities of their territories; another that looks at all of Mexico; and finally, one that takes on planetary horizons. In this sense, the Zapatista opening also works to refound a project of collective liberation that, in the face of late capitalist domination, is both credible and desirable. If the *Enough!* of 1994 opened the possibility of escaping a future in ruins, it soon became clear that this was not simply a question of resuscitating previous forms of revolutionary hope. It was necessary to seek unknown paths (or those left forgotten and denied).

The Zapatista opening is characterized precisely by this. It offers extremely valuable contributions for the formulation of new emancipatory perspectives— freed from the modernist and productivist, state-centric, and Eurocentric logics that contributed to the tragic revolutionary failures of the twentieth century. We seek to explore this dimension of the Zapatista opening in this book.

❀ ❀ ❀ ❀

The Zapatista opening is a challenge. The Zapatistas invite us, time and time again, to examine our own level of commitment, asking "And what about you?"[2]

The Zapatista opening forces a choice: Do we ignore it, pretend that it does not exist, contribute to its invisibility, pass judgment on its uselessness, offer up advice on how it might act more efficiently? *Or* do we approach it and join the collective effort to keep the crack from closing? As a Zapatista said when asked why she wants to see what lies on the other side of the wall, the crack allows us "to imagine everything that can be done tomorrow."[3]

In this regard, instead of feigning an impossible and undesirable neutrality, I acknowledge that I write this book from the experience of living in Chiapas, which—from the first moment I felt interpellated by the Zapatistas—radically changed the course of my life. This awakened me from the resignation imposed by the triumph of neoliberalism, allowing me to discover other worlds, to move away little by little from academic life, until I made the decision to largely give it up. I write this book, then, from the premise that I identify with the Zapatista struggle—or perhaps, that I look for myself in it.

Among the many doubts that arise as I write this book, one is that the Zapatistas have explained on multiple occasions what their struggle is about, and the reader may question why it is relevant to do so again, in a way that might seem to supplant their own word. For example, they organized the Zapatista Little School (*Escuelita Zapatista*) to share their experience, not only with words, but directly through interpersonal exchange, inviting visitors to live together with Zapatista families and communities.[4] On the other hand, during this same Little School, the teachers invited us to spread what we had learned from the Zapatista experience. So it is that I am now writing this book, as a student of the Little School, with the intention of sharing with others a bit of what I have learned over many years in Chiapas.

Either way, it is not easy to choose the right distance. It would be absurd to suggest that I am simply transmitting the word of the Zapatistas and deny that I am the one who writes these pages. It seems to me that it is best to bring together two distinct perspectives. In certain parts of the book I try to represent, in the most honest way possible, what I have understood about what the Zapatistas do and say. Of course, there is always the risk of failing to adequately understand and portray the multiple aspects of the Zapatista word and experience. Obviously, I do not intend to encompass all its aspects, and, in fact, some dimensions are barely present in the book. In other parts, after attending carefully to the Zapatistas' own word and experience, my point of view becomes more explicit, including about specific issues, doubts, and analyses that partially differ from theirs.

And although the expression of my point of view was reduced little by little in the successive versions of this book, my analysis can perhaps put the Zapatista experience in dialogue with others, in different calendars and geographies.[5]

Introduction

This is not to measure the Zapatista experience with criteria imported from other contexts but rather to suggest bridges between different experiences, memories, and traditions of thought, something relevant when we long to create a planetary network of rebellions and resistances.

One more clarification. Fifteen or twenty years ago, I probably would have relied on the following assertion by the late Subcomandante Marcos to justify what this book tries to do:[6] "Zapatismo is not a new political ideology or a rehash of old ideologies. 'Zapatismo' does not exist. It only serves, as bridges do, to cross from one side to the other. Therefore, in Zapatismo everyone fits, everyone who wants to cross from one side to the other. Everyone has their one side and their other side. There are no recipes, correct lines, strategies, tactics, laws, regulations, or universal slogans. There is only one desire: to build a better world, that is, a new one. In summary: Zapatismo belongs to no one and, therefore, belongs to everyone."[7] Back then, many marveled at the "lack of definition" claimed by Zapatismo. In this moment, it was indispensable if they were to build everything anew, avoid any sort of dogmatism, and be open to novelty. However, after a few years, they recognized that "this lack of definition cannot be maintained for long.... There must come a time when—having opened this plural, inclusive, tolerant world—the EZLN acquires its own identity."[8] Little by little, those features took shape: first in 2003 with the growing importance of building autonomy, and then in 2006 with the statement of principles in the "Sixth Declaration of the Lacandon Jungle." These principles include an uncompromising rejection of capitalism and a political path that distances itself from state institutions. As Subcomandante Marcos put it, "paths entail definitions and commitments."[9]

We should always reject definitions that create a univocal and immutable object, thereby imprisoning thought (and also practice). The Zapatista experience neither seeks definitions of this nature, nor can it be boxed in by them. Their multifaceted forms of struggle resist a single definition, as does their attempt to create a world in which many worlds fit, as well as their flair for transgressing absolute categories (Subcomandante Galeano's companion, the cat-dog, is emblematic). Ultimately, the Zapatista experience can only be understood as a trajectory of permanent transformation. For all these reasons, in this book I will try to not talk about "Zapatismo," as to avoid adding it to a long line of unfortunate "isms" and risk defining it in a univocal and categorical way. Instead, I use expressions such as "the Zapatista experience" or "the Zapatista struggle," which better reflect such transformation.

We should reject concepts with fixed and closed definitions but without discarding the use of *all* concepts or definitions, and without replacing the pretense of absolute knowledge with the glorification of not-knowing. Doing so would risk pushing a definitive conception of indefinition, and absolutizing not-knowing. Rather, not-knowing has to be understood as part of a knowing that is always incomplete and in constant tension with itself. Open and provisional concepts and definitions are indispensable tools, although they must be permanently questioned and reformulated (and, sometimes, abandoned). Thereby we can assert, against postmodernism, that not all interpretations are equally valid. On the contrary, there must be shared criteria of truth to evaluate the validity of any interpretation—although the controversies in this regard may never end.

This book does not pretend to offer a definitive history of the Zapatista experience. Despite that being an important task, I cannot undertake a properly historical study of the Zapatista struggle here. It is not the right place, and perhaps not the right time either. Thus, before going fully into the different chapters of the book, I offer a brief prologue to summarize the main moments of the Zapatistas' trajectory.

Chapter 1 will describe and analyze what we may consider as the basis of the Zapatista experience from 2003 to the present—the construction of autonomy in the rebel territories of Chiapas. The following chapters analyze the concepts and approaches that the Zapatistas have developed and shared. Chapter 2 covers the implications of a very "other" politics, below and to the left, that rejects both the centrality of the state and organizational models based on unity, homogeneity, and hegemony. Chapter 3 takes up the various formulations that comprise Zapatista anti-capitalism, especially their insistence on analyzing capitalism as a Fourth World War against humanity. Chapter 4 develops the implications of the Zapatista call to build "a world where many worlds fit." This led to a radical critique of modern European universalism, inviting us to conceive of a planetary community based on multiplicity. Chapter 5 emphasizes the importance of history and memory in the Zapatista word and experience, pointing to new conceptions of historical time.

In this book I will often refer to "the Zapatista word." For the Zapatistas, the word is not simply discourse; it is rooted in practice and implies commitment:

Introduction

"We believe that the word leaves traces, the traces chart paths, the paths entail definitions and commitments."[10] In fact, the word must itself be considered an action—an action that is inextricable from practice, that arises from it, and implies a commitment to other actions. There is a close link between the Zapatista experience and their word: you cannot understand one without the other. The relationship between theory and practice is similar. During the seminar "Critical Thought in the Face of the Capitalist Hydra," the Zapatistas repeatedly affirmed that theoretical reflection is indispensable for nurturing the struggle and to adequately understand the enemy ("we need concepts, theories, sciences"). Crucially, they also insisted on always connecting theory and practice: "neither theory without practice, nor practice without theory."[11]

The Zapatista word is a word in action, a concrete thinking and acting together that challenges the division between practice and theory ("the Zapatistas' meta-theory is our practice"), in the same way that it challenges the separation between thinking and feeling.[12] In fact, for the Zapatistas, there are seven senses, adding thinking and feeling to the five that are usually considered. They invite us to "feel with our brains and think with our hearts."[13] The Zapatista word links to what is done. Besides being analyzed and debated, it must be felt, so that definitions and commitments result.

Finally, this book seeks to understand how the Zapatistas' practices and trajectory brought consistency to their collective political thought. While this politics stems from their practices and trajectory, it also has implications and a contagious effect far beyond them. This is not a book of theory, much less a "theorization of Zapatismo." Instead, it is an effort to highlight the theoretical-practical achievements of the Zapatista experience. Anyone who attempts such an endeavor (me, in this case) has to confront it on the basis of their own experience, questioning and transforming themself in the process, as "To live is to search, to search for ourselves," not for what we are but for what we can become.[14]

San Cristóbal de Las Casas
November 17, 2018

Historical Prologue

Transformations of the EZLN

We begin with a review of some of the most well-known elements of the EZLN's history, highlighting the processes of transformation that shaped it before and after the January 1, 1994, uprising.

The first stage is remarkable in that, only ten years after the EZLN was founded, in 1983, by a handful of men and women, it had grown into a veritable army composed of Indigenous communities from the Canyons, Highlands, and northern area of Chiapas. But before discussing the EZLN's founding and growth, we must first review the previous decades of peasant struggle leading up to it.

Peasant and Indigenous struggles in Chiapas

It would be useful to consider five-hundred years of Indigenous resistance to colonial domination. But we will begin with the Indigenous Congress held in October 1974 in honor of the first bishop of Chiapas, Fray Bartolomé de Las Casas, which is widely recognized as a key moment in the recent processes of Indigenous organization in Chiapas.[1] Bishop Samuel Ruiz's condition for agreeing to lead the Congress was that it be organized by the Indigenous peoples themselves. To this end, the event was preceded by a long series of regional meetings, allowing for Indigenous communities to express and gather their word. In the end, the Congress brought together 1,230 Tsotsil, Tseltal, Ch'ol, and Tojolabal delegates (among others), who painted a picture of their common suffering, deeply rooted in a long history of shared grievances.

Central to this suffering was the brutal exploitation on the *fincas*, including keeping peons tied to the manor, debt bondage perpetuated through the owner's "company store," land invasions by farmers, corrupt officials' refusal to redistribute land as *ejidos*, discrimination against Indigenous peoples, and generating confusion over territorial delimitations to incite conflicts.[2] The Indigenous Congress organized their common demands into four areas: land, commerce, environment, and health. Without a doubt, it was a decisive moment, as the Indigenous peoples of Chiapas saw they shared the same problems and desires, and in doing so they became aware of their strength. As one Tseltal delegate put it, "Brother Bartolomé is no longer alive, so this Congress is in his name only. He's dead, and we don't expect another to come along. . . . All of us together must be the new Bartolomé. And we will achieve this when we are able to defend the organization, because there is strength in unity."[3]

Several independent peasant organizations emerged over the following years. In the Canyons of Chiapas there emerged the Quiptic Union of Ejidos. It was created in 1975 and, as it continued to grow, formed the Union of Unions in 1980, which brought together around 120 *ejidos*. In 1988 that became the Rural Association of Collective Interest (ARIC in Spanish). In 1975 the Independent Confederation of Agricultural Workers and Peasants (CIOAC) was formed in the Highlands of Chiapas; and in 1982, the Emiliano Zapata Peasant Organization (OCEZ) in the Central Valley and the Highlands.

The process of Indigenous organizing in Chiapas brought together several currents. First, the pastoral activity of Bishop Samuel Ruiz, inspired by liberation theology, beginning in 1968 with the Conference of the Latin American Episcopal Council (CELAM) in Medellín, Colombia.[4] Its guiding principle was the "preferential option for the poor"—both a critique of social oppression and a call for consciousness-raising and self-organization of the oppressed, understood as agents of their own history struggling for material, political, and cultural demands. This was followed by Indigenous theology, which recognized the word of God within Indigenous peoples' own cultures. This theology was then spread by a broad network of catechists and deacons, selected by their own communities. In the Chiapas Canyons, the Diocese's contribution to community organization emerged in the context of a recent process of new settlement. This theology looked to the story of Exodus, seeing the *fincas* as the equivalent of ancient Egypt and the Selva Lacandona as a new promised land ("God wants us to go find freedom, like the ancient Jewish people"). New villages constituted themselves and cohered through the confluence of Indigenous communities' tradition and Christian brotherhood.[5] In general, the pastoral work of Samuel Ruiz and his team, inspired by liberation theology, was central to the process of consciousness raising and organizing Indigenous communities. For many of those who joined the EZLN during its clandestine period, this was a decisive first step in their trajectories. As one person said, "The word of God helped us discover that we are human beings and deserve to be treated with dignity, that there was great social inequality.... It helped us start coming together and organizing to defend our rights."[6]

The next current is the arrival of militants from central and northern Mexico. Most of the so-called "Northerners" were invited by Samuel Ruiz himself, and they formed a Maoist organization called the Proletarian Line. Their activities focused on creating organizations such as the Union of Unions, and especially on developing productive projects and obtaining loans. Because they were constantly negotiating financing with state and federal governments, their ties to those in power became stronger and stronger. For example, one of Proletarian Line's leaders was Adolfo Orive, who was obsessed with creating a credit institution and managed to negotiate its financing with the federal government in 1982. Sixteen years later, he ended up advising Francisco Labastida, who was President Ernesto Zedillo's Secretary of the Interior. Another problem was the growing division between leaders, which led to a split within the Union of Unions in 1983 and the expulsion of its advisers.[7] This is the same year that the EZLN was founded, highlighting how this episode with the "Northerners" left a lot of mistrust toward those who arrived in the communities—ostensibly to support their struggles—who ended up doing little more than acting on personal rivalries and their own desires for power. The resulting disillusionment with struggles oriented toward negotiating with government authorities could very well have contributed to the search for other avenues, such as that of the EZLN.

In any case, the organizational process emerging in the 1970s grew out of the work of the Indigenous people themselves, based on their long history of oppression and resistance. Their intense mobilizations and land reclamations achieved significant results. Despite fierce repression, they managed to redistribute land formerly belonging to many *fincas* and to create new *ejidos*. Although large landholdings remained in some regions—especially in the environs of Altamirano and Las Margaritas, where a few families, such as that of General Absalón Castellanos, held on to several thousand hectares—arduous peasant struggles largely succeeded in dismantling the *finca* system. This is not to say that all agrarian demands had been resolved; on the contrary, a good many of them increasingly appeared insurmountable. State authorities refused to create new *ejidos* or expand *ejido* lands, despite peasants' incessant and exhausting trips to the state capital to comply with their bureaucratic demands. These legal efforts to obtain land failed to bear fruit, causing both desperation and increasing interest in the EZLN's proposals. Nonetheless, Subcomandante Marcos emphasized that the Indigenous people, who the first Zapatistas began to relate to, "were not blind people whose eyes we needed to open" but instead were part of "an Indigenous movement with a long tradition of struggle, with a great deal of experience, very committed, and very intelligent too."[8]

The founding and growth of the EZLN

The EZLN was founded on November 17, 1983, by a small group of militants belonging to the National Liberation Forces (FLN). This organization was founded in Monterrey in August 1969, after the Tlatelolco massacre convinced many organizations that armed struggle was the only possible way to confront the PRI dictatorship.[9] The National Liberation Forces followed this trajectory, guided by their Marxist-Leninist principles and admiration for the Cuban Revolution. After several years spent attempting to establish itself in Chiapas, a small group (three *mestizos* and three Indigenous, according to Subcomandante Marcos) entered the Lacandon Jungle and founded the Zapatista Army of National Liberation on November 17, 1983.[10]

In its first phase, between 1983 and 1985, this group learned to survive in the mountains and remained quite isolated, having hardly any contact whatsoever with the surrounding communities. The person who later became Subcomandante Marcos arrived in the summer of 1984, along with a female comrade and another Indigenous male comrade.[11] An important step was taken in 1985, when the guerrillas first openly entered a community in the Lacandon Jungle. From then on, they could intensify their clandestine recruitment work. Those who had already joined the organization worked to convince others from their families, communities, or other villages to join the insurgent forces that lived and trained in the camps—always with considerable discretion, and a great preoccupation for security. Or they might convince them to remain in their communities as "support bases," entailing a commitment to support and feed the insurgents.[12] A third option was to join the militias while remaining in the community and participating in intermittent military training in the camps.[13] Family and community ties were important here, as were religious ones, especially because of the influence of the catechists and deacons mentioned above and the spaces they had created through their pastoral activities. This all led to the "Zapatista boom" between 1988 and 1990. The number of combatants went from eighty to several thousand, and the membership of the EZLN went from being a handful of families to entire communities. Although many of the EZLN's members still also belonged to lawful organizations such as the Union of Unions, soon "Most of the villages in the Jungle and the Highlands were completely Zapatista."[14]

The organization grew so quickly that Subcomandante Marcos himself could hardly believe it.[15] Alongside all the other factors contributing to this, we should also mention the government's constant repression of popular struggles, especially during the governorships of Absalón Castellanos (there were 153 political assassinations and 503 illegal arrests between 1983 and 1988) and that of his successor, Patrocinio González. Another element is the fraudulent election in 1988, in which Carlos Salinas de Gortari won the presidency, closing the peaceful path toward change pursued by Cuauhtémoc Cárdenas. Many members of groups such as UU (Union of Unions) and ARIC (Rural Association of Collective Interest) had once supported this project, but between the electoral fraud and the corruption of their own leaders, half of all adherents defected between 1989 and 1993. As dissatisfaction with legal avenues grew, support for armed struggle increased.

Alongside the external factors favoring the EZLN's growth, there were also internal transformations, without which these external factors would have remained inconsequential. It was necessary for the original EZLN to transform itself enough for the Indigenous communities to be able to make it their own. Otherwise, it would not have lasted for long, much less grown as it did. Subcomandante Marcos recounts how the EZLN went from being "a revolutionary vanguard army to an army of the Indigenous communities," a process in which "the communities appropriated it and made it their own, placing it under their rule."[16] But to achieve this, the original militants who founded the EZLN had to enter into a process that transformed their initial schemas: "Our conception of reality was very square. And when we collided with reality, that square got quite dented. It was like this wheel over here. It began to roll and to be polished by its friction with the peoples. It ceased to have anything to do with the beginning. . . . We are the product of a hybridization, of a confrontation, of a clash in which—fortunately—we lost."[17] This is what Subcomandante Marcos calls "the first defeat of the EZLN," specifying that "if the EZLN had not accepted it, it would have isolated itself, it would have shrunk, it would have disappeared, and the EZLN that comes out on January 1, 1994, never would have been born in the first place."[18] He adds yet another element in a later interview, saying that the transformation that occurred during the EZLN's clandestine years is not only that of a guerrilla *foco* that became an Indigenous army, or the transformation of the original militants' square vision as it came into contact with the communities.[19] In addition to all this, they went from a vanguardist stance, as guides and teachers, to becoming the communities' students: "We were not teaching anyone to resist. Instead we became students in a school of resistance taught by those who had been doing it for five centuries."[20] This implied reversing the prior model in which they proposed solutions from above, and instead starting to build them "from below."[21] None of this is to say that the EZLN renounced the verticality of its military structure or disposed of its Marxist political formation. But yes, it touched off an internal transformation, which was necessary for the communities to appropriate and build the organization the way they did. There was undoubtedly an "Indianization of the EZLN" that disrupted its initial perspectives, overcame its *mestizo* cadres, and can be considered one of the fundamental bases of its subsequent transformations.[22] Indigenous peoples' organizational forms, their ways of being and of seeing the world, and their long traditions of struggle have been an essential component without which the Zapatistas' trajectory could not have had the creativity and growth that have characterized it.

The EZLN continued growing from 1989 onward, but it could no longer count on support or cover from organizations such as ARIC or the diocese—with the latter growing increasingly concerned about the Zapatistas' influence. Salinas de Gortari's neoliberal policies also added new reasons for people to mobilize. There was a crisis in the livestock market, as well as a drastic fall in coffee prices in 1989. INMECAFE (The Mexican Coffee Institute) would have provided a cushion, but it had been discontinued.[23] The biggest change came in 1992 with Salinas's reform of Article 27 of the Constitution. He proclaimed that this marked the end of agrarian reform, as it allowed *ejido* property to be converted into private property. It was a flagrant provocation that triggered massive protest. The level of mobilization achieved that year by the Indigenous peoples of Chiapas is illustrated by several initiatives, such as the Xi'nich March from Palenque to Mexico City, and the March of 10,000 Indigenous people in San Cristóbal on October 12. The latter marched under the banner of the Emiliano Zapata Independent National Peasant Alliance (ANCIEZ in Spanish), destroying the statue of the conqueror Diego de Mazariegos. Only years later did people learn that half of these protestors secretly belonged to the EZLN.[24]

That same year, a referendum organized in the Zapatista communities showed a clear majority in favor of the armed uprising, which led to a confrontation with the FLN, on whose leadership the EZLN continued to depend. At the Prado meeting in January 1993, the communities and the leadership of the EZLN imposed the decision for war on the leaders of the FLN—in the words of Subcomandante Marcos, "the Jungle won out over the city." This led to a restructuring and greater autonomy for the EZLN. It acquired a new governing body, the Indigenous Clandestine Revolutionary Committee, which was made up of Indigenous leaders from the different regions, who, now with the title of Comandantes, assumed political command of the EZLN.[25] The decision for war was undoubtedly determinant in consolidating the autonomy and Indianization of the organization founded ten years earlier.

The impact of the armed uprising

In the final days of 1993, some 4,500 Indigenous combatants took their positions and another 2,000 remained in reserve.[26] At dawn on January 1, EZLN military regiments occupied four cities in Chiapas: San Cristóbal de Las Casas (the historic capital), Ocosingo, Altamirano, and Las Margaritas. They also "passed through" Huixtán, Chanal, and Oxchuc. From the balcony of San Cristóbal's seat of municipal government, Subcomandante Marcos read the "First Declaration of the Lacandon Jungle"—a declaration of war against the federal army and a call to depose the usurper Salinas de Gortari. Surprise and disbelief reigned during the Feast of Saint Sylvester.[27] The federal army was slow to react, as its troops were either on leave or drunk and partying.[28] Meanwhile, the authorities tried to minimize events, with Chiapas Governor Elmar Setzer speaking of disturbances caused by "a total of about two hundred individuals, most of whom are monolingual."

Yet the shock waves were quickly felt around the entire country. The Chiapas elite—and especially the "coletos" of San Cristóbal—saw it as a manifestation emerging from the depths of the colonial era. They were witnessing their greatest fear—stemming from the great rebellion of the Highlands and northern Chiapas in 1712—that their capital might be overtaken by an Indian army. Nationally, the overwhelming force of the surprise uprising ruined the festivities of the president and his powerful guests who, that very night, were celebrating Mexico's official entry into the North American Free Trade Agreement (NAFTA), the culmination of the country's supposed integration into modernity's exclusive club. While Mexican elites were preparing to start a year devoted to their connections to the North, the Zapatistas' audacity forced an about-face, and the country awakened anchored to the South, to its peasant and Indigenous roots. The clash between the two countries—between "imaginary Mexico" and "deep Mexico" (to borrow a phrase from Guillermo Bonfil Batalla)—could hardly have been more explosive. In addition, the uprising quickly took on an even broader meaning as was perceived from many locations as a scream of "Enough is enough!" to neoliberalism, one of the first demonstrations of insubordination in the face of its planetary triumph, a bold gesture that broke the illusion of "the end of history," a cry that gave hope a place once again.[29]

What was the uprising's immediate objective? "The First Declaration of the Lacandon Jungle" called on the legislative and judicial powers to unseat the usurper on the presidential throne. It also called upon the people to freely elect new authorities and to join in saying "Enough!" to the poverty suffered by the "millions of dispossessed." The Zapatistas then called for a struggle for "work, land, housing, food, health, education, independence, freedom, democracy, justice, and peace" for all Mexicans.[30] Their stated military strategy was to move onward into the neighboring states of Oaxaca and Tabasco, and ideally toward the federal capital, in hopes of provoking a generalized popular uprising. Toward that end, the EZLN used its official newspaper, *Awaken Mexico* (*El Despertador Mexicano*), to publish the "revolutionary laws" it would apply in liberated territories. Among other things, these included confiscating the means of production and handing them over to local civic authorities; a general agrarian reform; the organization of free elections; as well as "The Women's Revolutionary Law"—the true revolution within the revolution.[31]

EZLN troops withdrew from San Cristóbal at dawn on January 2, prior to the federal army's arrival. They continued intense fighting around Rancho Nuevo, the headquarters of the 31st Military Zone but did not achieve their objective of taking it.[32] The unit that had taken Las Margaritas later lost a key officer, Subcomandante Pedro, the EZLN Chief of Staff, thereby preventing it from attacking the city of Comitán and the important military base located there.[33] Also on January 2, the units that had taken Ocosingo were unable to withdraw on time and were trapped in the city market, where the arrival of the federal army caused a terrible massacre with many civilians killed. Zapatista forces then retreated on January 3 to protect communities from the aerial bombings the federal army had commenced, especially in the area south of San Cristóbal.

On January 12, there were large demonstrations across the country demanding an end to the war. That same day, Salinas de Gortari ordered federal troops to cease fire. The EZLN's Command also announced a suspension of offensive operations. It began to take note of the broad movement of Mexican society that, although it failed to take up their call for revolt, showed itself to be receptive to the Zapatistas' message as it demanded peace. In the words of then Major Moisés, "People began to protest, saying 'Stop the war!' We had to recognize that it was civil society that was asking for this. And that's one of the things that stopped us. . . . We understood that we had to speak to the people, to explain what we want, what we're working toward, who we are."[34]

Thus, after twelve days of combat, the phase of Fire—for which the EZLN had prepared for ten years—came to a close. What began then was the phase of the Word, emphasizing dialogue with the federal government and, above all, discussion with civil society.[35] Zapatismo began a second transformation, a process that was just as important as that which occurred in the 1980s when the initial urban militants met the Indigenous communities. As Marcos explained, "There was a new clash, this time between the Zapatismo of 1983 (which had already changed by 1993 and had to be recreated again in 1994) and a new Zapatismo. . . . The armed Zapatismo born in 1994 became something new once it came into contact with civil Zapatismo across Mexico and the rest of the world, with people who think like us, who fight for the same things but who do so without weapons or ski masks."[36] It was a process of exploring new forms of political struggle, distinct from the armed struggle.

From the ceasefire to the March of the Color of the Earth (1994–2001)

It is impossible to delve into every detail of the Zapatistas' story, so here we will only highlight the principal moments in their struggle. Also, please bear in mind that the following chapters will elaborate the importance of the Zapatistas' principal initiatives.

The Zapatista Experience

The ceasefire on January 12, 1994, opened the phase of the word, including engagement with the federal government via the Cathedral Dialogues in San Cristóbal de las Casas. This commenced when the EZLN accepted Samuel Ruiz as mediator on the 13th of January; and, on the 18th, recognized Manuel Camacho Solís as the federal government's "true interlocutor."[37] The Zapatista delegation, composed of eighteen Indigenous comandantes plus Subcomandante Marcos, proceeded to meet with the government's delegation. Marcos began his first press conference by unfurling a large Mexican flag, forcing Manuel Camacho to join in, lest he appear less patriotic than the rebel chief. The dialogue took place between February 21 and March 2, 1994, at which point the EZLN suspended it, in order to consult their communities about the government's response to their demands. Ultimately it became impossible to continue this dialogue with the outgoing government, as Mexico's state-party system entered a period of acute decomposition when the PRI's presidential candidate, Luis Donaldo Colosio, was assassinated and later his secretary general José Ruíz Massieu, as well.

The EZLN began to prioritize building connections with civil society, especially with the "Second Declaration of the Lacandon Jungle" and its call for a National Democratic Convention. This took place from August 6 through 9, 1994, in the "Aguascalientes" of Guadalupe Tepeyac, which had been transformed for the occasion into a gigantic auditorium in the middle of the jungle, a space for sharing the word and searching for collective, civil paths toward democracy.[38] Around six thousand delegates from popular organizations across the country participated, and—although internal divisions prevented the Convention from becoming a permanent body—the meeting was emblematic of the intense social mobilization generated by the Zapatista uprising. Mobilization also continued in Chiapas, where many organizations took advantage of the situation by radicalizing their demands and, most importantly, occupying around 100,000 hectares of land during just the first three months of 1994. These organizations converged in January 1994 to form the State Council of Indigenous and Peasant Organizations (CEIOC), which subsequently joined with independent unions, civil associations, and the Women's Convention to form the Democratic State Assembly of the Chiapanecan People (AEDEPCH). All this organizing lent support to the gubernatorial campaign of Amado Avendaño, founder of the *El Tiempo* newspaper. After an attempt on Avedaño's life and an electoral fraud that handed the election to the PRI's candidate Robledo Rincón, the EZLN supported a strategy of civil insurrection, recognizing Avendaño as "the constitutional governor of Chiapas in rebellion."

Rincón's inauguration on December 8, 1994, is widely believed to have caused the breakdown of the truce that had been in effect since January. The EZLN initiated a military campaign in which, between December 11th and 18th, they broke the siege of the Canyons and carried out a "lightning" advance (without a clash with the federal army). Their troops entered into the Highlands and Northern regions of Chiapas and declared thirty "municipalities in rebellion" throughout their territory.[39] In the wake of all this, and with a deep economic crisis erupting in the first month of his term, President Ernesto Zedillo appeared to seek detente. He prepared for a return to a ceasefire by sending Esteban Moctezuma Barragán, the Secretary of the Interior, to meet with the EZLN General Command on January 15, 1995, near Guadalupe Tepeyac. But the government was actually preparing to attack. On February 9th, they staged a dramatic revelation of Subcomandante Marcos's presumed identity while, throughout Mexico, several people were arrested, accused of being linked to the EZLN. Most importantly, the federal army put its full force into searching the Jungle region for the Zapatista leaders. This episode came to be known as "the February betrayal," and it was a resounding failure. The EZLN comandantes and troops retreated into hard-to-reach areas and, after suffering through extreme conditions for various days, the federal army was forced to suspend a military occupation that, apart from failing to achieve its objectives, was widely repudiated across the country. Subcomandante Marcos wrote sarcastically to Moctezuma Barragán, saying, "You failed this time, Esteban M. Guajardo. Guadalupe Tepeyac was not Chinameca."[40]

Then, on March 10, 1995, and after much debate, Mexico's Congress approved the Law for Dialogue, Conciliation, and Dignified Peace in Chiapas, which the EZLN recognized as a valid basis upon which to resume dialogue with the government. It included guarantees for EZLN leaders and created the Commission of Concordance and Pacification (COCOPA), composed of legislators from all political parties. The law set the framework for a new round of dialogue, beginning in San Miguel, Ocosingo and then moving its headquarters to the rebel municipality of San Andrés Sakamch'en de los Pobres in the Chiapas Highlands. The Zapatistas hoped that, through the six rounds of dialogue proposed for San Andrés, they would emerge with a peace agreement that would put an end to the open conflict that began on January 1, 1994; and, moreover, that this would lay the basis for a new national project and a new constitution. In this way, the EZLN broke with the reigning scheme of two sides negotiating behind closed doors and instead transformed San Andrés into a venue for public debate with national ramifications. The delegation arrived alongside a hundred guests and advisors, representing wide swaths of Mexican civil society. Meanwhile, the National Indigenous Forum held meetings in January 1996 and transformed itself into the National Indigenous Congress (CNI in Spanish) the following October. Accordingly, "Indigenous rights and culture" was chosen as the topic for the first round of discussions in San Andrés, resulting in Accords signed by the EZLN and the federal government on February 16, 1996. The Accords recognize Indigenous peoples' right to autonomy, their own forms of government and normative systems, and control over their territories.

With the conflict moving in a positive direction during this initial phase of the San Andrés dialogues, the EZLN decided to organize a national and international *consulta* for August and September 1995.[41] They asked their supporters whether they should continue as a political-military organization or convert themselves into a civil society organization. About 1.3 million people participated, massively supporting the second option. In response, the "Fourth Declaration of the Lacandon Jungle," published on January 1, 1996, announced the creation of the Zapatista Front for National Liberation, a new type of political organization that aspired to be the civil and peaceful modality of Zapatismo. Yet meanwhile, significant obstacles emerged within the dialogue process, as the second round of negotiations dedicated to "Democracy and Justice" proved to be more difficult. The government's delegation was overwhelmed both by the depth of the EZLN's proposals—nourished as they were by their advisors and guests—and by the Forum on State Reform they held between June 30 and July 6, 1996. Discussions quickly hit a dead-end, especially since the rest of the process depended on the consolidation of the agreements made in the first round, which in turn required changes to Mexico's Constitution. Toward this end, the COCOPA submitted a definitive proposal on November 29, 1996: its recommendations on the constitutional reforms stemming from the San Andrés Accords on Indigenous Rights and Culture. Drafting the report itself required important mediation efforts between the two sides. The EZLN continued to have significant reservations, yet it nonetheless approved COCOPA's proposal. President Zedillo then proceeded to discard the recommendations made by this body of legislators and, in emitting his own observations, effectively rejected the document.

The president's decision ruptured the process that began on January 12, 1994. It broke off dialogue between the federal government and the EZLN and, with it, hopes of a negotiated end to the conflict. Under such circumstances, it was impossible for the EZLN to transform from a military organization into a civilian political organization. While the Zapatistas would surely continue pursuing nonmilitary options, it was now impossible for them to renounce their character as an army. A balance sheet of this first stage of the EZLN's public life would include difficulties—such as the National Democratic Convention, Amado Avendaño's government-in-rebellion and the break with the organizations grouped under the CEIOC and the AEDEPCH—errors that the EZLN has since recognized as "the products of our political clumsiness" and "authoritarian excesses of those who were the voice of the EZLN" causing "quarrels and resentment" instead of clarity and unity; as well as recognizing undeniable achievements (the main one being the signing of the San Andrés Accords).[42] Throughout, the most important aspect was their generative interaction with so-called "civil society," which provoked mobilizations, reflections, and transformations of the country's social forces. In particular, we should highlight the Intercontinental Encounter for Humanity and Against Neoliberalism, organized in the summer of 1996 in the five Zapatista Aguascalientes (La Realidad, Oventik, La Garrucha, Morelia, and Roberto Barrios). Apart from increasing pressure on the government as they engaged in the dialogues in San Andrés, it marked the beginning of Zapatismo's rising international impact.

For Zedillo's part, just as he was rejecting the COCOPA proposal, he was also generalizing the strategy of paramilitarization that began in the northern part of the state in 1995 while extending it into the Chiapas Highlands. It was meant to "deprive the fish of their water" by corroding the communities that provide the material base of the EZLN. Acting through party members at the head of various municipalities, the PRI's governing structure was directly aided by the military, creating armed groups comprised of Indigenous youth. These would force Zapatista families to flee their communities by attacking them, occupying their lands, and destroying their belongings.[43] Over ten thousand were displaced in the Highlands, mostly forced out of their communities in the municipality of Chenalhó and into camps in Polhó, where the Zapatista autonomous municipality is located. Others were displaced to San Cristóbal de las Casas. The most sinister moment within this panorama of generalized violence occurred in Acteal on December 22, 1997, when forty-five Indigenous Tsotsil people—most of whom were women and children—were brutally murdered while praying in a chapel. Responsibility for the massacre falls squarely on the state and its decision to respond to the Zapatista uprising with a counterinsurgency strategy. Chiapas Governor Roberto Albores Guillén carried out another act of aggression against the Zapatistas between April and June 1998 when he attempted to dismantle the autonomous municipalities of Ricardo Flores Magón, Tierra y Libertad (Land and Liberty), and San Juan de la Libertad and to weaken others by redrawing municipal boundaries.

These state and federal policies had some success. In some municipalities, the communities that form the Zapatista support base were weakened and the EZLN was trapped in a defensive posture, losing its earlier dynamism. In fact, for several years, the EZLN had to concentrate almost all its energy on a single goal: to use the constitutional reform proposed by COCOPA to gain recognition of the Indigenous rights embodied in the San Andrés Accords. They carried out stunning initiatives toward that end. In September 1997, a march of 1,111 Zapatista delegates arrived in Mexico City to participate in the Second Assembly of the National Indigenous Congress and to observe the founding Congress of the Zapatista Front for National Liberation (FZLN). (They did not participate directly since the EZLN was still an army, and therefore could not engage in this civilian organization that they proposed be formed).[44] In July 1998, they released the "Fifth Declaration of the Lacandon Jungle," announcing a national *consulta* on whether to accept the COCOPA proposal and to end the war of extermination against them. Votes were cast in March of the following year, with 2,500 Zapatista women and 2,500 men traveling across the country to promote participation in each and every municipality in Mexico. The initiative was a great success, both as an organizational effort and for the 2.8 million votes cast.[45] The government's wager that the EZLN would slowly die away had clearly failed. The PRI lost at the ballot box on July 2, 2000, and was forced to abandon the presidency, yet the Zapatistas continued in their territories. Zedillo had lost his war of oblivion against the EZLN. Marcos wrote to him saying, "You did everything you could to destroy us. All we had to do was resist."[46]

The PRI's seventy-one years of uninterrupted power had come to an end, and the EZLN signaled their willingness to resume dialogue on the very first day of Vicente Fox's presidency. They laid out various criteria for resuming talks, and Fox slowly complied. Twenty-three Indigenous comandantes set out alongside Subcomandante Marcos in a march to Mexico City that coincided with Fox's inauguration. Hope was in the air on February 24, 2001, as they set out on the March of the Color of the Earth from San Cristóbal de las Casas with the goal of arousing a broad national mobilization to recognize the San

Andrés Accords. They traveled for two weeks, greeted warmly by enthusiastic, multitudinous crowds in plazas and on highways. They visited twelve states across Mexico, held dozens of events, participated in the National Indigenous Congress in Nurio, Michoacán, and arrived in Mexico City's central plaza on March 11. Despite all manner of hurdles and tricks, the delegations from the CNI and EZLN entered the chambers of Congress for a momentous session, with Comandante Esther leading the appeal for the constitutional reforms proposed by COCOPA. The EZLN considered this to be a first step in the official recognition of the Indigenous part of the nation and therefore reinitiated contact with the federal government that very day.

As the Zapatista delegation returned to Chiapas, everyone agreed that the march was a huge victory, that its only conceivable outcome was the approval of the constitutional reforms that everyone had struggled for since 1996. All conditions pointed toward peace, and yet on April 28 all three major political parties (including the supposedly leftist PRD, Party of the Democratic Revolution) united in the Senate to approve a constitutional reform that had nothing to do with the COCOPA proposal. Their reform openly contradicted the San Andrés Accords, both in the letter of the law and its spirit, and instead harkened to a bygone era of clientelism and Indigenist assimilation.[47] The EZLN and CNI denounced this counter-reform as a betrayal. Nonetheless, despite being rejected in the ten states that are home to two-thirds of Mexico's Indigenous population, a majority of state Congresses approved the reform. Fox signed it into law on August 14 and, despite several Supreme Court challenges, the law was approved. All three branches of federal government thereby shared responsibility in the failure to comply with the San Andrés Accords, thereby definitively ending the period of dialogue with state institutions that had begun on January 12, 1994.

After 2003: Autonomy in practice and networks below

Despite the Zapatistas' best efforts and the success of the March of the Color of the Earth, the political class and their institutions stonewalled the constitutional reforms required by the San Andrés Accords. There would be no negotiated agreement ending the conflict initiated by the uprising of January 1, 1994, nor would the EZLN be able to transform into a civil political organization. The Zapatistas had to begin a new stage in their struggle. Instead of reducing their development over time to a contrast between periods of "fire" and periods of "the word," there is a third element woven throughout: "a third axis that acts like a spinal column," which is "the ongoing development of the organization of the Zapatista communities."[48] The communities' forms of organization were continually transforming during the ten years leading up to 1994, as they sought to balance the fire and the word. Moreover, as Subcomandante Marcos states, "The communities do not just sustain the EZLN . . . they are the path by which the EZLN moves."[49] With the strengthening of autonomy in 2003, this axis of popular organization became even more decisive than it had been before.

Given the rejection of constitutional reforms that would have recognized Indigenous peoples' autonomy, the EZLN chose to unilaterally put autonomy into practice, regardless of having been denied a legal framework to do so. Comandante Brus Li hinted at what would be officially declared later in the year when—during a public act held on January 1, 2003, in the central plaza of San Cristóbal de Las Casas ending with a ritual of "the new fire"—he said: "Let's not wait around for the bad government to give us permission. We should organize ourselves like true rebels and not wait for someone to give us permission to be autonomous. We'll govern ourselves . . . with or without the law."[50] On August 8, they announced the creation of five Good Government Councils (*Juntas de Buen Gobierno*), each corresponding to a region of Zapatista territory.[51] Their purpose was to coordinate the autonomous municipalities that had been declared in December 1994.

The formation of these councils responded to two main needs: The first was to prevent imbalances between autonomous municipalities, especially regarding the distribution of resources and solidarity projects coming from national and international civil society. Secondly, they clarified the separation between the EZLN's military structure and the civilian structures of autonomous self-government. In the "Sixth Declaration of the Lacandon Jungle," they recognized that the military side was excessively assertive, writing, "We saw that the EZLN, with its political-military component, was involving itself in decisions that belonged to the democratic authorities, 'civilians' as they say." This is why they decided "to begin separating the political-military from the autonomous and democratic aspects of organization in the Zapatista communities."[52] They therefore prohibited people with roles within the EZLN's command structure from taking on responsibilities within the autonomous municipalities or the Good Government Councils. They also announced the death of the "*Aguascalientes*" and birth of the "*Caracoles*," a new name for the political-cultural centers where the Good Government Councils would be based and where the EZLN would host their main activities. Evoking the symbol of the conch shell that the communities sounded to call one another together in case of emergency, the "Caracoles" are spaces of exchange between the worlds within and without. "They will be like doors for going into the communities and for the communities to leave. Like windows for seeing us and for us to look out. Like speakers for taking our word far, and for us to listen to what is far away."[53] Above all, the creation of the Good Government Councils was a step forward in building autonomy, which—as we will see in chapter 1—the Zapatistas have continued to center in their everyday work.

Despite the importance of autonomy, the EZLN risked falling into increasing isolation if it limited its activity to a territorialized construction. As they wrote in the "Sixth Declaration," "It is possible that we could lose everything we have if we remain as we are and do nothing more in order to move forward."[54] As they had learned from their repeated, futile attempts to advance through legal channels, they needed a new political initiative that rejected any negotiation with state institutions and the political class. This is why, when the "Sixth Declaration of the Lacandon Jungle" was released in June 2005, it did not call for the creation of a party or a unified organization. Instead, it called for a network of organizations and collectives capable of recognizing one another's differences, *and* their agreement on two basic principles: an explicitly anticapitalist stance and a political practice situated "below and to the left." As we will explore further in chapters 2 and 3, this means a politics outside state institutions, their electoral rituals, parties, and the political class. The "Sixth Declaration" also had an international dimension, proposing the formation of the "Zezta International" and a new Intercontinental Encounter.

Next was "The Other Campaign," beginning with six preparatory meetings held in the Caracol of La Garrucha in August 2005, and drawing hundreds of political organizations, unions, Indigenous peoples, collectives, and individuals. The campaign was launched when Subcomandante Marcos—transformed into "Delegate Zero"—set out on a tour of Mexico just as the presidential candidates were in the thick of their own campaigns. Instead of campaigning for votes, the Other Campaign was conceived as a space for Mexico-from-below to listen to one another's suffering and struggle, a first step in weaving together the network of resistance announced in the "Sixth Declaration." Once formed, this network would then create a "National Plan of Struggle." Four months into the campaign with its daily succession of intense encounters, Delegate Zero arrived in Atenco in the state of Mexico. The next day, in a brazen act of vengeance against the People's Front in Defense of Land—for their victory against a proposed new airport for Mexico City—Enrique Peña Nieto, the governor of Mexico State, orchestrated an attack against them that left two dead, two hundred arrested, and dozens raped by police. Subcomandante Marcos suspended the Other Campaign and decided to remain in Mexico City until all those arrested were freed.

Once conditions allowed for Delegate Zero to reinitiate his tour, he visited eleven more states in October and November. Then, between May and September of 2007, various Comandantes and Comandantas joined him at further events in central and southern Mexico. While all this certainly advanced the work of revealing the depth of Mexico-from-below and strengthening connections among its struggles, the repression in Atenco clearly dealt a severe blow to the Other Campaign. Meanwhile, the strident critiques of the PRD (Party of the Democratic Revolution) candidate Andrés Manuel López Obrador, delivered during the first phase of the campaign, led many sympathizers to distance themselves from Zapatismo, thereby consummating their divorce with the electoral left. While these critiques and the distancing of centrist supporters all predated the Other Campaign, the Zapatistas created further tension by rejecting electoral politics while rolling out an initiative that was parallel and possibly even in competition with the electoral calendar. This parallelism may have been uselessly confrontational. More importantly, the break was caused by the PRD when they betrayed the Indigenous struggle by voting for the counter-reform in 2001. Prior to that betrayal, the PRD had spent years refusing to condemn local elected officials from their party when they attacked Zapatista communities. As Subcomandante Marcos said, there can be no collaboration with those who are "our persecutors, our executioners, our murderers."[55]

The Zapatistas were also unable to carry out the international aspect of the "Sixth Declaration," which proposed a new intercontinental gathering. Nonetheless, they did organize three encounters between the Zapatistas and the Peoples of the World between 2006 and January 2008, dedicated to sharing their progress in building autonomy. Together with the CNI they also coordinated the Encounter of Indigenous Peoples of America in October 2007 in the Yaqui community of Vícam in Sonora state. Delegates from sixty-six Indigenous peoples participated, traveling from twelve different countries. Then, in December 2007, they held a Colloquium *In Memoriam* Andrés Aubry whose theme was

"Planet Earth: Antisystemic Movements." Subcomandante Marcos announced it would mark the end of two years of nonstop public activities—yet another large international event followed a year later: The World Festival of Dignified Rage. This marked the end of the a phase that began with the launch of the Other Campaign, which had notable advances but also failed to accomplish several of its objectives.

The General Command of the EZLN subsequently engaged in their longest period of silence to date, extending between January 2009 and December 2012. The Good Government Councils, on the other hand, publicly denounced an increasing number of attacks on Zapatista communities by paramilitaries and organizations manipulated by local, state, and federal governments. The Zapatistas continued strengthening their autonomy during these four years but their silence meant they did so without drawing attention to it, and neither did they debunk the rumors that began to spread about them. This included talk that the EZLN was falling into disarray and even that Marcos was morbidly ill or dead. While those on the outside suspected they were deteriorating, the Zapatistas were actually preparing.

The EZLN surprised the world with their mobilization on December 21, 2012—the day of the turnover from one Mayan long count cycle (*baktún*) to the next. Forty thousand Zapatistas occupied five cities across Chiapas, nearly the same ones they had occupied nineteen years earlier (San Cristóbal de Las Casas, Ocosingo, Altamirano, Las Margaritas, and Palenque). It was clearly an echo of January 1, 1994, but instead of crying out "Enough is enough!," everyone marched in a heavy, absolute silence. And instead of advancing military columns, this mobilization saw the serpentine advance of interminable lines of Zapatista men and women into the cities. Fists in the air, each of these "forty thousand male and female bosses (*jefes y jefas*) climbed across a stage erected for the occasion.[56] Adding further confusion to the surprise of it all, the EZLN released an enigmatic, short communiqué a few hours later, that read: "Did you listen? It is the sound of your world crumbling. It is the sound of our world resurging. The day that was day, was night. And night shall be the day that will be day." Without a doubt, it was their largest mobilization since the armed uprising, a powerful show of force, and in one fell swoop it debunked the rumors that Zapatismo had withered away. The Zapatistas clearly persisted, and they had never stopped working to strengthen their autonomy.

That day didn't just remind the world of their existence—it marked a new stage in the Zapatistas' path. Through a series of communiqués entitled

"Them and Us," released between January and March 2013, they announced new initiatives as well as updates to the "Sixth Declaration." They reiterated their commitment to the two principles of putting anticapitalism into practice and walking "below and to the left," away from state institutions. They also made two important adjustments: First, The Other Campaign and the Zezta International would be replaced by a single network of struggles and resistances called the Sexta (Sixth). In this way, they sought to create a greater connection between national and international activities, which the "Sixth Declaration" had initially separated. It was still important for their initiatives to be relevant to the Mexican context, but they also emphasized that they now had a different understanding of the connection between the national and international. They wrote that there would be only one terrain of struggle for the Sexta, saying "The territory for our work is now clearly delimited: the planet called 'Earth,' located in what's called the Solar System."[57] Their second adjustment was an invitation to pair the "No" that rejects capitalism and state-centric politics with a "Yes" asserting what we wish to collectively create. To explore it, they asked, "What world do we want? What is to be done? How? When? With whom?"

Within this new framework, they then offered three sessions of the "Zapatista Little School" between August 2013 and January 2014. Zapatista families hosted over five thousand participants in their homes for a few days, sharing with them the realities of everyday life in rebellious territory and teaching them the details of how they organize their autonomy. Zapatistas from each of the five Caracoles prepared "textbooks" for the event, containing an evaluation of their experiences of autonomy, its achievements, and its limits. It was a concrete and caring way of sharing everything they had accomplished in the twenty years since the uprising. Their next initiative was to reactivate the CNI and articulate it with the Sexta's networks via the World Festival of Resistance and Rebellion. The latter took place between December 2014 and January 2015, moving from Mexico City to Oventic, and passing through various CNI communities-in-struggle in Mexico State, Morelos, and the Yucatán along the way. Yet the EZLN was absent, having offered its spots in the caravan to the parents of the Ayotzinapa students disappeared on the tragic night of September 26, 2014, which plunged the country into such pain. In the following chapters we will discuss these and the many other initiatives the Zapatistas have continued to organize since their silent march in 2012. Among them are the international seminar, "Critical Thought in the Face of the Capitalist Hydra," in May 2015, the

CompArte for Humanity Festival in the summer of 2016 and then again in 2017 and 2018, and Zapatistas and ConSciences for Humanity from December 2016 to January 2017, and then again in December 2017.[58]

At this point we should quickly jump back in time to discuss another important change to the EZLN's organization. On May 2, 2014, shock troops from the Independent Union of Agricultural Workers and Peasants (CIOAC-Histórica in Spanish) entered La Realidad. The organization, which is at the service of state authorities and some members of the political class in Las Margaritas, ambushed and assassinated the Zapatista teacher Galeano and destroyed the local autonomous school and clinic. Galeano was a beloved community member. He had taken on many duties within the Zapatista organization over the years, most recently as the regional organizer of the Little School. At the time of his death, he was also a member of the Good Government Council. Because this grave attack was committed just a few meters from the Caracol and risked touching off an escalating cycle of violence, for the first time since its founding in 2003, the Good Government Council decided to suspend its activities and request that the EZLN manage the situation.

On May 24, during a public homage to the teacher Galeano, which was attended by thousands of people who had come from across the country, Subcomandante Marcos announced his own death, saying, "I declare that he who is known as Insurgent Subcomandante Marcos ceases to exist." Moments later he was resuscitated as Subcomandante Galeano.[59] In this way—and as the culmination of a sort of sacrificial ritual—each time he is named, the Subcomandante invokes and thereby prolongs the life of his fallen comrade. The personage of Marcos had been critiqued for some time, and during the event Marcos self-identified as a "clown." His death, announced in a speech entitled "Between Light and Shadow," marked a number of important replacements within the EZLN. First is the replacement of one generation by the next. Second is that the original core leaders from the urban middle class were replaced by a movement whose authorities are all Indigenous peasants. This includes the elevation of Moisés, a Tseltal Indigenous person, to the level of Subcomandante, military chief, and spokesperson of the EZLN a few months prior. And most importantly, third is the replacement of "revolutionary vanguardism" with the communities' everyday politics. Whereas Marcos was a charismatic leader, Galeano—described as "an extraordinary being," just like "thousands of other Zapatista women and men in the Indigenous communities"—would now be the name of Zapatismo's collective power.[60]

The final initiative we will mention here stems from the revitalization of the CNI begun in 2013. It was first proposed at the CNI's Fifth Congress, held in October 2016 on the twentieth anniversary of its founding, and this proposal was then put up for debate by each of the communities that constitute the Congress and was subsequently approved three months later. The agreement was to form a national-level Indigenous Council of Government (CIG). Council members were chosen by each Indigenous group within the Congress and were formally inducted in May 2017. The Council immediately named María de Jesús Patricio Martínez, known as "Marichuy," as their spokeswoman and began the work of collecting enough signatures for her to qualify to stand as an independent candidate in the 2018 presidential election. The proposal generated quite a bit of confusion and much debate, as many initially read the proposal as an abandonment of autonomy and a politics "from below and to the left." However, the CNI quickly clarified that their initiative was not a renunciation of past political positions, much less an attempt to gain an institutional post. Instead, they sought to enter the electoral field to draw attention to the attacks on Indigenous peoples' territories across all of Mexico, to strengthen the CNI, and to call on all Mexicans to multiply autonomous projects, to self-organize, and to disregard politicians' false promises. It was a call to "dismantle from below the power that is imposed on us from above."[61] Furthermore, inspired by the prevalence of the women on the Indigenous Council of Government within this initiative, in March 2018 the EZLN coordinated the International Encounter of Women Who Struggle in the Caracol of Morelia. It was entirely organized by Zapatista women, without any male participation whatsoever, and was an important moment for affirming women's capacities and ways of organizing themselves.

Networks to support the Indigenous Governing Council were mobilized between October 2017 and February 2018, but from the start the conditions imposed by the National Electoral Institute condemned them to failure. The Institute demanded that each of the required 890,000 signatures be collected using sophisticated digital equipment that was clearly inaccessible for a candidate whose social base was in communities that generally lack resources, especially internet access. Despite falling short, it was indeed an achievement to collect 300,000 signatures, considering that all other independent candidates were corrupt and simply purchased fake signatures. Marichuy's tour covered a large portion of the country, sparking political mobilizations, the formation of support networks, and generating admiration within sectors of society that had previously remained distant from Indigenous causes. These were all seeds of a growing connection between Indigenous and non-Indigenous struggles. This is why, when the Indigenous Governing Council Support Networks met in August 2018, the EZLN proposed that the Indigenous Governing Council be widened so as to "cease to be only Indigenous" or even "only national." They also proposed that its support networks grow into a planetary network of resistances and rebellions. Once again, the proposal was to expand from a long-lasting project of territorial autonomy toward a multiplication of initiatives—projects to strengthen connections between resistances and rebellions in struggle nationally and across the globe—thereby strengthening autonomy and politics from below.

Update to the Prologue: A new stage during tough times

The year 2018 was the start of a particularly difficult period, for Chiapas generally and for the Zapatista struggle in particular.[62] The Zapatistas warned of the change on December 31, 2018, while commemorating twenty-five years since the armed uprising. That day, instead of a joyous anniversary celebration, three thousand uniformed militia members entered the central plaza of the Caracol of La Realidad in seemingly endless columns, unarmed, with the clamor of their batons resounding to the rhythm of their double-step march on the ground.[63] It was an unusual demonstration that the EZLN's military, despite remaining in the background for some time, had by no means disappeared. With the stage set, the EZLN announced its position on Mexico's new President Andres Manuel López Obrador, who had assumed office only a month before. Subcomandante Moisés's harsh words confirmed that—despite what he had led thirty million voters to believe—the new president was not the bearer of hope for the Zapatistas, but just another "overseer" on the great plantation of globalized capitalism.[64] The Zapatista spokesperson repudiated the megaprojects López Obrador had announced, projects that will dispossess Indigenous territory and destroy their forms of life. He warned that, "Now we see that they are coming for us, the originary peoples."

Apart from the Interoceanic Corridor of the Isthmus of Tehuantepec (intended to be an alternative to the Panama Canal), Moisés centered his critiques on the misnamed "Mayan Train," the flagship project of López Obrador's presidency, which sought to connect Palenque in Chiapas with the Yucatán's principle tourist destinations. The president obstinately plowed ahead with the project during all six years of his administration—granting the army the concession for most of its construction—despite the fact that it intensifies tourism's well-documented ecological and social impacts.[65] Subcomandante Moisés considered it an offense and a mockery for him to baptize the train with the name of his ancestors and without asking Indigenous peoples' permission. He went on to express his intent with absolute clarity, saying, "We are not going to allow his project of destruction to pass through here"; "We are going to fight if necessary." Thus, the EZLN stated their orientation toward the new federal government with total clarity and has not changed it during the ensuing five years.

However, this message did not initiate a period of silence and closure—of the sort that have characterized the EZLN's long journey—or a return to armed struggle. Rather, it served to emphasize that the Zapatistas were prepared to give their lives to defend their territories and their autonomy. "We are going to continue building," said Subcomandante Moisés, clarifying that their wager would continue to be on the civilian construction of autonomy. In August 2019, in a communiqué titled "And, We Broke the Siege" (recalling the military maneuver of December 1994 in which they proclaimed the first Zapatista municipalities), the EZLN announced the creation of seven more Good Government Councils and four additional autonomous municipalities. Thus, Moisés affirmed that the construction of Zapatista autonomy continued to permanently expand and adapt.[66] In some cases, the creation of new Good Government Councils was due principally to the difficulties of moving within very large zones, which therefore were divided into two or three. In other cases, new autonomous communities were formed where none existed before, including in regions far from the principal Zapatista zones. For example, new municipalities were created near the Guatemala border in Motozintla and in Chicomuselo, where people have been resisting mining. Another Good Government Council was created in the new Caracol of Jacinto Canek, which is located on the grounds of CIDECI-Unitierra, on the periphery of San Cristóbal de Las Casas. This gave Zapatista autonomy greater visibility within a large urban area.

The same August 2019 communiqué announced a full series of national and international "encounters" (encuentros): a Forum in Defense of Territory and Mother Earth, the "Puy ta Cuxlejaltik" Film Festival, a new installation of the CompArte for Humanity Festival; The Second International Encounter of Women Who Struggle, as well as a call to resume discussions about forming a planetary network of resistances and rebellions. However, soon the Covid-19 pandemic presented a huge challenge, as it did for so many struggles across the world. The Zapatistas' response was immediate and clear. On March 16, 2020, the EZLN declared a red alert, recommended that the Good Government Councils close the Caracoles, and invited the peoples of the world to adopt "exceptional health measures" without abandoning their current struggles.[67] Over the following days, the Zapatista autonomous health authorities used audio messages to share information about the contagion and suggest preventive measures such as canceling meetings or quarantine for those returning from other regions. Their approach stood in contrast to that of President López Obrador, whose response, in spite of identifying politically as a "progressive," was more like that of Trump and Bolsonaro. Like them, he hugged his supporters, scorned preventative measures, and even showed off religious images that he said were his "bodyguards" against the virus. Like them, his priority was unimpeded economic activity, especially for megaprojects like the Mayan Train whose construction began at the height of the pandemic. We must therefore understand the Zapatistas' response within the context of countries that suffered—not from an excess of health measures—but from their absence, from their rulers' decision to sacrifice health on the altar of economic (ir)rationality. Above all, the Zapatistas' response to the pandemic helps us to understand what it means to take protective health measures in an autonomous and self-organized manner. Autonomous measures taken to confront the risk of contagion are quite different from those the state imposes unilaterally, including via policing and repressive measures.

In October 2020, at the height of the pandemic, the Zapatistas surprised the world again when they announced plans to travel to the five continents, beginning with Europe. They did so in a long text that began with its sixth part, titled "A Mountain on the High Seas," and ended on January 1, 2021, with a "Declaration for Life" signed by the EZLN and hundreds of organizations, collectives, and individuals from all over the planet.[68] Since 1994 many visitors from many countries have visited Chiapas to learn about the Zapatista experience, and this initiative launched a journey in the opposite direction, to visit these collectives all around the world. Up until then, no members of the EZLN had ever left Mexico, except for one man and one woman who participated in the Second Intercontinental Encounter for Humanity and Against Neoliberalism in 1996 in Catalonia. The primary goal of the initiative was to thank all those who had supported them since 1994, and to continue weaving connections among struggles from below. The idea of forming planetary networks of rebellions and resistance may very well begin to concretize itself with this voyage to the five continents.

The maritime delegation, named Squadron 421, because it was composed of four women, two men, and a non-binary person (*"unoa otroa"* in the Zapatistas' lexicon) was put in charge of the first part of the voyage. On May 3, 2021, they left from Isla Mujeres on board a boat called *The Mountain* to undertake a crossing that brought them to Vigo in Galicia, where they disembarked on June 23rd. The trip was conceived as a way of reliving the conquest of the Americas but in reverse (obviously not as an imposition, but "a consensual invasion" in agreement with the Europeans themselves). In fact, the Squadron's was a take on the arrival of Christopher Columbus to the island of Guanahani on October 12, 1492, when he plunged a cross into the ground and named the island San Salvador. This time, Marijosé was the first to step onto European soil ("It won't be a man, or a woman; it will be an other (*unoa otroa*))," giving the European lands a new name, this time in the Mayan language. They proclaimed, "In the name of Zapatista women, children, men, elders, and of course *otroas*, I declare that from now on this place, currently referred to as 'Europe' by those who live here, be called *Slumil K'ajxemk'op*, which means 'Rebellious Land,' or 'Land which does not give in or give up.' And that is how it will be known by its own people and by others for as long as there is at least someone here who does not surrender, sell out, or give up."[69]

The Squadron was present in Madrid on August 13, 2021, for the five-hundredth anniversary of the conquest of México-Tenochtitlán by the army of Hernán Cortés. They were present within the context of five centuries of struggle against colonial domination, a struggle common to all the Indigenous peoples of Abya Yala, a struggle the Zapatistas have taken up since the "First Declaration of the Lacandon Jungle" (and clandestinely since 1992). But they had a unique way of conceiving this struggle. First, they made clear that they were not interested in the Spanish state or the Catholic church apologizing for the conquest and colonization.[70] They wanted to avoid essentializing the whole western world, making it into a homogeneous bloc to be rejected in its totality, as this would only raise insurmountable barriers between struggles from below. For the Zapatistas, the totality of Europe cannot be reduced to the colonizers. On the contrary, understanding that it has undergone its own processes of internal colonization, we can then come together with those who have suffered from it. Besides, the colonized do not have to limit themselves to being victims, which is why their message to the people of Spain on August 13, 2021, was "You didn't conquer us. We continue to resist and rebel."[71] What really matters now is to stop the ongoing crimes against Indigenous peoples, those disguised as megaprojects (some of which are committed by giant European companies). In undertaking a reverse voyage of conquest, they were not trying to return to the past, or seeking some petty revenge, but rather striving to create the possibility of an other history.

What followed was complicated for a number of reasons. The main part of the Zapatista delegation had planned to travel by plane as soon as Squadron 421 landed, but they had to deal with a number of bureaucratic obstacles. The first of these was to get Mexican passports; then, at that very moment, the European Union began requiring vaccination certificates (from approved vaccines, not including the Chinese ones widely used in Mexico). The arrival of the airborne delegation had to therefore be postponed until September. But eventually around 180 Zapatista men and women, plus a delegation from the National Indigenous Congress, landed in Vienna, Austria, on September 14th. They divided themselves into twenty-eight teams of five people each and spent three months circulating through all corners of Europe, from England to Cyprus and from Portugal to Finland, visiting hundreds of collectives and spaces of struggle. They prioritized closed-door meetings to enable direct exchanges, rather than organizing public events or looking for coverage in the commercial or alternative media.

Thanks to this journey—and once all its teams had shared their experiences of it with one another—the Zapatistas now have an unparalleled knowledge of the struggles from below across Europe. Everywhere they went, they found people who took responsibility for housing and feeding them, caring for them and curing them if they got sick, transporting them from one place to another, and organizing their activities. All of this happened in hundreds of places, without major problems or serious incidents. While they are not as strong as they were in the 1990s, this is a significant achievement for the collectives supporting the Zapatista struggle. In fact, the Voyage for Life was a tremendous effort, both organizationally and in terms of fundraising. It was the fruit of over a year of work, including thousands of meetings among local collectives and regional, national, and Europe-wide coordinating bodies. The process had its tensions, sometimes quite sharp ones. Yet it also led to some positive connections, when collectives in the same region that had not previously had a relationship began working together, creating links they have since maintained. However, the difficulties that arose during the voyage were so great that, to date, a new structure connecting the various struggles has not emerged, nor have there been advances in the network of rebellions and resistances that the EZLN proposed in 2013.

In any case, the Journey for Life led to an enormous number of exchanges and encounters that left a lasting mark on those who lived them. Many seeds were sown, albeit at the cost of a sometimes-overwhelming organizational effort. And although we have not heard testimony about it, we can imagine that the voyage had effects inside Zapatista territories as well. Upon returning, the different teams synthesized their experiences and shared them with all the Zapatista communities. We can suppose that the direct knowledge of other regions of the world, a knowledge that was previously based only on the visits of "internationals" to the autonomous territories, transformed the way Zapatista men and women perceive the world and relate to other struggles.

In this context, the EZLN's position on the war in Ukraine is quite relevant. They denounced all capitalist wars and refused to support any state or government ("Neither Zelensky nor Putin"), first via a communiqué issued on March 2, 2022, and then through a mobilization in six cities across Chiapas on March 13th. But they also clearly stated that, in this war, "there is an aggressor: the Russian army" and a people suffering an invasion. One of the principal slogans of the March 13th march was "Russian army out of Ukraine."[72] From the very beginning, the EZLN knew to avoid the traps of Putin's propaganda and distanced itself from the tendency (widespread in Latin America) to mechanically reproduce anti-imperialist positions, thereby ignoring Russia's imperial actions. The EZLN came to this position, in large part, through its international networks, particularly in consultation with collectives both in Russia and in Ukraine.

Returning to the situation in Mexico and Chiapas, recent years have clearly been very difficult ones for the Zapatista struggle. The López Obrador government has succeeded in co-opting various Indigenous organizations, even leaders who had been part of the National Indigenous Congress and close to the EZLN. At the same time, many struggles that have not bowed to the federal government have suffered fierce repression. This is true of the People's Front in Defense of Land and Water, which opposes the construction of thermoelectric plants in the states of Morelos, Puebla, and Tlaxcala, as well as of the inhabitants of the Juan C. Bonilla municipality in the state of Puebla, who for months occupied a Bonafont bottling plant (property of Danone) and transformed it into the People's House until they were evicted by the National Guard. Paramilitary organizations like the Regional Organization of Coffee Producers of Ocosingo continue to carry out aggressions against Zapatista communities. Violence against Zapatistas in the Moisés y Gandhi region has been particularly pronounced, as they have been attacked with firearms, their homes and crops have been destroyed, and in September 2021 two members of the Good Government Council of the community of Patria Nueva were kidnapped.

More generally, Chiapas is in a chaotic situation, due to the corruption and inaction of state authorities who have allowed organized crime to grow to unprecedented levels. Whereas five years ago, a good part of Chiapas (especially the Highlands) was relatively free from the criminal organizations that have unleashed extreme violence across Mexico, this exceptionalism has been completely wiped off the map. Now, the large cartels that operate nationally, like Sinaloa and Jalisco New Generation, are vying for control of the state. While international trafficking was previously concentrated along the Pacific coast highway, today the cartels consider it critical to control the Pan-American highway, which runs through central Chiapas and through San Cristóbal de Las Casas. There, the cartels rely on local criminal organizations, exacerbating violence between them. There is a battle for control of key spaces, like markets and places where drug and arms traffickers operate, as well as migration routes from Central America. Drug traffickers even permeate the rural Indigenous areas, where they recruit young people and charge *derecho de piso* in the municipal capitals.[73] Large flows of money and the possibility of displaying material abundance to achieve social status create upheavals in community life and are another factor tempting youth to migrate to the US. These transformations extend their reach even into Zapatista communities, although there is no drug consumption or trafficking there.

The EZLN has warned about the social decomposition unleashed in Chiapas on multiple occasions, especially in a September 19, 2021, communiqué with the alarming title "Chiapas on the Verge of Civil War."[74] Alongside paramilitary violence, the document calls out the "mis-government" that prevails in the state, the alliance between the authorities and drug traffickers, and these officials' interest in promoting political destabilization. This all points to the conclusion that the growing power of organized crime is the most effective counterinsurgency tactic, accomplishing what past modalities (military intervention, paramilitarism, and the government's social assistance programs) have been unable to achieve. Facing persistent paramilitary aggressions, the growth of criminal organizations, generalized migration, the advance of megaprojects, and political decomposition across the state of Chiapas, it was necessary for

Zapatista autonomy to reorganize itself to adapt to such an extraordinarily difficult situation and defend itself more effectively.

A long, twenty-part communiqué released between October and December 2023 announced important changes, opening "a new stage" in the Zapatista struggle.[75] It begins enigmatically, with Nicaraguan poet Rubén Darío's rendition of the legend of Saint Francis of Assisi in "The motives of the wolf."[76] In it, the animal—who is briefly domesticated by the saint's preaching—tires of its mistreatment by humans and ends up returning to its old instincts. A later part in the communiqué announces the "death" of Subcomandante Galeano—a discrete and almost ironic passing, far from the public staging of the death of Subcomandante Marcos in 2014.[77] This time he was resurrected with the name and the rank of "Insurgent Captain Marcos," as he was first known during the years of clandestinity in the jungle. The rest of the communiqués insist on looking toward the future. They reiterate the importance of childhood and introduce the figure of Dení, a little girl who will live 120 years from now as the sixth-generation descendant of another Dení, now five years old, whose parents are Zapatistas. Subcomandante Moisés says, "We must look at that girl [who will live] in 120 years" and struggle for her, since "If we don't look at that girl . . . we won't understand what we are doing." This new stage is "about going through this and other storms that will come. It's about surviving the night, and reaching that morning, 120 years from now, where a girl begins to learn that being free is also being responsible for that freedom."[78] The Zapatistas thereby situate their path within a long temporal horizon, meaning the new stage cannot be evaluated according to its immediate effects. They write that "in the midst of collapse we have to look far away."

The communiqués' foremost announcement was a significant transformation of autonomy, with the disappearance of the Zapatista Autonomous Rebel Municipalities and Good Government Councils and the implementation of another organizational form, centered in "Local Autonomous Governments."[79] (There are further details regarding these changes at the end of chapter 1.) Beyond the "errors" of autonomy mentioned by Subcomandante Moisés, they have undertaken this reorganization to adapt to a context with many dangers, in particular the growing presence of organized crime.[80] In a more general sense, it is about resisting what the Zapatistas have called the storm (and the capitalist Hydra). As Subcomandante Moisés writes, "This new stage of autonomy is made to confront the worst of the Hydra, its most infamous bestiality and its destructive madness, their wars and business and military invasions."[81]

Furthermore, he also announced an internal transformation of the EZLN, writing "The structure and disposition of the EZLN have been reorganized in order to increase the defense and security of towns and mother earth in the event of aggressions.... We have prepared so that our towns survive, even isolated from each other."[82] This is not a return to armed struggle, but it does indicate greater attention to the requirements of defense, with all that that entails, in terms of cohesion and the ability to react. Clearly, the needs of self-defense and survival within a highly threatening context are at the heart of the new stage, designed to get through tough times.

CHAPTER 1

"Autonomy Is the People's Life Itself"
The Construction of Autonomy in the Zapatista Territories

With autonomy, we come to the heart of the Zapatista political project. "Autonomy" is a word the Zapatistas employ to synthesize their experiences and to name what they have been building in their rebel territories in Chiapas. The present chapter will focus on concrete aspects of Zapatista autonomy, leaving for the next chapter the broader implications of this idea that represents a path toward anticapitalist transformation that circumvents the state. What the Zapatistas have constructed in their territories demonstrates the possibility of creating, in the here and now, a reality distinct from the one imposed by the world of globalized money. Yet this is insufficient for the Zapatistas. Their construction of autonomous spaces should be understood as a part of a struggle that is both national and planetary, that is nothing less than a war between humanity and capitalism.

The idea of autonomy has been present since the first years of the Zapatista uprising, and it became central during the negotiation of the San Andrés Accords. In December 1994 the concrete first steps were taken, with the declaration of thirty "rebel municipalities," each proceeding to take shape over time. Autonomy was further organized and deepened in 2003, with the creation of the five Good Government Councils (referred to sometimes as *Juntas*). Between August 2013 and January 2014, during the three sessions of the Zapatista Little School (*Escuelita*), more than five thousand attendees learned directly from the Zapatistas about the successes and difficulties in building autonomy. These evaluations were published in their textbooks titled *Freedom According to the Zapatistas*, and are one of this chapter's principal sources.[1]

Zapatista autonomy is the fruit of the specific history that made it possible and explains its particular features. It could not have unfolded without the determination of those who had organized clandestinely over the span of ten years and then rose up in arms on January 1, 1994. The uprising opened the political space that the EZLN then transformed into the conditions for autonomy. The Zapatistas have been able to defend their autonomy only by maintaining their collective strength, and by continually inventing new strategies in the face of unrelenting counterinsurgency attacks.

Nourishing self-determined forms of life

While autonomy is best understood as a way of organizing government, we should begin by investigating the forms of life the Zapatistas seek to defend—that eschew capitalism's basic structures. However, despite the growth of their autonomy, the Zapatistas do not pretend to live entirely outside of capitalism. They maintain a clear awareness of how the constant pressure of the capitalist system blocks their ability to act, foments aggression against them, and influences their forms of life. Given all this adversity, their efforts to free themselves from the heteronomy of the commodity and to strengthen their self-determined forms of life are even more significant.

Community, land, and territory

We can understand the Indigenous peoples of Chiapas's forms of life through these three dimensions. Many of these people accommodate themselves to the encroachment of capitalist domination, which works to destroy their forms of life bit by bit, while others fight to defend them. This is true of the Zapatistas but not only them. Community is at the heart of these forms of life, together with the organizational forms and ways of being in and seeing the world that go along with it. The Indigenous community should not be understood as a timeless essence, unchanged since before the Spanish conquest; it has never stopped transforming and reformulating itself. For the Zapatistas, community is associated with both a respect for tradition as well as a critical distance from it, as we shall see later. In any case, communal organization is so incompatible with capitalist logic that all liberal and neoliberal reforms have tried to annihilate it. It is a way of being based on the premise that life can only be practiced collectively and built through reciprocity. This is exemplified by the community assembly as a place for speaking and elaborating decisions; by participation in the *cargos* (organizations in service to the community) that carry out these decisions; with mutual aid and collective work to protect communal resources; with celebrations and rituals; and, crucially, the different forms of collective land possession (both the *ejido* and communal land).[2]

The territory, understood both in its concrete and symbolic dimensions, including its inhabited and cultivated areas, as well as the forests and mountains (considered as water reservoirs, essential for the cycles of life), is what lends consistency and singularity to the community. It is the lifeworld without which it could not exist.[3] The land itself, insofar as it is cultivated (as *milpas* of corn, beans, and squash, or for other productive uses) cannot be separated from the totality of territory and from Mother Earth: understood as a force (*potencia*) of life no one can appropriate and, more to the point, that to which we all belong.

> First, for us, Zapatistas, Indigenous peoples of Mexico, of America, and of the world, the earth is our mother, life, memory, refuge of our ancestors, home of our culture and way of life. . . . Second, the earth for us is not simply the ground we walk upon, cultivate, where we raise our descendants. The earth is also the air that, producing wind, comes down and rises up from our mountains; the water of the springs, rivers, lakes, and the rains that turn into life through our crops; the trees and forests that give fruit and shade; the birds that dance in the wind and sing in the branches; the animals that grow, live, and feed beside us. The earth is everything that lives and dies. Third, the earth is not a commodity for us, in the same way that human beings are not commodities, nor are the memories or the greetings we give to and receive from our dead. The earth does not belong to us, we belong to it. . . . Fourth, we are warriors defending the earth, our mother, our life. For us, this is the final battle. If the earth dies, we die.[4]

This form of life—which is based in the community experience, rooted in its own territory, and considers itself part of Mother Earth—is a complete anomaly in the epoch of global capitalism. Defending this form of life requires an arduous struggle, and the Zapatista communities, along with many others throughout Mexico, have dedicated themselves to it. It is a struggle to oppose the neoliberal politics that, since President Carlos Salinas's changes to Article 27 of the Mexican Constitution, have enabled the liquidation of the collective ownership of land, and particularly the transformation of *ejidal* land into private property. It is also a struggle to resist the effects of the North American Free Trade Agreement, which has accelerated the destruction of the Mexican peasantry by overwhelming them with US imports. It requires an embodied defense of territories against mining, tourism, and energy and infrastructure projects—a war that in Chiapas and throughout Mexico has mobilized the Zapatistas together with the other peoples united in the National Indigenous Congress.[5]

The Zapatistas also try to halt the advance of agroindustrial production in their territories by revitalizing peasant agriculture. This means maintaining the traditional polyculture of the *milpa* while also cultivating vegetable gardens and organic coffee using new agroececological practices, eliminating chemical fertilizers and pesticides, and defending native seeds. The primary objective of this peasant agriculture is self-subsistence, both for the family and the community. In other words, it is the capacity to materially sustain the autonomous project.[6] Beyond just defending their territories through these practices, the Zapatistas were also able to extend them through the recuperations conducted during the 1994 uprising. A portion of this land was used to establish new settlements, mostly for young families who did not have *ejidal* or communal land.[7] Another portion of this recuperated land is used for experimenting with new forms of collective work, which is carried out in the communities as well as on a municipal and regional level. This collective work involves growing corn or other vegetables, or raising livestock. For example, a municipality could have thirty or fifty head of cattle, with everyone taking turns caring for them. This sort of collective work helps finance the political initiatives and encounters organized by the EZLN and, above all, to sustain all the various aspects of autonomy that will be discussed in the next section (education, health, and government).[8]

In this respect, the Zapatistas insist that their massive recuperations of land—their principal means of production—is the material basis that makes it possible to build autonomy.[9] This effort to expand the capacity for autonomous production is especially important within a context where self-sufficient production is the norm (not just of food but also traditional clothing and housing). This is something the Zapatistas pursue by creating all sorts of cooperatives, including bakeries, textiles, shoemaking, carpentry, metalworking, construction materials, and so on.

Autonomous health and education

One of the principal achievements of Zapatista autonomy is their self-organization of health and education, done without any institutional support whatsoever. I will speak only a little about the health system because it is beyond my expertise, however, I can mention that there are health promoters in every single community, that larger communities have a health house (*casa de salud*), each municipality has a microclinic, and each *Caracol* (regional center) has a clinic.[10] The latter provide general medical treatment as well as various specialized services, including the ability to perform surgeries. Volunteer doctors lend their services in solidarity, particularly for surgeries, but the most essential services are carried out by the Zapatista health promoters, who examine patients and treat the most common illnesses, such as gastrointestinal problems and respiratory infections. They also run tests, give eye exams, and provide dental care. More delicate cases are delegated to doctors, and patients with serious illnesses are transported to hospitals in a nearby city. Even when patients are sent outside the Zapatista health-care system, they still benefit from the autonomous health program, since health promoters accompany them to ensure they do not suffer the discrimination and negligence that Indigenous patients are so often subjected to in public hospitals.

Municipal and zone-level health commissions support the promoters, especially in obtaining medicines and organizing trainings. There are two principal challenges facing the autonomous health-care system: first is the need to better train new health promoters, and second is the scarcity of resources, despite the collective work through which Zapatista communities support their system of clinics, microclinics, and health promoters. Therefore, although the goal is for all treatment to be free for everyone (including non-Zapatistas), during hard times they request that patients provide a partial payment.

Autonomous health care brings together Western and traditional medicine. The former is fully assumed, but traditional medicine is also well-represented through the inclusion of midwives and bone-setters (*hueseros*), as well as through the health promoters' deep knowledge of how to use medicinal plants for a variety of curative and preventative purposes (for example, to periodically kill parasites in children and adults). The use of medicinal plants is an important aspect of autonomy, as it reduces dependence on pharmaceutical products. Another important factor is their holistic approach to health as well as sickness, a perspective rooted in Indigenous conceptions of the world. This leads them to put great emphasis on preventative health measures, especially vaccination campaigns and initiatives to improve nutrition and hygiene. Finally we can observe a partial de-specialization of health care, as the responsibility to care for health spreads throughout the social body. The health promoters in the communities continue to cultivate the land, and even those who work in the clinics and micro-clinics remain connected to the collective rhythms of rural life. Their responsibilities are the result of decisions made in community assemblies and across the entire Zapatista project, including its commissions and levels of autonomous government. Everyone works to create ways of caring for health that align with collective life in the Zapatista rebel Indigenous communities.

The Zapatistas have also created their own education system; they have conceived an entire pedagogical project, built hundreds of schools, and trained education promoters who serve the communities' children and youth. The first autonomous education projects began at the end of the 1990s and were further strengthened in 2003 with the creation of the Good Government Councils ("*Juntas*" for short), leading each zone to embark on its own process of building autonomous education. For example, most zones began with primary schools and later opened secondary schools, but the *Caracol* of Oventik decided to start with a secondary school instead, with the idea that it could train primary school promoters as well as enrich other autonomous projects. There were intensive collective mobilizations in every zone to build their respective education system, probably more so than for any other autonomous area. The results are astonishing. In 2013, just the Highlands, one of the five Zapatista zones, has 157 autonomous primary schools where 496 promoters instructed 4,886 students.[11]

Beyond the numbers, it is important to highlight the many actors involved in this mobilization for education: teachers and students, zone-level coordination groups, parents, community assemblies, education commissions within the autonomous municipalities and the Good Government Councils, and commissions within the EZLN, just to name a few. Being an education promoter is a duty (*cargo*) similar to the other responsibilities in the communities but it is not restricted to a limited period of time like the rest. The position is taken up as a service to one's community, and in turn this community takes responsibility for providing for the promoters' basic needs. It is therefore not a paid position. The community takes control over the education process through their assemblies, which are an essential space for interacting with the promoters. This is where the community and the promoters reciprocally make commitments to each other, where they work out their pedagogical approach, where they advise the promoter, and resolve the difficulties that are sure to arise.[12] Generally speaking, the most important achievement of autonomous education has been to get everyone, or almost everyone, involved in building an emergent educational experience, one that—within the struggle for autonomy—is permanently being reinvented and transformed. One way to say it is that autonomous education is education from us, for us, and by us.

The Zapatista educational experience does not entirely avoid reproducing conventional pedagogical models. It does not attempt to critique schooling itself or opt for deschooled learning. Instead, the community and heads of families look to appropriate the traditional model of schooling, both reproducing and reformulating it. However, the Zapatistas' practice is also an incisive subversion of this model. First of all, Zapatista schools radically distance themselves from the state's education system, in which teachers are typically not Indigenous and, when they come into this world, work to reproduce the discrimination characteristic of Mexico's internal colonialism. Furthermore, neoliberal reforms have subjected education to economic imperatives and the logic of modernization, turning it into a tool for the Mexico above to impose its will on the Mexico below, and especially for their ethnocidal destruction of the world of Indigenous communities. Contrary to this, autonomous education stems from the peoples' own life itself, which is rooted both in the communities' realities and in the Zapatista struggle to create other worlds.

Because education promoters interact closely with community assemblies, and because the communities directly involve themselves in moving the project along, education can arise from communities' life instead of contradicting it. We see evidence of this collaboration in the way the academic calendar is adapted to the rhythms of collective life. For example, breaks will coincide with the coffee harvest, which requires the participation of all family members, including children. Another example is the way learning comes from concrete reality, including the local environment, local health concerns, community values, the Zapatista struggle, and specific situations where mathematics, reading, and writing are needed. Most importantly, education is not separated from other forms of learning that occur in the communities, such as participation in assemblies. All this shows that there is no contradiction—but rather an interconnection—between learning in school and learning outside of it. This breaks with the classical model of education, where the school aspires to monopolize legitimate knowledge. If the school arises from the community, it will not forget that the community is also a school.

Another dimension relates to the role of education promoters. They are entrusted with the education task but with a very partial specialization. They are called "promoters" and not "teachers" because they are not considered specialists or professionals.[13] They still work the land to some extent and share the way of life of the rest of their community. Moreover, most are quite young, and their initial training is relatively brief, which ends up minimizing the distance between promoters and their students.[14] Finally, because autonomous education is hardly institutionalized and because of the many difficulties it must navigate, the work of teaching is constantly being reformulated. Nonetheless, this process of de-specializing and de-professionalizing education is a key to the Zapatistas subverting the conventional model.

Autonomous education is profoundly intercultural, despite not explicitly invoking this concept. Its basis is in the community's life itself, in its Indigenous languages and cultural practices, and yet it refuses to remain trapped within these dimensions. However, the Indigenous and the community are not its only horizons, since the Zapatista struggle has a national perspective as well as a planetary one. It takes up Mexican history as its own, while also joining in solidarity with the struggles of all the peoples of the world. It understands capitalism as a global, historical phenomenon and seeks to name all the different forms of domination suffered by humanity. It also valorizes and defends its own way of life and enthusiastically opens toward the other. Because of all this, the task of autonomous education is to confront and connect with different cultures, particularly between the Indigenous cosmovision and scientific knowledge.[15] In chapter 4 we will return to the dual task of reclaiming one's own roots and opening toward the other, as a part of an emancipatory project involving both Indigenous and non-Indigenous perspectives, the national and international, the struggle to build a world where many worlds fit.

Finally, it is important to recognize the difficulties autonomous education confronts. Building their system required considerable effort, undertaken with limited resources. While we should appreciate how the communities have mobilized around the project and the intense commitment of the education promoters, we should not ignore their difficulties. Now and again, the community does not follow through. The result is sometimes from a lack of commitment to education and sometimes simply because of a lack of resources. At times, following through is not even enough, especially when the promoters themselves have children. Other times their duties begin to feel like an excessive burden, as some begin to feel that they lack the training and experience needed to confront all the difficulties of teaching. Though promoters have a deep sense of responsibility, are supported by the people across the collective project for autonomous education, and are committed to contributing to the common struggle, occasionally they quit as a result of these difficulties.[16] If they reach this situation, many promoters are ashamed, believing that they have risked or setback the progress of autonomy. However, we can also see an advantage here: After a while, former education promoters might take on positions in other autonomous projects where their experience proves to be useful. This amounts to an unplanned rotation of tasks, reducing the dangers of specialization and the fossilization of the teaching corps, while also allowing for the wisdom acquired through teaching to be more broadly diffused and shared.

Despite the difficulties, autonomous education has had considerable success, building a self-determined educational system grounded in the collective effort of the promoters and the communities. It radically subverts the conventional model of schooling by collectively appropriating it, rooting it in community life, inventing new ways of teaching, and reinscribing it within anti-capitalist, autonomous, transformative, and liberatory struggle. Its greatest achievement is the generations of young people who have been raised in Zapatista schools. The communities' mobilization to build education has allowed them to benefit from the youth's rebellious energy. They are a new generation whose subjectivities are very different from previous ones, and that knows how to affirm its adhesion to the Zapatista struggle and its desire to transform it constantly.

Women's struggles and the transformation of gender relations

The transformation of women's lives is an essential dimension of the Zapatista struggle, not some secondary concern. Here we can see clearly how building autonomy means creating new ways of living, in the most concrete, everyday sense. Zapatista women's struggles date back much longer than the turn toward strengthening autonomy in 2003. Indeed, they began before the armed rebellion. For example, the Women´s Revolutionary Law—which Zapatista women and men consider to be a revolution within the revolution—was passed in 1993. The law was the result of many years of hard work, during which women leaders of the EZLN—like Comandanta Ramona and others—brought together Zapatista women's reflections (*la palabra*) on their situation and their demands, successfully legitimizing an explicitly gendered struggle within the organization.

Indigenous women's oppression in Chiapas was astounding, both on the *fincas*—where the landowners imposed absolute power (including the power to rape)—and in the communities—where, as Comandante David recognized during the San Andrés dialogues, "Among Indigenous people, as in other places, women's position is greatly inferior to men's. In Mexico, we, the men, are very *machista* and we don't consider women's circumstances. We don't want to give them the place they deserve in history. We don't want to allow them to fully participate in society."[17] Therefore, among the Women's Revolutionary Law's ten points are the right to freely choose a partner and the number of children one wants to bear, the prohibition of any form of domestic violence, the right to education, and the right to equal participation in all *cargos* and at every level of EZLN structure. All these were changes that opened a process of radical transformation in Indigenous women's lives.

The effects of their participation in the Zapatista struggle were first seen in the army. For many women, joining the insurgent troops was a way to escape the predetermined destiny of a forced marriage and uninterrupted pregnancies. Yet life in the camps had its own challenges. As Subcomandante Marcos explains, "Living in the mountains and serving as troop commanders, women were met with resistance from most male insurgents, who didn't want to take orders from a woman. . . . Invariably, men felt that they could lead better than their commander, if that 'it' was a 'she.'"[18] But this resistance did not stop women from taking on the highest responsibilities within the EZLN. Many communiques pay tribute to women rebels, like Major Ana María, who led the takeover of San Cristóbal de Las Casas on January 1, 1994, or some years later, when Maribel also rose to that same rank, commanding one of the five Zapatista zones. These women's prominent roles—together with the everyday determination of many other insurgent women, have been fundamental in transforming the position of women throughout the Zapatista experience.

The role of the *comandantas* is also notable. These are members of the Indigenous Clandestine Revolutionary Committee, the EZLN's political leadership body. Comandanta Ramona was an emblematic member and the only woman in the Zapatista delegation during the Cathedral Dialogues in San Cristobal de las Casas. Women's participation was more extensive during the San Andrés dialogues beginning the following year, including *comandantas* such as Trinidad, Andrea, Susana, Leticia, and Hortensia, among others. In 2001, at the closing of the March of the Color of the Earth, Comandanta Esther delivered the principal EZLN message from the podium of Congress. She underscored the triple oppression someone like her faces as a poor person, an Indigenous person, and as a woman.

Women's participation has grown during later events organized by the EZLN. For example, in May 2015 Comandantas Miriam, Rosalinda, and Dalia—accompanied by the youth Lizbeth and Selena—participated in the seminar entitled "Critical Thought in the Face of the Capitalist Hydra." In his intervention, appropriately entitled "The Vision of the Vanquished," Subcomandante Galeano expressed the male perspective on Zapatista women's struggles, commenting on both men's resistance to women's advancement and their ultimate defeat. He said that "In reviewing our history, I see it was marked by a defeat. . . . It must be made clear that [the women] fought against us and that they defeated us."[19] Another significant moment was the International Encounter of Women Who Struggle, held in the *Caracol* of Morelia in March 2018. Men were prohibited from attending, but more importantly, it was exclusively organized by Zapatista women—a decisive confirmation of their collective capabilities as women.

Beyond their participation in the liberation army, in EZLN leadership, and in grand public events, women are integrated into every level of government and area of autonomous activity. This integration was given special attention in the Little School with one of its textbooks especially dedicated to "Women's Participation in Autonomous Government." In it, women emphasize both the advances that have allowed them to play a larger role in the municipal and Good Government Councils, as well as the obstacles they still confront. They repeatedly note that women often try to refuse when called upon to participate in self-government. Sometimes this is because they anticipate their husbands will disapprove, and sometimes it is because they see themselves as incapable because they cannot read and write or for fear of speaking in public—a fear that is reinforced by men who mock or denigrate them when they do participate in an assembly or a meeting.[20] In addition to working to change men's attitudes, there are also efforts to overcome the reluctance of women themselves. A woman who formerly served on the *Junta* relates that, "There are times when the *compañera* herself doesn't want to do it. She says, 'I can't.'"[21] So they look for concrete solutions, such as putting two women in the same position so that they can help each other and boost each other's confidence.[22] Transforming perceptions internalized over a long history of oppression requires similarly long-term work. Two strategies have been fundamental here. There are women's collectives that run stores, farm, produce artisanry, etc. Beyond allowing women to learn to organize on their own and have their own resources, they are also spaces for building confidence and for collective reflection on their situation. As well, autonomous education plays a key role in transforming the collective understanding of women's roles. Youth gain an understanding of gender relations that differs greatly from that of former generations—not only through lessons and discussions in the classroom but also by seeing how the male and female promoters interact with one another.

Finally, on the occasion of the Little School, Zapatista women explained the extent to which the struggle has transformed gender relations in daily life. Despite some resistance from elders, the custom of parents arranging marriages, often at an early age, has been abandoned and consent is now the norm. However, they also complain that many women still marry quite young, when they would be better off studying and training.[23] In terms of birth control, progress seems to be more uneven. They say that "there are women who still have a ton of children," but there are also "some families nowadays that understand what the consequences are later, when they can't care for the family."[24] And, although younger generations clearly have fewer children than their parents and grandparents, for Zapatista women these sorts of decisions must be made together with their partners. Domestic violence has reduced considerably—though not completely—as a result of women's adamant demand that alcohol be completely prohibited in Zapatista territories. They write that "Incidents still occur in our communities because bad customs and habits still contaminate men's heads. *Machismo* continues to exist. Some still think, 'I am stronger and you must respect me.'"[25] The difference now is that, in such cases, women know they have every right to approach the autonomous justice bodies and that their situation will be addressed with care.

Women's political participation and their responsibilities within autonomy have caused important changes within families. Initially men were resistant to letting their wives attend meetings and assemblies, but this attitude is now openly condemned (some husbands continue nonetheless). Women's responsibilities—especially regarding health, education, the municipal and Good Government Councils—often require them to be absent from home for one or two weeks at a time, leaving their husbands no other option but to take on the housework and childcare. While some men push back, most accept what just a few years earlier would have been considered an unbearable transgression against what were perceived as traditional gender roles.

These changes are synthesized into a painting created by a collective of male and female education promoters in Oventik and presented at the Morelia *caracol* during CompArte 2018. In the center is an enormous double spiral conch shell, containing several symbols of daily life in autonomy: A man and a woman emerge symmetrically from the shell's mouth, each holding their own staff (*bastón de mando*), because—as the explanation accompanying the painting says—"both have the right to govern, not only men, but also women." While the woman wields a machete in her other hand, the man carries a tortilla maker. The painting inverts the objects traditionally associated with each gender, because "both have the freedom and right to do something in the fields and at home, so there is not a division of labor."[26]

Despite significant obstacles still to be overcome, there have been radical changes in a relatively short period of time. Raising consciousness about women's rights and the recognition of their dignity and ability to participate in all aspects of autonomy have led to widespread, concrete changes in the roles and responsibilities of family and community life. Moreover, there is an even deeper transformation in the younger generations who, thanks to this struggle, can now develop the full potential of their personalities without fear. This is particularly true for the newest generation—not those born right before or after the uprising, but the children of those who were born then, who are today barely a few years old. Subcomandante Galeano depicts this generation, in all its unbound potential, through the figure of Defensa Zapatista, the young girl who is the protagonist of his more recent writings. The Subcomandante admonishes Defensa's playmate Pedrito, saying "What we must do is warn Pedrito that the Zapatista women he'll be dealing with in a few years will be even more *other*, and that it wouldn't hurt to adopt a defensive position."[27]

Two additional observations: Zapatista women did not learn to fight because they discovered feminist thought but it was from their own desire to escape from their crushing conditions of oppression. Their practices and ways of seeing differ in many ways from the various waves of feminism that are rooted in urban worlds and whose thought emerges from modernity. Their fight as women is not limited to the rights of the individual as such but is instead articulated around the collective rights of communities. Above all, Zapatista women insist that the struggle is for both women and men, saying, "It is very important that not only women participate, but also men."[28] One aspect of this assertion is that gender relations can only change if men actively participate in the process, and it also means that the struggle for equality between men and women cannot be disconnected from the common struggle for emancipation.

For Zapatista women, the struggle for gender equality is neither more nor less important than the anticapitalist struggle as a whole; the two simply cannot be separated.

Finally, the Zapatista women's struggle relates to tradition in a particular way. While men often invoke tradition to justify their resistance to the changes brought by women and to preserve their privileges, women have been more open to changing supposedly intransigent traditions. Taking to the podium of Mexico's Congress, Comandanta Esther spoke in the name of Indigenous women when she said that, "We, women, know which customs and traditions are good and which are bad."[29] For these women, it is not about rejecting the bases for the community but instead sustaining it while also profoundly transforming it. This is a fundamental aspect of autonomy, that it is not the continuation of an existing form of life but an ongoing construction now in the making. In fact, the transformation of gender relations is one of autonomy's most notable aspects, manifested in the most personal and everyday aspects of their forms of life. We might even say that autonomy is the invention of a new life—and there is no doubt that women have even more reasons than men to fight for it.

Leaving the world of money?

Despite knowing full well that it is still not possible to fully escape from the reality of the capitalist system, the Zapatistas fight day after day to deepen and defend forms of life that, at their core, are not fundamentally determined by capitalism. Here, I want to focus on their relation to money. The denunciation of the world of money is omnipresent in the Zapatista word.[30] For example, during a meeting at the Zapatista Little School a teacher showed us two bags, one with corn and the other with coins. The lesson was that the first signified life; the second, death.

Zapatista men and women clearly understand what is needed for the rebel territories to become a world fully liberated from capitalist barbarism, which surrounds them, attacks them, and tries—by every possible means—to put an end to their antisystemic project. My votán—the "guardian" in charge of me during my stay at the Little School—was clear about this outside pressure while also emphasizing autonomy's achievements. He said, "Can we say that we are outside the system? No, we can't. We are still living within the system, so we need money, for now."[31] In fact, money continues to be indispensable for accessing some necessary capitalist commodities that they do not yet have the capacity to make through their own productive activity (which is to say there are some capitalist means of production that are not completely destructive and superfluous—means of production that, for now, are still in capitalists' hands). But it is important to emphasize that the "for now" of my *votán* charts a path toward a world without money, a world in which money, as a universal equivalent, will cease to be necessary.

Meanwhile, there is a process of relative de-monetization within Zapatista autonomy, which favors collective practices and forms of organizing that do not require money. Subcomandante Moisés notes that "rarely do we handle money."[32] Most importantly, the autonomous health and education systems described previously function without resorting to salaries. In both areas, promoters complete their tasks without pay, but they can count on the community's commitment to guarantee that their food and other basic needs are met. This happens in various ways. For example, if an education promoter has their own *milpa*, community members will maintain it while the promoter is occupied with teaching.[33] There are slightly different situations in each zone's clinics, but the health promoters are similarly supported through collective work arrangements.[34] It is also important to underscore that—because it is carried out by the students and promoters themselves—administrative and maintenance work in schools is also de-specialized.

The same holds true for the work in autonomous self-government that we will discuss later in the chapter. Because those who hold these *cargos*—whether at a community level, on the municipal councils, or in the Good Government Councils—do not receive a wage or any other sort of material support, there is a great difference between them and those with positions in the Mexican constitutional political system. Even members of local governments in rural areas make as much as one hundred times the minimum wage. Meanwhile, the Zapatistas remind us that autonomous authorities "don't work for money but out of commitment."[35] Overall, then, the autonomous political system manages to function without resorting to salaries and with barely any money—in radical contrast to the colossal expenses the constitutional Mexican system incurs each time it holds elections, among many other costs.

We will also see below that autonomous justice is imparted totally free of charge, without using money even to pay fines (a type of penalty that has been completely done away with). The Zapatistas explain that, in the hundreds of cases resolved through autonomous justice, there is always a better solution than those involving money. They explicitly say that autonomous justice is about finding "non-economic" solutions.[36]

How can they do this? First, autonomous governments carry out their tasks in a simple manner, without relying on a large body of professional bureaucrats. This is only possible because they reject the absurd complexity of a world dominated by the abstractions of value and the state, and concentrate on the problems that really have to do with the organization of collective life. Secondly, autonomy can work without paying salaries because it works through a process of de-specializing politics. Those who hold office (*cargo*) continue with their usual productive activities during this time and do not require collective funds for their personal or family upkeep. However, autonomous government does have certain expenses. Those most frequently mentioned are transportation (from their communities to the seat of the autonomous government, or for traveling to evaluate a situation or a project). These costs are negligible, laughable when compared to the budgets of constitutional governments, but at the humble scale of life in Indigenous communities, even these costs are high and impossible to cover individually. Thus, one of the functions of the collective work described above is to cover the costs generated by autonomous government.

To sum up, the education, health, justice, and self-government projects within Zapatista autonomy have all enjoyed significant success without resorting to wage labor or other monetized forms, instead prioritizing contributions from collective work. This does not mean that Zapatista communities do not need money, nor does it deny that they face significant challenges, especially due the lack of monetary and productive resources.[37] It does mean that they have found—through the power (*potencia*) of their own activity—the most significant support for collectively determined forms of life. Compare this with the situation of *campesinos* who accept government programs, especially counterinsurgent ones that promote dependence on monetary handouts. Suffice it to say that a considerable part of the handouts from programs such as *Oportunidades* (state-run social assistance) end up paying for junk food and cellphones. The programs themselves are schools of consumption, strengthening a dependency on money that cannot be satisfied by traditional agriculture. This in turn encourages market-based agriculture or migration in search of wages.

It is a battle to build autonomy, and this battle pits the community's vitality—forms of life they have defined and strengthened autonomously, by their own activity—against that which still eludes them, since all the means of production are controlled by the world of capital. The struggle is a process of walking away from the world of money, from the economy. Autonomy means escaping from the productivist mandate, the logic of quantification, and from competitive subjectivities. As such, it is a concrete way of preserving an ethics of living well (*buen vivir*), which the Zapatistas usually call "a dignified life" and sometimes "a good life."[38] It is an ethics that privileges the qualitative aspects of life, that cannot comprehend individual existence outside of its relation with the collective and with Mother Earth, that manages to break free from the coercion of the abstract and increasingly accelerated time of the capitalist world.

Organization of autonomous government

The three levels of government and autonomous justice

Political organization in the autonomous territories brings together these three levels: the communities, the autonomous rebel municipalities (MAREZ in Spanish, of which there are twenty-seven, each containing dozens of communities), and the zones (each of which includes between three and seven autonomous municipalities).[39] At each level there are assemblies and corresponding authorities who are designated for two or three years and responsible for carrying out the assemblies' decisions. The [municipal] agent corresponds to the community assembly; the municipal council corresponds to the municipal assembly; and the Good Government Council corresponds to the assembly of the zone. The practice of holding community assemblies is deeply rooted in Indigenous tradition, and exists among non-Zapatistas as well. The governing structures of the autonomous municipalities exist alongside the official municipal institutions and, in fact, the autonomous municipalities and the constitutionally recognized or "official" ones coexist in more or less the same territories (but sometimes with slightly distinct boundaries). Finally, the *Juntas* are a distinctive innovation of Zapatista autonomy, created in 2003.

Besides coordinating the activities and projects of the various municipalities, the *Juntas* are the conduit between Zapatista territories and the outside world. They are open to receive the appeals of both Zapatistas and non-Zapatistas seeking to resolve problems, and they also receive visitors looking to learn more about autonomy. They work to ensure coexistence between Zapatistas and non-Zapatistas, and they try to resolve conflicts provoked by the constitutional (i.e., official government) authorities—all within a context of incessant counterinsurgency operations. The projects of the different areas of autonomy (health, education, communication, production, etc.) are coordinated by their respective collectives, and they are supported by both the Good Government and the municipal councils as they work toward (always needed) improvements. The councils—working together with the assemblies—are generally responsible for the following: proposing new projects to help cope with the difficulties of collective life; promoting the participation of women and addressing obstacles to it; and defending the territories, preserving the environment, as well as improving their own productive capacities.

The autonomous authorities also maintain their own civil registry—a record of births, deaths, and marriages—and it is their responsibility to impart justice, at all three levels.[40] This work is done by the agent or community assembly, ensuring it remains as close as possible to everyday life in the community. If they are unable to resolve the situation, and especially when there are repeat offenses, the matter is passed on to the municipality or to the *Junta*. This also happens when the situation involves people from different communities or municipalities, or a dispute between Zapatistas and non-Zapatistas. Community-level problems taken up by autonomous justice include the theft of chickens or other animals, conflicts about the boundaries between parcels of land, illegal logging, prohibited sale of wild animals or fish, drunkenness, domestic violence, and divorce. Theft and agrarian disputes are examples of more serious issues that would be brought to the municipal level. The municipal authorities also intervene in their territories to stop drug and lumber trafficking. The *Juntas* take up problems that cannot be resolved at the municipal level, very exceptional issues such as homicide as well as any tensions that arise with members of other organizations. When the hostility of the state and federal governments prevents a local situation from being resolved through autonomous justice, the *Junta* may instead choose to issue a public denunciation.

Beyond operating without fees or corruption, autonomous justice differs from official justice in its very logic. It is a justice of mediation that brings the parties together, listens to them, investigates if necessary, and encourages them to reach an agreement that will permit a reconciliation and restore the conditions of community life. As one Zapatista said, "Here, there's mediation. You can talk, investigate, ask both parties, and there's reconciliation." What happens is "just reasoning with people, taking them into account, and investigating their problem," so that "both parties end up in agreement . . . and the issue is resolved." The mediating role of the authorities is important because their legitimacy acts as a powerful incentive to reach an agreement. The idea is not so much about determining crimes and punishments but rather recognizing errors and problems that harm the fabric of community life, and finding solutions to heal the wound. In the words of those who impart it, autonomous justice is all about "how to resolve problems, so as to arrive at a good and peaceful solution." Therefore, Zapatista justice implies a radical critique of the prison, since prison solves nothing and just adds more problems on top of those that already exist. (It affects the lives of the entire family, and besides, prison is simply a school for crime.) Though they may decide to detain someone while an accusation against them is being investigated, or if they seem to be dangerous (mostly when the person is intoxicated), incarceration as a punishment does not exist. Following a logic of reconciliation, they seek to *repair* the harm, accepted as such by the victim(s). This implies restitution or, when this is not possible, "repairing the damage" in a non-monetary way, such as via workdays for the victims (or for the community when it is the affected party). For example, in the case of homicide, the guilty party cedes land to the family of the deceased or commits to work for them for several years. It is worth mentioning the exceptional-yet-significant case of a Guatemalan migrant trafficker (*coyote*) who was arrested by the autonomous authorities. He was sentenced to a few months of community work, participating in the construction of a bridge to access the San José del Río hospital, and once he finished, he thanked the Zapatistas for having taught him the craft of an *albañil*.[41]

In summary, autonomous justice is based on mediation and seeks an agreement among the parties to restore the possibility of collective life. In contrast with the inefficiency, impunity, and corruption that characterize Mexican official justice, it makes sense that many non-Zapatistas prefer to bring their issues there. It is decisively better because, as well as never involving money, its autonomous authorities operate on the basis of their knowledge of life in the Indigenous communities. More broadly, Zapatista autonomy is an example of the radical de-specialization of the administration of justice. Far from the ritualized, highly specialized, extremely codified justice of the state, autonomous justice is imparted by ordinary people who have no specific training or experience in this area, and yet they manage to fulfill the task to the benefit of their communities. The state's justice, draped in the solemnity of its institutions, separates itself from its citizens so that it may better subordinate and impose its authority over those who are subject to its procedures. Autonomous justice remains immanent and rooted in the simplicity of ordinary action. On the one hand, collective bodies endowed with legitimacy are needed for mediation. On the other hand, the burdensome, oppressive apparatus of Law and state justice may be eliminated, reincorporating the resolution of "problems" into the fabric of collective life.

Authorities and assemblies

Zapatista autonomy is characterized by its articulation of assemblies and authorities. Assemblies are fundamental (without implying that absolutely everything is decided horizontally), and the authorities, it is said, "govern by obeying" them. The interaction between the two is different at each level. In the community, the assembly is particularly important. All men and women participate, and even the youngest children attend. The youth have a voice there from an early age—in some zones as early as twelve years old, and by fifteen or sixteen, they participate in decision making.[42] The assemblies meet frequently to deal with community affairs, while the agent carries out their decisions and functions as a liaison with the municipal authorities. At the municipal and zone levels, the assemblies meet less frequently, which means the role of the municipal and Good Government Councils becomes more important.

As for the relationships between the assembly and authorities at the zone level, the Good Government Council can make certain decisions on specific issues or act in emergency situations, but for more important issues (especially concerning the projects in the distinct areas of health, education, agroecology, etc.) it is necessary to consult the zone's general assembly. This assembly is considered the maximum authority in each zone, and it meets for several days every two or three months and calls extraordinary assemblies when necessary. The assembly includes all the municipal authorities of the region, representatives of the communities, and those responsible for the various areas of autonomy. Sometimes, the assembly makes decisions and instructs the *Junta* to carry them out, but if it concerns important projects, or if they do not reach a clear agreement, the issue has to be returned to the communities for consultation.[43] Then it is the job of the representatives to gather the opinions of their respective communities, ensuring that their agreement, rejection, or proposals for modifications are taken into account in the next assembly. If necessary, the assembly debates and elaborates a new proposal that is again sent back to the communities. Various comings and goings may be necessary before a project, a regulation, or a work plan is fully approved. This procedure is not always respected, as there are instances when the *Juntas* have made decisions without sufficient consultation. According to the teacher Fidel, "A plan that isn't analyzed and debated by the communities will fail. This has happened to us," he admits. That is why "now all projects are discussed and debated."[44]

This sort of decision making is based on the principle of governing by obeying (*mandar obedeciendo*), which requires multiple interactions between numerous governing bodies. There are various commissions, including the supervisory commission (*comisión de vigilancia*), which is responsible for verifying the accounts of the Good Government Council each month and then completing a more thorough review every year or six months. It is also important to highlight the role of the Clandestine Revolutionary Indigenous Committee alongside the *Juntas*.[45] During their first years, it seemed from the outside that the *Juntas* were the maximum governing bodies in each of the autonomous zones, but they are part of a web of multiple governing bodies. The teacher Marisol explains, "We trust in the *Junta,* but to be certain we have to be vigilant."[46] She expresses a clear awareness of the risks of separation (and possibly of substitution) inherent in any delegation of collective decision making capacity. This is even true when dealing with a government of the people, one that emanates from them, whose authorities are not remunerated for carrying out their responsibilities, who are revocable, and who understand their work as a service to the collectivity. In fact, any body that concentrates decision-making, even if it is partial, controlled, and temporary, can fall into the temptation to make decisions without always sufficiently consulting—even if this is only for lack of time and energy.[47] Therefore, an important tool in the ever-present struggle against the potential failures of self-government is to create many, complementary, interacting governing bodies.

We must now shift toward considering how they conceive the role of the authorities. Their mandates are called *cargos*: a responsibility taken up as a service to the community, without remuneration. No one nominates themselves for these positions; the communities nominate those they consider capable of exercising them. They take on these responsibilities in an ethic of service to the collectivity, an ethic synthesized into the seven principles of governing by obeying, which each contrast service with coercive notions of power. They include "serve others, don't serve yourself," "look below, not above," "propose, don't impose," and "convince, don't defeat." They articulate what is very much a lived ethic, rooted in the experience of the communities, whose members know that they cannot exist unless everyone contributes to their reproduction. In this sense, to take on a responsibility is an active way of making the community. Besides, the *cargos* are always carried out by a team and without much specialization. They are under the control of the commissions mentioned above and the population as a whole, since their terms of office are not renewable and their mandates are revocable at any moment "if the authorities don't do their work well."

Another important element is that those who exercise a mandate (*mandato*) continue to participate as ordinary members of their communities.[48] They do not consider their selection to be evidence of their superior capacities or extraordinary personal talents. Zapatistas can truly say that those on the *Juntas* "aren't specialists in anything, let alone in politics."[49] This nonspecialization means that authority is exercised from a position of "not knowing." The members of the councils and the *Juntas* are quick to acknowledge that they do not know how to carry out the task that is delegated to them. ("No one is an expert in politics, and we all have to learn.") Furthermore, they insist that governing from a position of "not knowing" is what allows someone to be a "good authority"—a person whose authority is exercised through listening and learning from everyone, knowing how to recognize their own errors, and allowing the community to guide them in the carrying out of decisions. In the Zapatista experience, entrusting tasks to those who have no training in governing is the concrete basis on which "governing by obeying" can flourish. It is also a strong defense against the danger of a distance between rulers and the ruled.

Governing by obeying and a non-alienated mode of delegation

Now we can try and close in on the meaning of "governing by obeying." It may come as a surprise that the relationship of authority to the people continues to be defined in terms of "governing" and "obeying," maintaining a dichotomy that the logic of self-government should dissolve. However, governing by obeying implies a paradoxical conjunction of two relationships (governing/obeying) that, when combined, subverts the meaning of each: The authorities can only govern to the extent that they obey the will of the communities. The government does not exercise "power-over," it cannot impose its own decisions, cannot override the will of the people. Nor can we speak of a true separation between the government and the people if it is the people who decide, and the authorities simply carry out their decisions, acting as the mere instrument of their self-government. This disconcerting formulation of "governing by obeying" is incompatible with state power, as the state is a mechanism of separation that dispossesses the collective of their capacity to organize and decide, concentrating that expropriated power within an apparatus or group acting according to their own interests.

On the other hand, the principle of governing by obeying demands we discard purely horizontalist readings of Zapatista autonomy, instead recognizing that not all decisions are made in assemblies, and that the role of authorities is indeed important. The Little School's teachers emphasized this point when they clarified the basic definition of governing by obeying, saying "There is a moment when the people lead and the government obeys, and there is a moment when the people obey and the government leads."[50] These two opposing relationships are not completely separate, yet one side or the other predominates in different moments: The government *obeys* because it must consult and then do what the people request; the government *leads* because it must carry out and ensure compliance with the decisions that have been agreed upon through collective deliberation. Also, in urgent situations, it must take measures without being able to consult; for example, when responding to the conflict with the Mexican state and the paramilitary groups it fosters.

The role of the authorities is taken on as a duty of oversight and initiative. According to the Little School teacher Jacobo, "The authorities take the lead. They orient and motivate, but they don't decide or impose. It's the people who decide."[51] While the municipal and Good Government Councils can only implement what has been debated and approved by the assemblies, we cannot ignore or underestimate the special role of the authorities in the elaboration of these decisions. This role probably extends beyond the first moment when a new initiative is proposed. Throughout the ensuing process, there remains a certain asymmetry between those who promote the projects they have proposed, and those who may discuss, modify, and even reject a proposal but without putting in the same effort as the authorities.

We should recognize the specific role of those who the collective temporarily entrusts with the task of "being an authority"—an authority without authoritarianism. They should not impose but instead motivate, acting as the pivot that allows for strengthening the capacity for collective action. Therefore, it is not a "power-over" that a segment of the collective hoards and wields over the rest, nor is it a perfect horizontality that risks dissolving due to lack of initiatives or the capacity to materialize them.[52] My observation of the Zapatista experience, as it has developed until now, reveals a tension between two log-ics: On the one hand, decision-making capacity fundamentally resides in the assemblies; on the other, those who take on a rotating, revocable *cargo* have the duty to initiate and promote projects, and in this way mediate between the collectivity and their capacity for self-government. There is a double risk here, of doing all this either too much or not enough.

Finally, governing by obeying entails a very "other" conception of delega-tion. To understand it, we can contrast forms of delegation that are alienated forms (*disociativo*) with those that are not (or are to the least extent possible). Alienated forms are those that, together with other aspects of social reality, reproduce a *separation* between the governing and the governed, between the dominating and the dominated, and seize collective power (*potencia*) for the benefit of the former. This is how classic forms of representation operate in the modern state. Even democracy (today's market variety) works method-ically to organize the effective absence of the represented. It is a device for dispossessing the people of their collective capacity to organize themselves and decide, in order to concentrate this "power-over" within a separate group and a bureaucratic apparatus. As for unalienated forms of rule, although they involve delegation (it is not a question of pure, direct democracy), they seek to limit, as far as possible, the separation between the rulers and ruled instead of consolidating it. To this end, they strive to implement concrete mechanisms to prevent this alienation and keep the effective use of collective power-to (*poten-cia*) in the hands of all.

That said, we should be clear about how the alienated and nonalienated modes of delegation differ. The Zapatista experience highlights the follow-ing attributes: short mandates that are not renewable and revocable at any moment; a lack of personalization by exercising positions together as a team; reviews conducted by other levels of self-government; limiting the concen-tration of decision-making authority; an ethic of collectivity; and the ability to listen. Above all, the effective de-specialization of political tasks is crucial. Instead of being hoarded by a specific group (be it the political class, a mon-eyed caste, or personalities that amass a certain prestige), they must have the widest circulation possible. As the Zapatistas say, "We must all take our turn being the government."[53] As mentioned earlier, this means refusing to select authorities based on an evaluation of their individual abilities. Instead, the (quite challenging) precondition for the full de-specialization of politics is to assume that the authorities do not know (much) more than anyone else.[54]

Moreover, this "not knowing" makes it even more important that the authorities know how to listen and consult: The fact that those who govern do not have any more governing ability than anyone else is the basis for governing by obeying and establishes one of the strongest defenses against the danger of separation of the rulers from the ruled.

Another decisive condition to avoid this danger is to prevent the authorities' way of life from starting to differ from the rest. For this reason the members of the Good Government Councils (located in the *Caracoles*, regional centers that may be quite far from the villages where members of the Council live) carry out their work in ten or fifteen-day rotations. This helps minimize the interruption to their everyday activities, so they can continue attending to their families and land. It is an indispensable condition for guaranteeing the general accessibility of political work and for preventing a separation between ordinary life and the lifestyles of those who assume a particular role in the organization of collective life, if even for a brief time and in a restricted way.

There is always a risk that the alienation between rulers and the ruled reappears. A genuine politics of autonomy depends on the practical mechanisms it must continually invent to fight against this tendency and maintain a dispersion of the functions of authority. Clearly the differentiation between alienated and nonalienated forms of delegation is never complete, but it is an important distinction, nonetheless. We could even argue that herein lies the key difference between a state politics based on the dispossession of collective "power-to" and its crystallization as "power-over" on the one hand, and on the other a non-state politics that does not alienate the rulers from the ruled, instead striving to ensure that the exercise of authority remains a manifestation of the collective capacities of all.

Difficulties in the process of autonomy

While the Zapatistas value autonomy's progress, they refuse any sort of self-congratulatory posture. Although their experience may inspire other struggles, they refuse to offer it as a model, and they urge people not to idealize Zapatismo. It is impressive to see how much space in the Little School's textbooks is dedicated to difficulties, errors, and limits in the process of building autonomy.

Many of autonomy's foremost difficulties are consequences of the violent counterinsurgency they face. After the massive deployment of the federal army, followed by the most intense period of paramilitary activity between 1996 and 2000, less-visible yet equally pernicious forms have prevailed—all seeking to foment division and conflict within the communities. Exploiting the fact that the land recuperated by the EZLN has not been legally regularized and recognized, peasant groups and other organizations—with support from governmental authorities—invade these lands, destroying property and homes in an attempt to evict Zapatistas from their communities. Social programs, whose presence has increased in and around Zapatista territory, have also been used as a tool of counterinsurgency. They offer economic projects, houses, and other support to goad Zapatistas into leaving the organization (since the first rule of autonomy is to not accept any support from the "bad government").[55] Although the EZLN continually denounces the false promises and deceitful nature of government programs—which are designed to impose social control and de-structure peasant labor and community organization—they are nonetheless hard to resist. Moreover, another important difficulty that Zapatista women and men mention is their own lack of resources; although their domestic needs are met, autonomy presses on in permanent struggle against limited resources.[56] This struggle has not prevented autonomy's impressive achievements, which can be understood as the art of doing much with little, but it requires an enormous effort from the Zapatista support bases, which may generate a certain fragility.

Building autonomy within the context of a counterinsurgent siege, and with limited resources, is an arduous task. Zapatista men and women confront these difficulties with tenacity and a great deal of determination, with everyday heroism, sustained by their conviction in the justice of their cause, and by the satisfaction of creating by themselves the world that they want. There is also a notable element of joy in collective action, as well as a feeling of recovered dignity and pride in the successes of autonomy. However, there are cases where the burden of work feels unsustainable, given that tasks like domestic production, collective work, responsibilities in the commissions or as autonomous authorities, assemblies, and meetings of all kinds are always piling up. All this can even lead to illness, increasing exhaustion even more, to the point where people renounce their membership in the EZLN.[57]

The EZLN has openly admitted that there have been departures over the years.[58] There are various reasons: in addition to excessive fatigue, other factors can cause people to become discouraged, such as interpersonal conflict or other relationships that weaken one's feeling of belonging. For example, marrying a non-Zapatista is not incompatible with membership in the EZLN, but it can surely make it more difficult to reconcile the demands of the struggle with family life. Departures may have various consequences: While some former members develop openly anti-Zapatista attitudes, a good number of those who leave the organization maintain good relations with their former *compañeros*. More than a few continue to share the ideals of the Zapatista struggle and lament having to abandon it, and some even attempt to rejoin the organization later.[59] The departures need to be acknowledged, as well as the exhaustion—which is inevitable in a struggle lasting so many years and under such adverse circumstances. At the same time, this is offset by new generations growing up in Zapatista families.

Migration is another issue. Beginning in the year 2000 migration to the United States, which had scarcely existed in Chiapas previously, became a massive phenomenon. The Zapatistas were not immune to the "American dream" that was spreading among the youth in Indigenous communities. Besides questions of economic need, there is also the desire to experience other ways of living. At first, Zapatista leaders (*responsables*) considered migration to be a betrayal of the collective project. Later they assumed a more flexible posture, considering migration to be a temporary experience that, for practical reasons, required suspending the migrant's membership in the organization and reincorporating upon return. Simultaneously, and perhaps due to a better understanding of the journey's risks and the working and living conditions of the undocumented, it seems that northward migration is no longer as attractive.[60] Instead, another option for those suffering economic hardship—above all the youth without enough land—is short-term migration to the tourism centers of the Yucatan peninsula, for periods anywhere from a couple weeks to two or three months per year. In any case, the Zapatistas continue to analyze the consequences and extent of the problem.[61]

Now to return to the difficulties of autonomy itself, especially the practice of governing by obeying. We already mentioned various risks: making incorrect decisions, decisions lacking a sufficient basis in consensus, and a renewed separation between those who take on positions in government and the rest of the community members. When he affirms that "We must always stick close to the people," a former member of the Good Government Council recognizes that the opposite situation may occur. Instead of "sticking close," the government and the people can become divided.[62] A particularly serious case occurred in the autonomous municipality of San Andrés Sak'amch'en de los Pobres, which was one of the first formed in 1995. It is the only autonomous council that was able to install itself in what had formerly been the building of the official municipality in the center of the town. In this unique context the autonomous municipal council agreed to collaborate with the official authorities to remodel the central plaza (*zócalo*). The costs ended up being exorbitant and, above all, disconnected from the real needs of the communities.[63] Their error was denounced, those responsible were recalled, the San Andrés council was sanctioned, and for a few years they could not receive economic support for the municipality. While this case is exceptional, it is a reminder of just how severe mistakes can be within an autonomous self-government. There is no guarantee that mistakes won't happen: understanding *cargos* as a service to the collective is not a guarantee; nor are mechanisms for consulting the communities; nor the collegial nature of the municipal and Good Government Councils; nor the interactions between the various levels of autonomous government; and not even the existence of oversight commissions. Even if the capacity to propose projects and move them forward is carefully delegated to people with temporary and revocable positions, there is still the risk that those who take on these positions will distance themselves from the actual wishes of the people, despite having made a commitment to governing by obeying. No system of (self) government is without this risk. That is why it is necessary to know how to identify it, and to create mechanisms for fighting against it.

Another aspect to consider is the relation between the civil organization of autonomy and the political-military structure of the EZLN. In 2003, when the Good Government Councils were created, it was made clear that the autonomous governments are civilian bodies separated from the organizational structure of the EZLN, which is why neither military commanders nor the members of the Clandestine Revolutionary Indigenous Committee (CCRI) can occupy positions in autonomous government.[64] Despite this, in his report on the first year of the Good Government Councils, Subcomandante Marcos openly criticized the misguided interventions of the CCRI into matters of autonomy, writing, "Accompaniment has sometimes turned into management, advice into orders . . . and support into a hindrance. . . . The fact that the EZLN is a political-military and clandestine organization still corrupts processes that should and must be democratic. In some *Juntas* and *Caracoles* it has happened that CCRI *comandantes* take decisions that are not theirs to make and meddle in problems of the *Junta*. Governing by obeying is a tendency that keeps bumping into walls that we ourselves erect."[65]

There have been efforts to correct this situation and avoid imposing, and the report offered in the "Sixth Declaration of the Lacandon Jungle" is less severe ("The leadership of the EZLN no longer jumps in to give orders," and instead "accompanies and supports"). Ten years later, the situation had notably improved, and the Little School textbooks mention the presence of the CCRI *beside* the Councils: "They orient us. They don't give orders. They just support us."[66] This means that the *Juntas* are not subordinate to the political direction of the EZLN, but we should not minimize the role of the *comandantes* either. We can easily understand their importance if we consider the moral authority of the members of the CCRI, as well as the experience they have accumulated through so many years of political involvement.

It is therefore important to highlight the two structures that have sustained the advances of the Zapatista experience: one is the civil organization of autonomy; and the other is the EZLN as a political-military organization. While autonomy was being strengthened, especially since 2003, the power previously concentrated in the leadership of the EZLN was progressively returned to the Zapatista support bases and their self-government bodies. This project is still ongoing, and although its general orientation is clear, certain tensions remain. While autonomy is based on the principle of governing by obeying and seeks the broadest possible participation in decision making, it must also reckon with the openly vertical character of the EZLN as an organization. For example, the "Sixth Declaration of the Lacandon Jungle" recognizes that "the political-military part of the EZLN is not democratic, because it is an army." Therefore, building Zapatista autonomy has required articulating a vertical structure together with a more horizontal form of organization.[67] The change of balance between the EZLN as a political-military organization and the civilian organization of autonomy entails a progressive shift from the verticality of the chain of command toward more democratic forms. It is not easy to break with attitudes and practices forged during a long formation that is saturated in military discipline.[68] The building of autonomy has allowed for enormous advances in this regard, but this continues to be one of its biggest challenges, as it entails a process of collective re-education, internal democratization, and struggle against all forms of authoritarianism. It is a matter of extending the ability to "express opinions, study, analyze, propose, discuss, and decide" within every area, in a truly collective way, and without impositions.[69] The new generations of Zapatistas, who have not had to prepare for war and have grown up within autonomy, seem to be very capable of carrying this process forward and overcoming its obstacles so that, within all of autonomy's spaces, everyone feels that their lives are guided by their own decisions.

Despite the great difficulties, the advances of autonomy are extraordinary. They demonstrate that it is possible to immediately begin the work of building a reality distinct from that imposed under the rule of capital and the state. Zapatista autonomy opens up a space where we can breathe, amid the storm that is engulfing the entire planet. But the Zapatistas also clearly see the limits of what they have built. They know that autonomy is fragile and incomplete, as it faces the pressure that the capitalist system exerts against all attempts to escape its grasp. They know it is impossible to strengthen autonomy without the ability to resist all kinds of attacks. In fact, Zapatista autonomy would not have been possible without the armed uprising of January 1, 1994, and the territorial and political space it created. We cannot forget that autonomy, despite being a civilian process, continues to depend on the EZLN's capacity for self-defense. This was confirmed after the assassination of the teacher Galeano in May 2014, when the Good Government Council of La Realidad suspended activities and called on the EZLN to take command. That is why the Zapatistas insist that creating and resisting are two inseparable dimensions of the same process of autonomy.[70] Resisting without building something new is sterile, and it would be naive to believe it is possible to build another reality without having to defend it from systematic attacks.

Autonomy means experimenting with forms of self-government, following a logic of dispersion of political tasks. It seeks modes of delegation that avoid alienating (*disociación*) the governed from those who govern. It also means that the tasks of governing return to a scale that is infinitely smaller and with radically different characteristics than under government in the capitalist world. In fact, what is called "government" within Zapatista autonomy is an ensemble of tremendously modest tasks that are completely alien to modern governmentality (that is, the management of populations) and its arcane administrative structures. An astute observer might have been describing the activities of the Good Government Council when he wrote: "The whole sham of state-mysteries and state-pretensions was done away with by councils, mostly consisting of simple peasants . . . doing their work publicly, simply, under the most difficult and complicated circumstances . . . acting in broad daylight, with no pretensions to infallibility, not hiding themselves behind circumlocution offices, not ashamed to confess blunders by correcting them. Making the public functions—military, political, administrative—into real community functions, instead of the hidden attributes of a trained caste." This is actually Marx's description of the Paris Commune in 1871, a description that—except for a few words (I replaced "Commune" with "councils" and "workers" with "peasants" or "community")— is perfectly suitable to the simplicity with which those in Zapatista autonomous government carry out their task.[71]

On the other hand, nothing would be gained if self-government meant simply doing for ourselves the same things that others used to do for us. If practiced in the world of commodities, self-government would amount to little more than imposing the laws of the Economy onto ourselves. So in no way is this about developing a government to merely administer things as they are. Or simply to cope with the contradictions of a world system that, with its compulsory productivism, drags us ever-closer to annihilation. Self-government can only be emancipatory if it mobilizes collective capacities to enable forms of life liberated from capitalist destruction. Therefore, we have to emphasize that Zapatista autonomy is both the invention of a practice of self-government, and the unfolding of *self-determined forms of life*. For the Zapatistas, autonomy means doing *for* themselves but also *from* themselves, based on forms of life that they take up as their own.

This is what makes up that "small slice of freedom" (to take an expression from Subcomandante Moisés), at once humble and extraordinary, that is Zapatista autonomy.[72] At the end of the Little School, whose entry-level course was titled "Freedom According to the Zapatistas," one of the teachers asked us, "And you, do you feel free?"[73] For the Zapatistas, the answer is clear. For the rest of us, not so much. Maybe the practice of this freedom—that is, the collective action that allows self-determined forms of life to flourish—is what provides the motivation and patient determination necessary to walk, day in and day out, the difficult path of becoming autonomous.[74]

Thus, for the Zapatistas, autonomy is not limited to a single dimension such as levels of government or the organization of production. Instead it encompasses all aspects of life. They could even say that "autonomy is the possibility of a new life," and that "autonomy is the people's life itself."[75] These new ways of living and feeling also entail new subjectivities, manifested with particular force in the spirit of struggle and transformational energy of the younger generations of Zapatistas. They are among autonomy's greatest successes, and its greatest promise.

Postscript on the reorganization of autonomy

As previously mentioned, the new stage in the Zapatista struggle that was announced at the end of 2023 is characterized by a significant reorganization of autonomy.[76] While the autonomous municipalities (MAREZ in Spanish) and the Good Government Councils disappeared, another organizational form was born—one whose "principal basis," the new "nucleus of all autonomy," is Local Autonomous Governments (GAL in Spanish). These are formed in each community, "coordinated by autonomous agents and commissioners, and are subject to the assembly of the town."[77] Furthermore, the Local Autonomous Governments can coordinate at the regional level, forming "Collectives of Zapatista Autonomous Government" (CGAZ), and they can call assemblies of community authorities to reach agreements of mutual interest. In turn, the CGAZ can join together to form "Assemblies of Collectives of Zapatista Autonomous Governments" (ACGAZ) that have their headquarters in the Caracoles and—when the GAL and CGAZ deem it necessary—can convene zone-level assemblies.

This reorganization eliminates the municipal level of autonomy that was created in 1994, replacing it with coordinating bodies at the so-called "regional" level.[78] At the broader "zone" level, the councils of elected authorities known as the Good Government Councils have been eliminated, and we can consider the ACGAZ to be a new modality of what were previously known as zone-level assemblies. And while autonomy continues to be organized at three levels, the balance between them has shifted considerably. The local, community level has a more decisive role, while at supra-local levels the new organizing forms are simpler: The councils of elected authorities have been eliminated and replaced by coordinating structures in the form of assemblies and meetings of local authorities. Importantly, these regional and zone-level articulations only meet and act at the request of the GALs and remain under their command.

There are two reasons for this reorganization. The first is to adapt to a context with many dangers (especially the growing presence of organized crime) and to give greater attention to the need for self-defense. The second is in response to self-critiques of how autonomy has operated up until now.

Subcomandante Moisés brings these two reasons together when he writes that the prior form of autonomy "proved that it will no longer be useful for what is to come. In addition to the inherent flaws."[79] This was a critique of how autonomy had become "pyramidal." Besides cases of "poor administration of people's resources" (that were sanctioned), Subcomandante Moisés explains that the principal defect is that the authorities were "already falling into wanting to decide themselves, the authorities." Furthermore, "The proposals from authorities did not go down as they were to the people, nor do the opinions of the people reach the authorities." In short, the authorities and the communities "have distanced themselves," they have become "separated." Subcomandante Moisés concludes that the structure was too vertical, something that may work in the military but not in the civilian realm. The reorganization is presented as a way to "cut the pyramid," or rather, to "turn it upside down."

Another important aspect of the new stage is explained in the final part of the communiqué, titled "The Common and Non-Property." Alongside the present modes of labor—individual work on *ejido* or communal land for family subsistence, and collective work (mainly on land recuperated in 1994) to finance autonomous government and projects—they propose a new way of using recuperated land: "to establish extensions of the recovered land as common. That is, without property. Neither private, nor *ejidal*, nor communal, nor federal, nor state, nor business, nor anything. A non-ownership of land."[80] Concretely, this land will not be permanently granted to anyone but will instead be lent in turn to those who desire to work it for a period of time, whether or not they are Zapatistas—which requires agreements among inhabitants of different organizational affiliations, based on compliance with the "rules of common use" mentioned in the communiqué. This initiative likely seeks to overcome a serious threat to recuperated land: Because they were never legalized, the government incites other organizations to attack the Zapatistas living there by offering them material benefits in exchange for laying claim to the land. This proposal for shared and consensual land use among Zapatistas and non-Zapatistas may be a way to reduce the aggression and conflicts that have continued to multiply over the years.

Beyond these immediate circumstances, the proposal is based on a critique of not just private property, but on all forms of property legalized by the state, including the *ejido*, the legacy of the Mexican Revolution. Their call for non-property opens a window toward a new relationship to the land and new practices, yet to be invented. In addition, "A few hectares of this Non-Property will be proposed to sister nations in other geographies of the world. We are going to invite them to come and work those lands, with their own hands and knowledge."[81]

What does this evaluation—which led to the elimination of the autonomous municipalities and the Good Government Councils—mean for the analysis of autonomy presented in this chapter? At this point, it is still a difficult question to answer. First of all, what Subcomandante Moisés shared at the end of 2023 are only "conclusions from the critical analysis of MAREZ and JBG" (the autonomous municipalities and the Good Government Councils). We still await the chance to learn about these evaluations in greater detail, perhaps including the opinions of those who have participated in autonomous councils, as we did during the Little School. Second, one might wonder how the various factors leading to the elimination of the autonomous municipalities and Good Government Councils interacted with each other. How decisive were the critiques of autonomy? Remember that there were already many errors mentioned in the Little School's notebooks, meaning that those participating in autonomy have long been aware of the risk of authorities separating from the communities. Or was the need to adapt to an extremely threatening context the more decisive factor? And should we also consider other factors? Because building autonomy is such a difficult process, it would be naive to pretend that the EZLN has the same strength and territorial presence that it had in 1994 or 2003. Furthermore, an antisystemic rebellion will inevitably suffer some degree of exhaustion after sustaining a struggle for three decades, amid nonstop counterinsurgent aggression and an ever-worsening systemic crisis.

In any case, the changes announced by the EZLN at the end of 2023 lead us to emphasize even more the difficulties of autonomy. At the same time, though, they highlight Zapatista autonomy's exceptional ability to resist, despite all the factors that make this process a fragile one. (Recognizing that fragility arises from the very capacity to resist, and that strength can be found in fragility— meaning it is not a question of separating the good from the bad.)

We have already mentioned several difficulties facing autonomy in this chapter, including the constant aggressions against it, the difficulty of building an other world within such an adverse context and with such limited material resources, the errors of autonomous authorities, and the verticalism of the EZLN (something the Zapatistas themselves recognize, emphasizing that the military dimension could prevent the growth of civil autonomy and the horizontality it requires). The heavy burden of all the work that Zapatista resistance requires is another cause of fragility, increasing the instances in which people can no longer bear the exhaustion and choose to leave the organization. Other reasons might include migration and the tensions that come with any process of transformation.

We must also recognize all the aspects of resistance, why the Zapatista experience has managed to persist throughout its three decades of public life—something that defies logic, and borders on the improbable (or the impossible made possible). We should remember that they continue to be an armed force, so—even though they have done everything possible to avoid using their weapons—one aspect is their capacity for self-defense. Another is their constant political inventiveness, allowing them to weave together alliances and cultivate networks of solidarity. They have garnered a level of national and international support that—while less than that of the first years after the uprising—remains to this day, continuing to manifest its strength during the moments of greatest danger and to participate in important initiatives such as the Journey for Life to Europe. Above all, the Zapatista support bases exercise a degree of determination and tenacity that goes beyond the art of resistance rooted in Indigenous peoples' history. It is sustained by their conviction in the justice of their struggle, by the sensations of a reclaimed dignity brought about by self-governing and creating by themselves the world they deserve.

As previously mentioned, two structures sustain the advances of the Zapatista experience: One is the civilian organization of autonomy, and the other is the political-military organization of EZLN. The strengthening of autonomy, especially since 2003, has entailed a partial process of redirecting the power previously concentrated in the leadership of the EZLN toward the Zapatista support bases and their civilian bodies of government. But nobody said this process was complete. Perhaps the new stage will introduce another dynamic, with a greater presence of the military aspect (bearing in mind this does not mean a return to armed struggle). In any case, maybe the EZLN's verticality, as a political-military organization, has been a decisive factor in the construction and persistence of autonomy, while also creating difficulties that have accentuated its fragility.

CHAPTER 2

"We Can Govern Ourselves"
A Very Other Politics from Below and to the Left

Besides developing a practice of radical autonomy in the rebel territories of Chiapas, Zapatista men and women have generated a very other conception of politics. Its distinctive character began with their rejection of taking power, and later expanded into a generalized critique of "politics from above": the politics of the state and its institutions, of political parties and their electoral calendars, as well as the politics of revolutionary vanguards that claimed to guide the masses toward salvation. Instead of traditional politics that think from above, the Zapatistas' proposals give form to a "politics from below," moving away from the state and hegemonic logics. Politics from below are rooted in the dignity of those who struggle to reclaim their capacity for self-government outside of established institutional frameworks.

The collective power-to (*potencia*) that comes from self-determination allows for the construction of autonomous spaces, given that it accumulates enough strength to create and defend them. In this chapter we will reflect on autonomy as an expression of the "other politics" that Zapatista men and women propose and practice: a politics from below that seeks to build other worlds outside the state-form and the logic of hegemony.

Leaving behind politics from above

Not taking power?
One of the Zapatista positions that has generated the most surprise and debate is their reiterated rejection of taking power. As early as February 2nd, 1994, when asked about the goal of their uprising, Subcomandante Marcos

responded, "Taking power? No, something more difficult: a new world."[1] Later, in May 1996, the invitation to the Intercontinental Encounter for Humanity and Against Neoliberalism called for the "construction of a new political culture. This political culture will arise from a new way of viewing power. The issue isn't taking power but revolutionizing the relationship between those who exercise power and those who suffer its consequences."[2] The same year, he took a slightly different approach to explaining the need to create something new instead of conquering what exists: "It isn't necessary to conquer the world. It's enough that we make it anew. Us. Now."[3] On other occasions, the EZLN has stated that its objective is "to create a political practice that doesn't seek to take power but to organize society."[4] This is a principle also taken up by the FZLN, the Zapatista Front of National Liberation, which defined itself as a "political force that does not aspire to take power, a force that isn't a political party, a force that can organize citizens' demands and proposals. . . . A political force that does not struggle for political power, but for a democracy where those who govern, govern by obeying."[5] Instead of conquering spaces and gaining positions within the structures of political power, the goal is to gain a greater capacity for organizing society, so that those who govern are forced to obey.

The repeated rejection of taking power has drawn the Zapatista word toward the vocabulary of rebellion, rather than revolution.[6] Interviewed by Julio Scherer when the March of the Color of the Earth arrived in Mexico City in March 2001, Subcomandante Marcos explained that the Zapatistas define themselves as "social rebels" and not as "revolutionaries": "We identify ourselves more as rebels who want social change. I mean, the classic definition of the revolutionary doesn't fit us . . . because a revolutionary seeks to fundamentally transform things from above, not from below, like the social rebel. The revolutionary says: 'We are going to create a rebellion, take power, and transform things from above.' The social rebel doesn't. The social rebel makes demands and goes about transforming the world from below, without having to consider the question of power."[7] A year later, he took up a similar idea, counterposing the revolutionary who is obsessed with sitting in the seat of power with the rebel who instead seeks out other rebels to file down the legs of the chair, so that nobody can sit in it. (This is a clear allusion to the famous photo of Zapata and Villa in the National Palace in December 1914[8]):

The Revolutionary (like that, with capital letters) . . . waits for the day when he arrives at the seat of Power. He knocks off the one sitting there with a single blow, scrunches his face as if he were constipated, and says to the others and to himself: "History (like that, with a capital H), has been fulfilled. Everything, absolutely everything now makes sense. I am in the Seat (like that, with a capital S) and I am the fulfillment of time." . . . On the other hand, the rebel (like that, no caps), when he sees an ordinary chair, analyzes it thoroughly, then goes and puts another chair next to it, and another, and another, and in a short while, it has become a *tertulia* [gathering] because more rebels (like that, no caps) have arrived and the coffee, tobacco, and word begin to swirl and mix. . . . And then there's the variation: when the rebel bumps into the Seat of Power (like that, with a capital S and a capital P), he looks at it carefully, analyzes it but instead of sitting there goes and gets a fingernail file, and with heroic patience begins sawing at the legs, until they are so fragile they will break when someone sits down. Which happens almost immediately.[9]

This insistence on rebellion rather than revolution is a constant in the Zapatista experience, from proclaiming the autonomous *rebellious* Zapatista municipalities, to the World Festival of Resistances of Rebellions, among many other examples. In the rebellion/resistance duality, the first word refers to the "no"— what is rejected, while the second refers to the "yes"—what is being built.[10] And, we should note that the word that is discarded (revolution) is the one that has to do with taking power.

Debates over the Zapatistas' stance on power largely stem from the polarized reception of John Holloway's book, *Change the World without Taking Power*. This exact formulation has not been used by the EZLN, although we do find an expression that is close (but inverted), when Subcomandante Marcos affirms that the Zapatistas do not "repeat the formula according to which, to change the world, it is necessary to take power."[11] It is important to clarify that Holloway's book doesn't set forth the Zapatistas' theory, as some believed or claimed to believe but rather proposes Holloway's own conceptualization based on his reading of Zapatismo. Without getting into either an analysis of Holloway's book, or the debate it provoked, I will only mention the important distinction between power over (*poder sobre*) and power to do (*poder hacer*), which reflects the distinction between power (*poder*) and power-to (*potencia*). The first implies a relation of domination, while the second refers to the individual or collective capacity to act and to create. This helps us understand that the renunciation of taking power does not condemn us to impotence. Holloway affirms that it is self-defeating to change the world by creating another "power over." Even a "counterpower" opposed to the reigning power would consolidate new relations of domination. Rather, we should pursue the path of an anti-power that eliminates any relationship of domination, in order to thereby liberate the collective capacity (*potencia*) to act. In reaction to these proposals, many have reiterated the absolute necessity of the state as an instrument of social transformation, while others reject the notion of anti-power and advocate for the formation of a counterpower.[12]

The abstract nature of the debate has generated more confusion than clarity. In fact, when speaking about "power," we often talk without knowing what exactly we are referring to. Two distinct dimensions of power can be identified in the Zapatista word. In the first place, when the EZLN rejects taking power, this does not imply that they abandon the field of politics, or that they reject all forms of political engagement. It only indicates that they turn their backs on the power *of the state*. That is why the Zapatistas' proposals are oriented toward creating an other politics no longer centered in the state. Secondly, the question of power can also refer to the way the struggle is organized. In that respect, the history of the EZLN can be read as a journey progressively moving away from thinking and acting "from above," in order to assume an other way that builds "from below." Subcomandante Marcos spelled out "the shift in the EZLN's position on the issue of power," saying, "The issue of defining power has left a great mark on the Zapatista path. We had realized—and this 'we' includes the communities, not just the first group [of urban revolutionaries]—that solutions, like everything else in this world, are built from the bottom up. And previously our entire proposal, and that of the orthodox Left up until then, was the reverse: It is from above that the problems of those below will be resolved."[13]

Therefore, more than the question of "power" per se, what is important is the Zapatista understanding of the state, on the one hand, and of modes of organizing, on the other. The distinction between anti-power and counterpower does not really help to clarify the Zapatista position. As we will see below, the Zapatistas reject the existence of any type of "above" at the expense of those "below"—which means distancing themselves from any sort of "power over." To appeal to notions of "anti-power" or "anti-politics" to describe the Zapatista experience runs the risk of idealizing it, since its actual path has never been free of verticality. This is true not only for the military aspect but for their process of building autonomy as well.

In fact, the Zapatistas' positions on power can be understood as a critique of the political tradition from which the first members of the EZLN came, what they identify as "the orthodox Left." This Left's foundational model was the Russian Revolution of October 1917, encapsulated in the insurrection through which the Bolshevik leaders took state power. We can see the Zapatistas' critique of this conception—shared by all the Marxist-Leninist Lefts of the world—in the following formulation: "We think that the issue of power has to be rethought, instead of repeating the formula that in order to change the world it is first necessary to take power, and once in power, organize it to best serve everyone, which is to say, to best serve whoever is in power, i.e., me."[14]

This two-stage revolutionary schema is denounced as an illusion. The social transformation justifying the conquest of power does not end up happening, and in its place, we find the logic of a state apparatus that seeks its own reproduction. Here, the Zapatista critique again coincides with Marx, who characterized the state as a "monstrous abortion of society" that impedes the people's own authentic social life.[15] To affirm—as Marx did—that an insurgent people "cannot simply lay hold of the ready-made state machinery and wield it for its own purposes" but must "destroy state power" and institute a regime of "local autonomy" that can "restore to the social body all the forces hitherto absorbed by the state parasite feeding upon, and clogging the free movement of, society"[16] is even more pertinent today, when we can see the tragic results caused by revolutionary struggles' obsession with state power throughout the twentieth century. Through their critique of their own political tradition, the Zapatistas discarded the idea that taking state power is an indispensable instrument of social transformation.

The other aspect of the issue of power has to do with the organization of political struggle. The Zapatistas' rejection of organizational forms that impose solutions from above led to their critique of vanguardism, another feature of their own political tradition. As early as January 20, 1994, the Zapatistas affirmed, "We are not trying to be the historical vanguard, the one, only, and true."[17] Subsequently, they have continued to reject acting as a vanguard that possesses the truth and uses it to direct everyone else, like the parties who imagined themselves the guardians of the revolutionary essence of the proletariat. For example, when Marcos was pronounced dead in May 2014, he insisted that the Zapatista path led to the replacement of "revolutionary vanguardism by ruling by obeying" (*mandar obedeciendo*). It was a move "from those Above taking Power to creating power below; from professional politics to everyday politics; from the leaders to the people."[18] Thus, through their process of self-transformation, the Zapatistas broke away from vanguardism, the focus on state power, and the idea of a politics designed by professionals and leaders—that is, the pillars of the classical revolutionary tradition. To invent new approaches, the EZLN had to distance itself from the model that ended in crisis with the fall of the Soviet bloc. Discarding the vocabulary of revolution in favor of rebellion is part of this process. In fact, the term "revolution" had been emptied of hopefulness by the historical experience that associated it with the vanguard party and the exercise of state power, ending in criminal perversion. If they hoped to move forward, it was therefore indispensable that they critique that political tradition. The EZLN did so by insisting on rejecting state power and vanguardist logics—that is, rejecting a politics that tried to build "from above." They had to also renounce the preeminence of the word *revolution*, without abandoning all horizons of emancipation.

What is to be done (with the state)?

What is the EZLN's analysis of the state? As we will see in the following chapter, in calling neoliberalism the Fourth World War, the Zapatistas emphasize the subordination of nation-states to transnational economic forces. Rather than implying their physical disappearance, this analysis argues that states' sovereignty is increasingly negated. They have consistently held this longstanding position, but they have introduced an important inflection to it. Initially, the Zapatista posture seemed like that of the alter-globalization movement, seeking to restore the state as a shield against the market. In 1996, Subcomandante Marcos indicated, "The Zapatistas think that in Mexico (attention: in Mexico) the recovery and defense of national sovereignty is part of an anti-neoliberal revolution. . . . They think that it's necessary to defend the nation-state against globalization."[19] This does not mean that they sought state power, nor is it a defense of the nation-state, instead, there is a double linkage. On the one hand, the defense of national sovereignty is joined to the call to construct an "international of hope" and to regard dignity as a "country without nationality that . . . ridicules borders, customs, and wars."[20] Secondly, they both abandon the struggle for state power and emphasize society's struggle for its own self-organization. In sum, the EZLN defends the state against neoliberal globalization but also defends society against the state and calls for the mobilization of the multitude beyond national borders.

Their vision changed notably in later years. In 2001, Subcomandante Marcos explained the Zapatistas' rejection of state power, saying "We know that the seat of power is empty. . . . The center of power is no longer in nation-states." Therefore, "the conquest of state power is pointless."[21] They reject the conquest of state power not so much because it is harmful but because it is useless. They reject it, not because of the risk of abuse of power but because institutions that are structurally subordinate to the market are in fact impotent. In "Seven Thoughts in May 2003," Subcomandante Marcos elaborates what these brief comments hinted at.[22] Here, the diagnosis of the nation-state is more dismal than ever. Lying on the battlefield of the Fourth World War, "It is in its death throes, waiting for someone to come to the rescue." He points to "its present exhaustion (almost to the point of disappearance)" and insists that the national political class destroyed the basis of the nation-state, which is why "looking to it as an 'ally' in the resistance struggle is an exercise . . . in nostalgia." Finally, the nation-state is on the verge of extinction, while "its hologram remains, fed by dogmas struggling to fill a void that globalization, even if it doesn't produce it, only exacerbates." This includes the hegemonic nation-state, the US, which "only exists on television," and the flag it flew for a moment in Iraq is also a hologram. The nation-state continues to make a show of strength but is in fact nothing more than an empty image. It's clear, then, that the Zapatistas have no intention to revive the dead. At the same time, they also demystify the old nation-state. Although the decision-making capacity of its political class allowed for a medium-term vision and a certain autonomy from economic power, the political class ultimately still served the capitalist class. Military dictatorships betray the true face of the old nation-state, "a bloodthirsty, animalistic face." Today the disappearance of national states is a fait accompli, and nostalgia is pointless. When struggling against neoliberal capitalism, it is better to assume that the defense or restoration of the nation-state is not a viable option.

So, if nation-states are empty places, where does real power lie? The Zapatistas respond:

We use "the society of Power" to name the ruling clique that has displaced the political class from basic decision making. This is a group that not only holds economic power, and not only in a single nation. Rather than cohering organically . . . the "society of Power" is defined by shared objectives and common methods. Still in the process of formation and consolidation, the "society of Power" tries to fill the hole left by the nation states and their political classes. The "society of Power" controls financial institutions (and through them, entire countries), the media, industrial and commercial corporations, universities, armies, and public and private police forces. The "society of Power" would prefer a world state with a supranational government but doesn't work to build it.[23]

True power no longer resides in political power but rather in the economy. The ruling clique is composed of the dominant actors in business and finance, and also those who hold crucial positions in international organizations, security forces, and education. And we could argue that the rulers of key countries also belong to the "society of Power," considering the fact that, in neoliberal times, the boundary between the private sector and public office is ever more permeable. The society of Power includes the capital holders of the 150 transnational corporations that control half the world economy, plus a handful of high functionaries and "experts" who circulate through those corporations, international organizations, and national governments. Above all, the society of Power does not constitute an organic body or—even less—a unified one. While they share common values and interests, their members are locked in brutal competition for control of resources and markets. That is why Subcomandante Marcos clarifies that the society of Power doesn't comprise a supranational government, let alone the conspiratorial fantasy of a world state.[24] Yes, the directives that the society of Power imposes on the world derive from shared class objectives, but these are in tension with the divergent interests at its core, contributing to the chaos we see across the world.

We return now to the state, designated by Subcomandante Marcos in his 2011 letters to Luis Villoro, as an "empty place," a "hologram," and even a "cadaver." There he insists that it is "impossible . . . to salvage or regenerate the wreckage of the nation state . . . because the foundations of that state have been destroyed."[25] His diagnosis has become ever more radical, and during the seminar "Critical Thought in the Face of the Capitalist Hydra," in May 2015, the question was posed yet again: "Has the nation state, the state as we know it, remained untouched by this system's war? Or are we faced with a hologram, an image of what was, a cardboard cut-out where different characters stick on their faces for the annual photo? Perhaps it is neither one nor the other. The nation state is no longer what it was, but does it continue to exert some sort of resistance against supranational powers?"[26]

Here again, the EZLN questions its earlier analysis and—given that

"understanding the character of the state is a necessary and urgent task"—
indicates its willingness to modify its position in the face of new evidence.
In that spirit, here are some aspects of the neoliberal state to reflect upon.[27]
First is delegitimization: Neoliberal ideology discredits state interventionism,
attributing to it all the ills it proposes to correct. Second is the shrinking of the
state's direct participation in production via privatization and the elimination
of social spending, or the welfare state. Third is the colonization of the state
itself by economic logics—everything from education to health care to public
administration is run like a business. Finally, and above all, is its subordination
to transnational capital, due to several mechanisms, including the power of
transnational corporations to secure the deregulation of financial markets and
the unhindered movement of capital. Meanwhile, public indebtedness transforms states into debtors dependent on the market and the ratings agencies,
obliging them to align their policies with those the dominant economic actors
deem advisable. Ultimately, all this means that they have been stripped of their
fundamental sovereignty, thus the metaphor of the hologram. At the same
time, the supposed disappearance of the nation-state is a dubious assertion
since nation-states continue to play a determinant role in the world (dis)order.
In the first place, they ensure that territories and populations continue to be
subjected to the economy's domination. States are therefore decisive actors in
the commodification of the world. Their role in social control is also indispensable, not only through repression (which grows ever greater), but also through
various forms of discipline: from education and the promotion of national
mythologies to the distractions and illusions that the electoral system recre-
ates periodically for millions of people (the crisis of representative democracy
notwithstanding).

In short, when asking whether the state is fading away, or if it instead retains
an important role of its own, the answer has to consider two facets. On the
one hand, as long as it conforms to the dominant logics of the economy, the
state plays a decisive role in molding territories and controlling populations,
i.e., it continues to be an actor of singular importance in globalized capitalism.
However, if it separates itself at all from economic orthodoxy, its structurally
subordinate position is manifest immediately insofar as it must submit to the
blackmail of firms relocating, capital flight, and rising interest rates that make
the debt burden unsustainable. That is all to say that, in the logic of capitalist
domination, the state is not an empty place but an important cog in the system.
On the other hand, from an antisystemic perspective, it is an empty place from

which, more than ever, it is impossible to carry out a transformation that breaks with capitalist logics.

Finally, despite some initial oscillations, the Zapatistas' word-thought with respect to the state is now quite clear.[28] First, the twentieth century demonstrated that—far from being an instrument of revolutionary transformation—the state has systematically hindered it. Second, the ongoing transnationalization of neoliberal capitalism has transformed the state into an empty place: it can only play an active role to the extent that it responds to dominant economic interests, as powerful mechanisms prevent it from taking antisystemic action to domesticate or channel the forces of capital. Thus, it is little more than an exercise in nostalgia to think that it is possible to use the state to fight against the most harmful effects of capitalist globalization. Neither is it possible to return to the prior form of Keynesian capitalism, in which state intervention through investment and social spending compensated for a lack of private initiative. For Subcomandantes Galeano and Moisés, the "attempt to return to the old system," to "the welfare state," to "Keynes' benefactor state" is "an impossible leap backwards."[29] It is impossible because Keynesian policies were not abandoned due to an ideological choice but out of structural necessity, as increasing global competition and a falling rate of profit caused a crisis in the valorization of capital.[30] As a structurally-determined process, the passage from Keynesianism to neoliberal capitalism is not a process that can simply be run in reverse. The conclusion is clear: we can't use the state to protect ourselves from the destructive impact of capitalism, much less build another world. It is both impossible and undesirable to use the state against capitalism.[31] The other politics we are trying to construct can only be a politics without the state.

In this context, it is important to note that the Zapatistas came to discuss the anarchist tradition—something they did not do initially. In 2011's "Ethics and Politics," Subcomandante Marcos acknowledges "the heroic effort by anarchist and libertarian collectives to remove themselves from the logic of the capitalist market" and makes a stirring homage to the thought of Tomás Segovia, citing, at length, writings in which he indicates the incompatibility between the left and the people, and between the left and power. He writes that "the Left is, above all, Power's other . . . 'The people' . . . are by definition those who are not in power. . . . It's impossible to argue that the desire for Power is the desire of 'the people.'"[32] Some years later, in a text mentioned during the "Critical Thought in the Face of the Capitalist Hydra" seminar, Subcomandante Marcos again declared his "admiration for anarchist thought," while clarifying that "it's clear that we are not anarchists, but their approach provokes and nourishes, it makes you think. Believe me, orthodox critical thought, for lack of a better term, has a lot to learn from anarchist thought. To give you an example, the current critique of the state is something that anarchist thought has been developing for some time."[33] As Marcos indicates, the EZLN does not come from an anarchist tradition, but from a Marxist-Leninist one that they subjected to a profound revision. It is therefore significant that, especially regarding organizational forms and the critique of the state *as such*, the EZLN's positions have strong affinities with anarchist thought. It is an important achievement of the Zapatista experience to have created the theoretical and practical space for a convergence between Marxist and anarchist traditions, suggesting that the strength of today's anticapitalist struggles depends on overcoming this historical division.

Below versus above

The Zapatista word synthesizes many of the issues discussed here into the duality of above and below. This approach was already present before the January 1, 1994, uprising, as a previous text announced the clash of a wind blowing from above with another blowing from below, as well as the storm that would follow.[34] In a famous 2001 television interview with Julio Scherer, Marcos framed this duality as an opposition between the rebel and the revolutionary, in which the latter seeks to "transform things from above, not from below."[35] This duality became even more important after 2005 when "The Sixth Declaration of the Lacandon Jungle" defined the Zapatista struggle in opposition to politics from above, the politics of parties and the state. It said "'No' to making agreements from above to be imposed below. . . . 'No' to seeking gifts, positions, advantages, or public positions from Power or those who aspire to it," and called instead "to go beyond the election calendar, not to try to resolve from above the problems of our Nation, but to build FROM BELOW AND FOR BELOW, an alternative to neoliberal destruction, a left alternative for Mexico." Since then, positioning oneself "below and to the left" has been one of the essential criteria for anyone to join the Zapatistas' Other Campaign and the other initiatives that have emerged from "The Sixth Declaration."

The duality of above and below actually has two dimensions. "Them and Us," a 2013 text that updates the "Sixth Declaration," identifies the opposition between below and above as a fundamental tension within the Zapatistas' analytic gaze:

We Zapatistas know that this great line that we have drawn across the geography of the world is in no way conventional. We know that this "above" and "below" bothers, irritates, and disturbs some. . . . Differences are persecuted, marginalized, ignored, disdained, repressed, displaced, and exploited, yes. But we see a greater difference that passes across all of those differences: that of above and below, the haves and the have-nots. And we see that there is something fundamental in this great difference: Those above are above on the backs of those below; the "haves" have because they dispossess those who don't. We believe that being above or below determines our gaze, our words, what we hear, our steps, our pains, and our struggles.[36]

The opposition between above and below essentially refers to economic and social inequality, to the class difference between those who have everything and those who have nothing. Similarly, Subcomandante Moisés defined the encounter between Indigenous peoples organized in La Realidad in August 2014 as a meeting of those below, "the poor, exploited workers of the countryside and the city," who have for centuries suffered injustice, misery, and inequality, while above were the landowners, and now "the capitalist system."[37] The "bottom" is a social concept; it is those who are poor and suffering. However, the same document also suggests another meaning, by insisting that the meeting was between "the popular grassroots" rather than "representatives" or "leaders," which refers not so much to an economic difference as to a difference of power. Subcomandante Moisés insists that above is where political parties are, saying "Our backs have been made into stairs for politicians to climb to power. They have worn out our backs, those mafiosos, by going up and down so much." The above is built at the expense of those below, not only through money but also through power.

In this sense, the opposition between above and below is also an opposition between two conceptions of politics, coinciding with (and revealing the true meaning of) the opposition between left and right. "Politics from above" is a struggle for state power, for space in its institutions, parties, and electoral calendars.[38] "Politics from below" recognizes that there is nothing to hope for from governmental positions, nothing to expect from parties and electoral routines. The same opposition appears again in the affirmation that

Those who are going to remain standing in the end will be those who realized that solutions do not come from above, but are built from below;

those who did not and do not bet on the illusions sold by a political class that stinks like a corpse; those who did not follow the calendar from above or adapt their geography to that calendar by converting a social movement into a voter registration drive; those who, facing the battle, did not remain isolated, immobile, waiting for the political class's new clown show in the electoral circus, but rather built a collective alternative of freedom, justice, work and peace..[39]

Or, as Zapatistas say elsewhere: "When are they going to understand that there are individuals, groups, collectives, organizations, movements who are not interested in changing what is above or renewing (that is, recycling) a political class that is nothing more than a parasite? We do not want to change tyrants, owners, masters, or supreme saviors, but to have none."[40] "Them and Us" also emphasizes this opposition between above and below by calling out the "you" who, without being part of "them"—the real bosses—submit to the "spectacle of politics from above." The contrast between "you" and "us" could not be clearer:

> You look up, we look down. You look for ways to make yourselves comfortable; we look for ways to serve. You look for ways to lead, we look for ways to accompany. You look at how much you earn, we at how much is lost. You look for what is, we look for what could be. You see numbers, we see people . . . You speak, we listen . . . You look at the many, we at the few. You see impassable walls, we see the cracks. You look at possibilities, we look at what was impossible until the eve of its possibility. You search for mirrors, we look for windows. You and us are not the same.[41]

We see that there are two aspects of the opposition between above and below, one that is more class-related and the other more political. The two overlap significantly, first of all because both "aboves"—the society of Power (the power of those with money) and the political class (the power of the state)—are closely linked, if not fused. Secondly, they overlap because politics from below is a struggle of the poor, waged outside of state institutions. However, the two aspects of the opposition between above and below do not necessarily coincide since the poor sometimes choose the path of politics from above.

While above and below have both a political and a social/economic dimension, the dichotomy also has a broader meaning, pointing to a critique of all forms of domination. This includes domination reproduced within anti-systemic struggles, and even within the EZLN itself. For example, "The Sixth Declaration" offers the self-critique that "it is not right for the military to be above and for the democracy [that is, the community] to be below." And if one fights against what is above, it is precisely to put an end to the ability of anyone to exert domination: "In order to save humanity and the battered house in which it lives, someone has to leave, and that has to be those on top. And we don't mean banishing those people. We are talking about destroying the social relations that make it possible for someone to be on top at the cost of someone being below."[42] This illustrates the most general meaning of above: it refers to any relationship in which someone is on top at the expense of others who are below. In other words, it is any relationship of domination, such as patriarchal relationships between men and women. And while the above can only exist at the expense of those below, when those on the bottom assert themselves, they struggle for a below that has no above. Politics from below seeks to end the opposition between above and below. It fights for a world "without above and below."[43]

One more clarification. Contrary to dominant values, the Zapatista word identifies with the small, the insignificant, the despised, what is not looked at or seen. In the text "Below and to the Left," while talking ironically about "the transmissions of the Zapatista Intergalactic Television System," Subcomandante Marcos mentions that "contrary to the Olympic motto of 'faster, higher, stronger,' in our Zapatista Olympics we instead raise the banner of 'slower, lower, weaker.'"[44] In this way, the Zapatista word seeks to reverse the competitive and quantitative mentality that predominates in the capitalist world and instead inserts politics "from below and to the left" into an ethic that attends to the lowly and the poor. The "below" reclaimed here is that which is considered weak or insignificant from the dominant point of view. This below contains women—although Subcomandante Marcos challenges their supposed weakness—and Indigenous people, "the smallest of them all."[45] It contains children ignored by classical politics, but who the Zapatistas see as having a role to play.[46] In this below, there are beetles like Don Durito, whom the insurgents' boots could well have crushed without even realizing it. These are the belows whose dignity the Zapatistas seek to make visible. Yet, in celebrating the small, the Zapatista word does not suggest they should remain under any above, crushed and subjected by the strongest. Nor does it intend to praise the humble so that they bow before the great, those who are above. The Zapatista ethic of the small and the humble never leads to submitting to the powerful but rather to confronting them. It seeks to make visible what the gaze that looks upward cannot see. It aims to prevent anyone, even—or especially—those who fight from below and to the left, from placing themselves above others. Humility is required but not of those who aspire to be above, only of those who aspire to be equals. That is, those below.

Politics from below: Self-organization and self-government

Now that we have identified that the Zapatistas are distancing themselves from taking state power (through force of arms or through elections), from the political class, parties, electoral calendars, and state institutions, it is time to analyze the "other" politics that they propose. The two main axes of these politics are everyday people's capacity for self-organization and, to the extent to which this grows, the creation of autonomous spaces. It is also an ethical politics and one based in the recognition of shared dignity. Finally, rather than treating politics as a distinct activity, it has to be reintegrated into everyday life.

Getting organized without THE organization

During their first years in public, the EZLN maintained an openness toward dialogue with the state and political parties. They agreed to talks with the federal government, first at the Cathedral in San Cristóbal de Las Casas and later in the town of San Andrés Sakamch'en de los Pobres. After signing the San Andrés Accords, they pushed for the state to integrate these agreements into the Constitution. In 1994, the EZLN supported Amado Avendaño's electoral campaign for governor of Chiapas and later supported him as "governor in rebellion." Regarding national politics, they said, "in response to the appeals of the National Democratic Convention, we call on the people of Mexico to participate in a civic, electoral struggle—which is not the only struggle, but the most immediate one—to vote against the state-party system."[47] While clearly downplaying the proposal, the EZLN's position was the result of decisions made by the National Democratic Convention, and it should be understood within a context where a defeat for the PRI was considered to likely be an opening for the Zapatistas. In any case, the breach of the San Andrés Accords by all three branches of government clearly showed that nothing would come from dialogue with the state, nor from seeking recognition of the constitutional rights of Indigenous peoples. Moreover, their betrayal by the three principal political parties in 2001 and the general decline of Mexican politics over the following years confirm the futility of electoral struggle and alliances on that terrain.

While the Zapatistas have indeed decided to stop participating in elections, they do not demand everyone else abstain from voting. Rather, they are indifferent to the issue. As Subcomandante Moisés explained in 2015, "We don't call for people to vote, nor do we call for them not to vote. It just doesn't interest us. . . . Whether you vote or not, get organized."[48] Their continual call to organize is the important part, not whether to vote or abstain. To strengthen politics from below, "We never tire of saying 'Organize yourselves.' Let's organize ourselves. Each person, from where they are, must struggle to organize themselves."[49] This is why it caused so much surprise and concern when they proposed that the spokeswoman of the Indigenous Council of Government run as an independent candidate in the 2018 presidential elections. It seemed like they were breaking with their longstanding position regarding politics from above. However, after the initial confusion, it became clear they were not competing in elections to tally votes or win positions in government. Instead, they sought to carry out an offensive attack on enemy terrain, to focus attention on the plight of Indigenous peoples and to show that another path is possible, an alternative to breakdown of institutional politics. It is the path of politics from below, of self-organization, of autonomy.

The most important thing is, quite simply, to get organized. But how? The answer may seem paradoxical. While the EZLN comes out of a certain organizing tradition, they have never tried to spread their own model. After the initial uprising, they never called on others to join them in armed struggle. After the first months of 1994, Subcomandante Marcos explained that the objective of the Zapatista armed forces was to "disappear," since they are "soldiers who are soldiers so that one day no one has to be a soldier."[50] Their 1995 *consulta* (referendum) put the question to all Mexican men and women: Should the EZLN disappear as a military organization? Even though conditions did not allow them to disappear, they have never again engaged in armed struggle. On the contrary, in "The Sixth Declaration of the Lacandon Jungle" as well as their later initiatives, they continue to insist they are a "civil and peaceful movement," even specifying that "the EZLN continues, therefore, in its resolve to not establish any kind of secret relations with either national political-military organizations or those from other countries." This is not to minimize the importance of the January 1st, 1994, uprising, which allowed them to exist and to have a voice. In the words of Major Ana María, we are "the voice that takes up arms to make itself heard."[51] Above all, the uprising opened the necessary political space for them to build their autonomy. And although the Zapatistas' trajectory has progressed from a military to a civil project, this progression is still incomplete. They have found it necessary to *remain armed despite not using their arms* to prevent and limit all manner of attacks against Zapatista communities, including by the military, paramilitaries, and organizations allied with the government.

By virtue of being an armed organization, the EZLN has a vertical structure. As mentioned above, "The Sixth Declaration" openly recognizes this, saying "it's not democratic, because it is an army." This is one reason that the EZLN does not call on others to re-create its military model. Ever since January 20, 1994, they have stated that the change they seek "will not be under the unified command of a single, homogenous grouping and the boss (*caudillo*) that directs it." This is because the EZLN does not seek to "absorb every single Mexican into its project and process," nor does it seek to "become a historic vanguard—the one, the only, the true."[52] Similarly, after having convened the National Democratic Convention, the EZLN refused to preside over it, saying "this is a convention seeking peaceful pathways to change; in no way whatsoever should an armed group preside over it."[53] They went on to say that "it's not our time. This isn't the moment for guns. We will step aside, but we will not leave." Beyond just stepping aside, they declared themselves subordinate to "the civil, peaceful mobilizations" that were occurring, writing "we subordinate ourselves to them, even if it means we cease to represent an alternative." Lastly, they said, "we do not wish to—nor can we—take on the role that some ask of us: to be those from whom all positions emanate, from which all paths depart, those with all the answers, all the truths." That is, they do not seek "the dubious honor of being the greatest historic vanguard among all the other vanguards we have to endure." All this is to say that they distanced themselves from the practices of the very political tradition that gave rise to the EZLN, practices encapsulated in the notion of the vanguard.

In his interview with J. Scherer, Subcomandante Marcos said that the EZLN "began to create an inclusive discourse, based on the understanding that there is a trick hidden in hegemony, the mistake of trying again and again to efface the other through homogeneity and hegemony," which is why "we're fundamentally breaking with the twentieth century and its great battle of hegemonies."[54] A few years later he said, "In its relations with other groups, collectives, organizations, peoples and individuals—and even with other realities, both those that are organized and those that aren't—the EZLN has plainly refused to hegemonize and homogenize. Not even within the Indigenous movement, which is our primary identity, have we accepted the role of a vanguard that represents the totality of the Indigenous movement in Mexico.... It is not, nor has it ever been, the EZLN's goal to create a movement under its hegemony and homogenized to its pace, ways, and no-ways."[55]

The concepts of vanguard and hegemony are nearly identical. For example, in "Them and Us" they write, "the Zapatistas reiterate our rejection of any attempt at hegemony, that is to say, any vanguardism."[56] This is a fundamental way to differentiate between politics from below and from above. In the classical conception, politics is about creating hegemony and imposing it upon others, whether through state power or within parties and other organizations. An other politics, which refuses to allow any above to be imposed on any below, requires a radical break with the logic of hegemony.

We also see this logic at play in what the EZLN calls the myth of unity. This is particularly pernicious, as the leader or group still imposes hegemony on others, but under the guise of common sense. "Them and Us," where the Zapatista define "The Sexta," says:

> All of you know that it is not our intention to build a great big organization with a central governing body, a centralized command, or a boss—be it an individual or a particular group. Our analysis of the dominant system—of its workings, its strengths and weaknesses—has led us to believe and to emphasize that unified action is possible if we respect what we call the "*modos*" [manner, ways of doing things] of each of us. And these things we call "*modos*" are nothing but the knowledges that each of us, individual or collective, have of our own geography and calendar. That is, of our pains and struggles. We are convinced that any attempt at homogeneity is no more than a fascist effort at domination, regardless of whether it is hidden in revolutionary, esoteric, religious, or any other language. When one speaks of "unity" they elide the fact that "unity" occurs under the leadership of someone or something, be it individual or collective. Not only are differences sacrificed on the false altar of "unity," but it hides all the small worlds that survive despite suffering under tyranny and injustice.[57]

Obviously, the EZLN does not always make good on their intention to break with the strategy of hegemony. They recognized as much in the conclusion to the World Festival of Dignified Rage:

> Here's our story: the EZLN was tempted by hegemony and homogeneity. Not only after the uprising but also before. There was the temptation to impose ways (*modos*) and identities, to say Zapatismo was the only truth. And the communities were the first to stop this, to teach us that it's not like that, to say "That's not the way," that we can't substitute one dominion for another, that we must convince and not defeat those who are like us but are not us. They taught us that there are many worlds and that mutual respect is both possible and necessary. And we're not talking about the respect that is demanded from us by those who attack us, but respect for those who have other ways but the same determination for freedom, for justice, for democracy. And so what we want to tell you is that this plurality, so similar in rage and so different in feeling, is the path and the destination that we want and propose to you.[58]

Politics from below seeks to organize without hegemony or homogenization, despite all its difficulties. In the first place, it means organizing without leaders and, on a deeper level, without anyone acting like they are greater than the rest. After repeatedly critiquing the figure of "Marcos" over many years, this critique became even more radical during the period that began on December 21, 2012 (the day of the Zapatista March, where "forty thousand bosses" climbed onto the stage).[59] May 24, 2014, was the ritual death of "Marcos," who was replaced by the EZLN's new military chief and spokesperson, now Indigenous, Subcomandante Moisés. Above all, this symbolized the replacement of the charismatic leader by the collective strength of the communities, represented by the teacher Galeano. The end of the speech announcing the disappearance of "Marcos" is the most pointed: "It is our conviction and our practice that to rebel and to struggle, neither leaders nor bosses nor messiahs nor saviors are necessary. To struggle, one only needs to have a few scruples, a bit of dignity, and a lot of organization."[60]

To organize without hegemonizing or homogenizing is to recognize that, across antisystemic movements, there are different ways of seeing and acting, different paths and ways to walk them. These differences should be accepted and respected, instead of trying to silence them through submission or uniformity.

Writing in 2007, Subcomandante Marcos said, "The *antisystemic* movement that we want to create in Mexico begins with a basic premise: We must work together with the other, with those who are different, and in doing so we must share our hopes and agonies, recognizing that the capitalist system is responsible for this unjust situation. This, we believe, is only possible through a mutual understanding that then grows into respect."[61] This is why their 2006 evaluation of the Other Campaign was so modest, emphasizing they had achieved no more than "a roll call, a series of introductions where each said who they were, where they were at, how they saw our country and the world, what they wanted, and how they wanted to do it."[62] It was a small but considerable step, because a politics that seeks to learn how to *build upon differences* must begin with those who are different finding one another, and getting to know one another, so that they may then struggle together. Overcoming the myth of unity means being able to understand heterogeneity as a strength:

> In the *Sexta* we Zapatistas reiterate our rejection of any attempt at hegemony—that is to say, any vanguardism—whether it places us at the forefront or alongside or, as we've found ourselves over the course of these long centuries, in the rearguard.[63] If with the *Sexta* we search for our kin in sorrows and struggles, regardless of the calendars and geographies that distance us, it is because we know well that the Ruler cannot be defeated with only one way of thinking, one force, one leadership (however revolutionary, consequential, radical, clever, numerous, powerful, daring, etc. it may be). We have learned from our dead that diversity and difference are not a weakness for those below but rather a strength from which to birth—upon the ashes of the old—the new world that we want, that we need, that we deserve. We know well that we are not the only ones who imagine this world. But in our dream this world is not one but many different, diverse worlds. And in their diversity lies their strength.[64]

They also reiterate that the *Sexta* (which replaces the national Other Campaign and the Zezta Internazional around the world) "was convoked by the Zapatistas. To convoke is not to unite. We don't intend to unite under a single leadership, be it Zapatista or any other. . . . Our destiny is the same, but the richness of the *Sexta* is difference, heterogeneity, the autonomy of distinct ways (*modos*) of walking. That is its strength."[65] In the same vein, a proposal was made in the summer of

2018 to increase the membership of the Indigenous Council of Government and to allow people who are neither Indigenous nor Mexican to join. This proposal was for "a Council that neither absorbs nor annuls differences but rather gives each of us the chance to be with others who share the same struggle."[66]

The work of building together, amid all our differences and heterogeneity, is much harder than acting according to the logic of the One, which raises the question: What to do so that these differences truly are enriching, and not a source of division or an obstacle in the struggle to organize collectively? "Them and Us" offers many suggestions. First is the importance of a strong collectivist ethic, which requires an effort to combat individualist forms of subjectivity. This includes the tendency to speak rather than listen, to assert rather than question, to hold one's own point of view to be superior, and to be eager for it to win out over others'. These are all attitudes that undermine antisystemic movements. Counter to this—and in an attempt to harmonize the construction of a "we" with respect for difference—"Them and Us" stresses the importance of the gaze (*la mirada*), saying "We, the Zapatistas, say that to gaze is a form of asking."[67] To gaze is to refrain from the temptation to make categorical, definitive affirmations. To gaze is to grant the other time to explain their reasoning or unreasonableness, distinct from our own. It is the space of "maybe," the space for allowing our own beliefs to become less absolute. In a few words, it is a space where judgment is suspended, an opening toward the other's differences ("it is in this gaze where alterity and the other appear"). It is what allows us to accept difference as such, as something we do not share and may even find upsetting or annoying.[68] The art of listening is no less important, which is why the Other Campaign was conceived as a space where, across Mexico's geography, those who suffer and struggle can listen to one another. This is an indispensable step toward weaving a network from below, and it is in stark contrast with politics from above, of politicians giving speech after speech, making promise after promise. It is impossible to do politics from below, to renounce hegemony and build a heterogeneous "we," without the art of listening.

Organizing amid heterogeneity also requires a certain *proportionality*, a concept that the Zapatistas borrowed from Ivan Illich through the mediation of Jean Robert during the World Festival of Dignified Rage:

With "The Sixth Declaration," we Zapatistas did not propose to organize and lead all of Mexico, much less the entire world. In it we said, "Here we are, this is what we are, this is what we want, and this is how we think we need to do it." We recognize our limits, our possibilities, our proportionality. . . . We say that everyone has their space, their history, their struggle, their dream, their proportionality. And then we say, "Let's make a deal to fight together for everything and for each person and each thing." By making a deal among our respective proportionalities and the country that results from them, the world we achieve will be made up of the dreams of each and every dispossessed person. . . . Well, we are worried about this world being a clone of the current world, or a GMO or a photocopy of this world that currently horrifies us, that we repudiate. We are worried, in other words, about that world not having democracy, or justice, or freedom. So we want to tell you, to ask you, to not turn our strength into a weakness. Being so many and so different will allow us to build something new. We want to tell you—to ask—that the new may also be different.[69]

"Proportionality," read in its Zapatista sense, is an invitation to be aware of the limits of who we are and what we can do, an invitation to recognize where our own space ends and that of others begins. It is an invitation to accept being incomplete, leaving a place for other men, women, and nonbinary people (*otroas*). It is a prerequisite for uniting through difference, for weaving alliances "between our respective proportionalities," for building a heterogeneous "we" that recognizes "to each their own" and that even abides the "I"s (as long as they know their proportion).

Lastly, the Zapatistas' resounding call to organize also rejects two extremes. On one hand, they reject "the myth of unity at all costs," especially within a single and unified organization that is the keeper of the truth and that reproduces the power of the vanguard, self-proclaimed to lead the masses, who are assumed to be incapable of their own liberation. On the other hand, we find other erstwhile allies to the powerful: the merely individual rebellions that—as Subcomandante Marcos wrote—are "so poignantly useless."[70] In the space between these two options lies the opportunity to build a collective force from non-unity, through an enormous heterogeneity of understandings, traditions, and ways of being. Of course, this does not require accepting all differences, all positions, every way of being (*modo*). Instead, following the two basic principles of the *Sexta*, we need an anticapitalist struggle that dismantles the path toward the state. And we must not validate ways of being that fail to respect difference. Yet even our basic criteria of building together by assuming heterogeneity is difficult enough. It demands an ethic of collectivity that can counteract the swollen egos bolstered by modernity's competitive individualism. It demands we practice the arts of gazing and listening, holding at bay our tendency to speak and judge according to absolute certainties. It demands the sense of proportionality required to demarcate our own possibilities while respecting others' spaces, all without exaggerating differences at the behest of our common struggle.

Specifically, this means organizing among a multitude of collectives and with all sorts of groups, assuming difference while seeking to weave together connections, so that we may learn from each other, support each other, and together build a planetary antisystemic force. This is what the Zapatistas have proposed since 1996—when they called for "an intercontinental network of resistance, for humanity and against neoliberalism"—through 2018, when they convened an international meeting "of networks of resistance and rebellion."[71] (We can picture this tapestry as a rhizomatic network, while also critiquing the concept's co-optation in business literature, which sees networks as a source of flexibility, adaptability, and efficiency.) Neither the Other Campaign nor the *Sexta* have ever proposed a coordinating structure, but perhaps that is a step that should be taken. In fact, the EZLN invited debate around the idea of creating a "coordinating committee or federation of networks." They obviously sought to avoid "a centralized and vertical command," as well as the mistake of allowing a lack of initiative to weaken collective capacity. The trick is to find an organizing form that can concretize and amplify collective power (*potencia*), without supplanting or quashing it. This highlights the fact that the ability to organize collectively is not solely about finding the right coordinating structure. Such structures are indeed useful but, above all, collective strength emerges from the many groups that constitute the collective. Organizing is the ability to *act* from a shared perspective—a common understanding not only of our enemy but of what we want, and of how we want to go about making it happen.

Ethical politics, politics of dignity

The Zapatistas' other politics is built on an ethical foundation. In "Seven Thoughts in May of 2003," Subcomandante Marcos says, "Practice, in our case, carries a heavy moral, ethical burden. That is, we try to act (not always successfully) in accordance—not only with a theoretical analysis—but also, and above all, according to what we consider to be our duty. We try to be consistent, always. Perhaps that is why we are not 'pragmatic' (which is another way of saying 'action without theory or principles').[72] They constantly reaffirm the ethical character of Zapatismo, treating "consistency in what we think and say" as a guiding compass, even when it means sacrificing efficiency or forfeiting a potential advantage.[73] How do they do it? And what criteria allows them to link ethics and politics, given that the latter tends to be the arena of instrumental rationality, where the ends justify any means for obtaining them? It cannot simply be a question of good intentions or personal purity. "Ethics and Politics," the epistolary exchange between Subcomandante Marcos and Luis Villoro, explains the most conclusive criteria. In each letter, we find—implicitly or explicitly—the opposition between politics from above and from below. The former is the space of simulacra and lies ("To lie greatly and do so with impunity, that is Power"), trickery and betrayal, petty interests, and factional battles.[74] We can see the lesson here in all its severity: for politics from above—guided as it is by the logic of hegemony—ethics is impossible. Therefore, if you wish to join politics and ethics together, you must leave the realm of power behind. This link can only be forged below, within this left from below that is "Power's other," to use Tomás Segovia's expression.

Subcomandante Marcos also highlights the way Luis Villoro differentiates between morality and ethics, writing "You, Don Luis, have said that 'Social morality is only the first level of ethics, a precritical one. Ethics begins when the subject distances themself from the existing forms of morality and questions the validity of its rules and behavior. They notice that social morality does not live up to the virtues it proclaims.'" Acting according to one's principles is therefore the heart of ethics, and this can only be so if those principles are not an imposed duty or an ideologized routine but an intentional commitment consistent with one's own life path. Ethics requires respect for the Zapatista principle of "each in their own way" (*cada quien su modo*), but it cannot be an individual quest. What is good for a person can only be so if their existence as part of a collective reality is taken into account, as no individual can survive—much less achieve their potential—without the relations that bind them to a community or collective. Therefore, using ethics as a compass for politics from below is nothing other than the search for a good life for all, in keeping with our sense of dignity. This is the ethical demand animating struggles from below, insurgencies against the imposition of humiliating, impoverished forms of life, struggling to create a full, beautiful, joyous life for all. This demand is called dignity.

Dignity is central to Zapatista word-thought. Subcomandante Marcos explained that, back in their clandestine period, "dignity started to become a very strong word," explaining that "It's not a contribution from us, the urban element but a contribution from the communities." With it, "the revolution became fundamentally moral. Ethical. More than the redistribution of wealth or expropriation of the means of production, the revolution becomes the possibility for a human to have a space of dignity . . . for dignity to be achieved, respected."[75] The concept is not unheard of in the Marxist tradition, as the *Communist Manifesto* includes dignity among the values that capitalism destroys: the bourgeoisie "has reduced dignity to exchange value . . . and has left remaining no other nexus between man and man than naked self interest." Dignity is also quite present in the thought of Ernesto Che Guevara. It is significant that the importance of dignity for the EZLN stems from its Indigenous component, and not its early urban militants, who had a more classical understanding of politics. (It should also make us wonder about the richness of Indigenous cultural values that is surely inadequately translated into the word "dignity.")[76] In any case, the concept has become omnipresent within the Zapatista struggle. For instance, the Zapatistas named their 2001 mobilization the March for Indigenous Dignity. Comandante Tacho amusingly reflects on the headaches this word caused the federal government's representatives during the San Andrés dialogues: "They told us they were hard at work studying what this 'dignity' means, that they were doing consultations and making investigations into dignity. The only sense they could make of it was that dignity meant serving others. So they asked us what dignity meant to us, and we told them to keep up their research. It made us laugh, and we laughed right in their faces. . . . We told them that once we sign a peace agreement, then we'll finally tell them what dignity means to us."[77]

Dignity always runs the risk of becoming a rhetorical device bolstering an empty unanimity, which is why it is so important to connect it with struggle. In fact, in today's world, dignity cannot be detached from the battle against that which negates it. As Subcomandante Marcos explained, "There is still no dignity. Dignity is yet to be. Dignity is the struggle for the world to finally become dignified."[78] Dignity is the struggle against the negation of dignity; dignity denied rebels against its denial. Understood in this sense, it is clear why the Zapatistas insist on the Indigenous dimension of the struggle for dignity. For them it is primarily a struggle to reverse five centuries of colonial subjugation and humiliation. Moreover, from the Zapatistas' perspective, dignity is not an essence—an element of one's being—but a relational concept. Just as it entails not repudiating the other, it is premised on the certainty of not being repudiated. Above all, it entails seeing oneself without also seeing the shadow of the other's repudiation in this reflexive gaze. Shared dignity therefore allows seeing the other respectfully while also being seen respectfully—and seeing oneself without shame. Dignity is an interpersonal relation based in the full recognition of both oneself and the other. It is a way of signaling social relations that are respectful of difference, that give them their place without denying them as differences. Marcos continues in the speech quoted above, saying:

> Dignity is a bridge. It needs two sides that are different, distinct, and distant. They become one through their bridging without ceasing to be different and distinct—although they are now less distant. When dignity's bridge is extended, the "we" that we are can speak, as can the other who we are not. The one and the other are there on the bridge that is dignity. The one isn't bigger or better than the other, nor is the other bigger or better than the one. Dignity demands they become a *we*. But dignity is not about everyone becoming *us*. For dignity to exist, the other has to be there, because we are always in relation to the other. And the other is other-ly in relation to us. Dignity is therefore a gaze. It is a gaze cast upon ourselves that also sees the other looking upon themselves and upon us. Dignity is therefore recognition and respect. Recognition of what we are and respect for that which we are, yes but also recognition of what the other is and respect for what they are. Dignity is therefore a bridge and a gaze and recognition and respect.[79]

Dignity opposes the repudiation and humiliation that Indigenous peoples, in particular, have suffered. Dignity is denied through injustice, through the degrading living conditions that most people suffer in today's world. Through the indifference of its calculating selfishness and dehumanizing relations, capitalist society dissolves dignity. This is why we can equate the struggle for dignity with the various ways that humanity rebels against capitalism. The Zapatistas created the concept of "dignified rage"—naming their worldwide festival in 2008 after it—to identify this rebellious dignity that struggles against that which denies it. (In the mirror that is dignity, "People see each other as equals. And if they are not equal, they rebel.")[80] Those who take up the struggle for dignity are inevitably enraged by the prevailing reality. Confronting that which denies it, dignity cannot express itself as anything other than rage, as rejection of the intolerable but it cannot remain limited to such negativity. It cannot be rage alone. It must become dignified rage that struggles to recuperate denied dignity, knowing that it can only regain it with dignity. At the same time, apart from being a rebellion that rejects ongoing oppression, dignified rage also seeks to build another world where human life can be lived in complete dignity. In this sense, when the Zapatistas speak of "dignity," they are naming both the struggle against capitalism and the struggle for a world free of the tyranny humanity is subject to. Dignity synthesizes the significance of politics from below, as an ethical politics in pursuit of a dignified life for all. It wants "every man and woman, wherever they are, to have a dignified life, so that they are all satisfied with whatever their concept of dignity entails. This is the world the Zapatistas want, so that we may all live with dignity."[81]

The politics from below begins with the recognition of shared dignity for all (noting that those who attempt to subject or humiliate others can only do so by sacrificing their own dignity). This is in stark contrast to politics from above, which is premised on the incapacity of ordinary humans, who are understood either as ignorant or as victims. This leads to a politics of compassion—or what the Zapatistas call "evangelizer syndrome"—which is a frequent practice of those who, armed with the best of intentions, attempt to help the poor Indians by teaching them what they need to do to end their poverty.[82] We find the same scheme at work with politicians who aspire to be the people's savior, as well as the vanguards who attempt to lead them into a glorious future. Yet in each case the result is the consolidation of power *over* the people. Politics from below, on the other hand, is premised on the dignity and capacity of all. Marcos writes, "We have learned to trust people, the people, our people. We know that you no longer need anyone to lead you, that you are equipped with your own structures for fighting and winning, that you take your own destinies into your hands and that you do it better than governments that impose themselves from without."[83] By beginning with shared dignity, they immediately thwart the ambitions of both the state apparatus and vanguards. This is what gives them the opportunity to experiment with self-organization and self-government, understanding that the only true emancipation is *self-emancipation*. In this sense, dignity is but another name for collective ability, the capacity of organized people to struggle and act on their own behalf. Politics from below is a path traveled through the shared dignity of those who struggle against the denial of their dignity.

Something else to consider is that we cannot break with classical politics without creating a new orientation toward the word. The living, concrete, incarnate word must replace discourses delivered from on high, those laden with vanguardist certainty, looking to impose themselves by dint of their generality and the prestige of their theory. Much has been said about Subcomandante Marcos's talents as an author, but the word is not a literary matter or merely a personal one. Instead, the very unique use of the word we find in the Zapatistas' communiques—first in baroque postscripts and later in extensive accounts of all sorts—should be understood as constitutive of a very other conception of politics. We find a break with conventional (and rather dull) forms of political discourse through the use of humor, irony, and the mingling of genres. For example, when the symposium in memory of Andrés Aubry began in 2007, Subcomandante Marcos, surrounded by intellectual celebrities (Immanuel Wallerstein at his side), began his portion by recounting the romances of Elías Contreras, one of the characters from his stories, as well as the current dance crazes in Indigenous communities and his own "elephant-like grace." After having recalled the wise saying "If I can't dance, I don't want to be part of your revolution," he concluded by saying that, "We need to find some way of connecting theory to love, music, and dance."[84] This breaks with the customary solemnity of political discourse, which benefits the typical revolutionary leader, whose supposed prestige is based in part on their claims of superior reasoning and theoretical certainties. By proclaiming its incompleteness, its errors, and its missteps ("We messed up, we always mess up"; "We declare that we're a mess!"), the Zapatista movement refuses once again to define itself as a new orthodoxy, sure to apprehend the Truth.[85]

Subcomandante Marcos treats his own personage with humor and irony. He often describes himself through his interactions with Indigenous children like Eva, Heriberto, Olivio, Yeniperr, and many others, attempting to play the role of a reasonable adult capable of controlling their overflowing energy. But these stories invariably conclude with the defeat of the EZLN's military commander by the mischief of these spritely creatures, such as when la Toñita takes revenge on the Sup by throwing his machete in the toilet.[86] Similarly, we find in his writings a struggle to deconstruct the figure of the strongman leader (*caudillo*). In general, the Zapatista word elaborates an ethics of the small and a poetics of defeat that are constitutive parts of a politics from below. To that end, it is worth clarifying once more that this is not some sort of defeatism or penchant for self-deprecation. Instead, it is a way of undoing authority figures to appreciate the nobility of the humble and the hidden wisdom of those who seem to know nothing. (For example, when Elías Contreras, in his deep discomfort with all things sexual, surprises Magdalena with his delicate perspicacity.[87]) This is not about seeming weak or defeated in the eyes of the oppressor but about defeating *in ourselves* that which aspires to a position of superiority.

"This business of making a new world is a very serious thing and, if we don't laugh, we'll end up with a world so square that we won't have a way to get around to the other side," said Marcos.[88] To that end, it's important to find a way to reunite the struggle and the *fiesta*, the political and the poetic, thought and the senses, the head and the heart, anticapitalism and dance. If we are struggling for a full life, in all its joyous beauty, we cannot construct it through a process that denies these very aspects. The struggle against separation cannot be carried out through divided and dichotomous forms. In this sense, throughout the struggle against separation—especially against a politics separate from lived experience—we must constantly reinvent a concrete and creative word, a word capable of re-unifying all the dimensions of human life.

Autonomy: A politics against the state

Politics from below is a process of self-organization, based on shared dignity and the power of collective activity (*hacer*). Autonomy, understood as a way of self-governing in keeping with peoples' own forms of life, is the expression *par excellence* of an other politics. We have already discussed the Zapatistas' autonomous practices in their territories, and now we must continue on this path by exploring what autonomy implies, in its opposition to state-centric politics.

The notion of autonomy—literally, the act of establishing one's own norms—has varied and even divergent meanings. So what kind of autonomy are we talking about exactly? That is, autonomy for whom? With respect to what and for what? Clearly the autonomy we are discussing here is not the freedom of the individual subject—one of modernity's founding myths—but is instead primarily a collective autonomy (without necessarily conflicting with individual autonomy). In practice, a collective asserts autonomy when it rejects what it considers to be external imposition, so that its own forms of organization may prevail. In this sense, autonomy combines a negative aspect (rejecting an external imposition) and a positive one (affirming their own rules). But this still says nothing about concrete autonomous practices, which depend on the rules the collective adopts and their relationship with those they reject.

There are a wide range of autonomies. There are integrated autonomies, whose rules differ very little from those of the sovereignty they withdrew from, except that these rules are now applied by new people. This is the case when autonomy is simply understood as the decentralization of state power. In contrast, antagonistic autonomies are those whose rules differ strongly from those they reject. We can also distinguish "inconsistent autonomies"—which reject domination imposed from without only to better impose domination from within—from more consequential autonomies—which reject external imposition to prevent *any* form of domination within. We could also contrast "closed" and even segregationist autonomies—based on identity categories that impose an absolute divide between the autonomous collectivity and the surrounding world—with "open autonomies" that are fundamentally relational, understanding autonomy itself to be constituted through its relations with other collectivities.

In the case of the Zapatistas, we should remember that they have built their autonomy without enjoying legal recognition; that they aim to withdraw from the state and from capitalism; and that they seek to couch their self-government project within a broader emancipatory struggle. Given all this, we could characterize their autonomy as consequential, deeply antagonistic, and open. It could also be characterized as a "rebellious" autonomy (after all, their self-government structures are called the "Zapatista Rebel Autonomous Municipalities"), and an "antisystemic" one.

This is why Zapatista autonomy is not just a local project or only an undertaking for Indigenous peoples, but we can understand how people may have initially (mis)understood the struggle for autonomy as limited to Indigenous peoples. For example, the EZLN demanded that "We Indigenous people must be permitted to organize and govern ourselves autonomously."[89] Also, the San Andrés Accords referred to Convention 169 of the International Labour Organization, which defines autonomy as the "concrete expression" of the "right of Indigenous peoples to free determination." As they have continued along their path, autonomy has become more and more important for the Zapatistas, and while this is in part due to a growing movement for Indigenous rights (as well their recognition internationally), this was never the full extent of the Zapatistas' struggle. Much less has their struggle been limited to debates over institutional interpretations of Indigenous autonomy. They made this clear when signing the San Andrés Accords, saying, "As for the autonomy [of Indigenous peoples], the EZLN understands this within the context of a much wider, more diverse national struggle, as part of the autonomization of all of civil society. The EZLN knows perfectly well that we will not topple the *ancien regime* with Indigenous autonomy alone but only with the autonomy—as well as the independence and the liberty—of the entire Mexican people."[90] Nearly two decades later, a teacher in the Zapatista Little School made similar remarks, saying, "We, the millions of Mexicans, can create our autonomies."[91] María de Jesús Patricio Martínez echoed these words in Tehuacán in November 2017, saying "the Indigenous Council of Government is a call to govern ourselves in our territories."[92] In fact, autonomy is a form of collective organization that all the peoples of Mexico and the world can share. It is not a purely local proposal, something small by necessity. Certainly it must be built *locally*, rooted in the particular ways of living and inhabiting a certain territory. But it is also a *generalizable* proposal that can be implemented in specific ways anywhere in the world.

Autonomy stems from shared dignity and the power of collective activity, creating forms of self-government based on people's own ways of living. It operates through a political logic diametrically opposed to that of the state. Eloisa, a teacher in the Zapatista Little School, offered a powerful lesson synthesizing autonomy, saying "They're scared we might see that we can govern ourselves."[93] Her precept recognizes both the current dominance of politics from above as well as their fragility, since the discovery of autonomy exposes the disastrous uselessness of those on top. It also suggests that autonomy requires dismissing (*destituir*) those on top, that is, leaving their power without foundation. For now, we underline that the teacher Eloisa's most important lesson during the Little School, which synthesizes the experience of building autonomy is this: "We can govern ourselves." With this declaration she overturns the premise of the modern state and flies in the face of Hegel. For the illustrious philosopher, the people are defined by their inability to govern themselves, as the people "do not know what they want," given that they lack "deep knowledge and insight" and therefore must depend on "state officials," those who "necessarily have deeper and more comprehensive insight into the workings and needs of the state."[94] Yet in practice, and counter to the principles of formal democracy, we see that the power of all manner of experts has only grown, subjugating the will of the people ever more. Within this context, formal democracy's mechanisms for electing rulers and representatives only energize and legitimate an apparatus that dispossesses the people of their ability to decide and to act.

Going back in time to one of the first theories of the modern state, we encounter the frontispiece of Thomas Hobbes's *Leviathan* (1651). In this engraving, town and country appear emptied of inhabitants, who are all bound together within the gigantic body of the Sovereign who dominates the land. It illustrates the claim that the people do not exist except during the fleeting moment when they alienate their sovereign power, ceding it to him who incarnates the State.[95] Giorgio Agamben concludes his analysis of this image and the political philosophy it synthesizes writing, "If we call '*ademia*' (from *dēmos*, the Greek term for people) the absence of a people, then the Hobbesian state—like every state—lives in a condition of perennial *ademia*."[96] In fact, *ademia* is the substance of the state, even when it dresses itself in "democratic" clothing—democracy understood in the severely restricted sense of the right to elect rulers and representatives. We might even understand the state as a mechanism for capturing the collective capacity to decide and to do (which it defines as sovereignty, locating it within the people as to better guarantee that they are dispossessed of it). The state is therefore a machine created to (re)produce the absence of the people, to consolidate the separation between rulers and ruled to better impose heteronomous norms of life, which today are those of the economy.

Autonomy is exactly the opposite of this state-centric politics. As we see in the lesson of the teacher Eloisa, it is based on the ability of everyone to govern themselves—to decide for themselves and organize themselves. It stems from the art of self-activity and shared dignity. It rejects all suspicion of ignorance and incompetence, which are used to justify the concentration of power among those who pretend to know what is best for others. Autonomy is the unfolding of the ability to "govern ourselves," according to people's own forms of life. This is the only way to break *ademia*, the absence of the people, which is fundamental to the state-form. As the teacher Jacobo said during the Zapatista Little School, "We believe in true democracy"—an expression we may consider a synonym of "governing ourselves."[97] Autonomy is another name for (true) democracy, which can only consist of people exercising their capacity for self-government, not in the right to elect those who deprive them of it. In politics from above, that of the state, *ademia* reigns, but in politics from below there can be real democracy, which is to say self-government. This is why autonomy is a politics against the state. For this reason, the Zapatista Good Government Councils can be considered *non-state forms of government*.

There are a few more aspects of political autonomy that we find in the Zapatista experience. First, it can be seen as a politics of processuality, as autonomy is not built by applying predefined recipes. The Zapatistas insist that they have never had any sort of manual telling them what to do.[98] Instead of attempting to spell out generalized, abstract solutions, they understand the experience of self-government as a process of constant trial and error that— through practice itself—attempts to find specific and concrete solutions to problems. They say, "Each thing we do is like taking a step forward. We have to see if it works, and if not, we have to change it."[99] As the famous slogan synthesizing the Zapatista method goes, the politics of autonomy "walks by asking questions" (*caminar preguntando*). Walking by asking questions means that the path is not set beforehand but rather made by walking. We advance without a predefined solution, without knowing for sure where we are headed. Questions and doubts arise with each step. Accepting them as such, instead of applying preconceived notions, allows us to discover how to proceed. Obviously, those doing the walking do not have to reinvent the world with each step; they can also rely on their accumulated experience and ethical criteria. But to walk by asking questions implies a relation between practice and theory in which the former cannot be subordinate to the latter. It means that the process of becoming will prevail over any kind of rigid, predetermined truth, established once and for all. This is how autonomy walks.

We were also told by a teacher at the Little School that autonomy "has no end," demonstrating a healthy consciousness of the incompleteness of the experience, no matter its progress. But it says more: the construction of autonomy will never be perfected and finished. By adopting this attitude, the Zapatistas refuse to aspire to create some ideal society where, on one sunny morning, they will proclaim the mission is accomplished, that their plans have been fully implemented. Instead, such a proclamation would certainly spell the death of autonomy, so it is quite literally vital to recognize that the project has no end. We must recognize that autonomy can never be fully accomplished, and by doing so we avoid the danger of pursuing a normative utopia, of seeking the perfect realization of pre-defined and abstract principles. We must admit there can be no ideal collective reality that is free from any risk of conflict. Even a world where autonomies spanned the entire globe would have its tensions and misunderstandings between a diversity of collectives, each with different interpretations of what good life is. Moreover, the Zapatista experience shows the importance of constantly modifying autonomy's organizational forms, in order to better struggle against the ever-present danger of separation of rulers and ruled, and the risk of petrification of institutions.

The Zapatistas' ability to maintain fluidity within their organizing forms is remarkable. Across their various areas of activity (education, health, etc.) as well as their levels of government, they continuously modify their practices to respond to the difficulties that are always arising.[100] There are never fixed arrangements or fetishism of the instituted, instead there is a restlessness that is laden with dissatisfaction, the pursuit of errors, and efforts to rectify them. Instead of stubbornly defending what has been established, autonomy is a process-based politics that incessantly builds and transforms its collective organizing structures, all while battling whatever puts them at risk. Conscious of the unnecessary danger of attempting to achieve some fully realized and supposedly ideal form, autonomy is a politics without end.

Autonomy is also a politics of multiplicity that rejects any abstract, general, *a priori* solutions and instead commences from the singularities of concrete situations. This is why there is no single form of Zapatista autonomous government. Not only are its methods permanently changing but they also differ between one municipality, or Caracol, and another. The method for resolving difficulties is found in the process, and they adapt to the particularity of each situation.[101] If autonomy is a politics that is rooted in the specificity of a territory and the ways of inhabiting it that those living there have created, this politics from below is also necessarily a politics of multiplicity. Uniform solutions are only conceivable through the distant, abstract, contemptuous gaze of those using the state's centralizing logic. Autonomy's logic assumes that there will never be a single solution to a widespread problem, that there are multiple options in processes of becoming, produced by the variety of concrete situations autonomy must attend to. (And this is why the aspiration of autonomous politics is "a world where many worlds fit.") Nonetheless, it is important to clarify that the Zapatistas' understanding of autonomy as a politics of multiplicity in no way leads them to consider singularities as absolute and to attempt to isolate them from one another. Autonomy is not autarchy, nor does it seek to isolate itself behind fortified walls, shunning contact with the other worlds that exist within this world. On the contrary, autonomous spaces thrive by weaving their freely developed forms of life together with other geographies. Autonomy is a politics of singularity and also one of free association between many local singularities. In sum, autonomy is a politics of concrete particularities, anchored in lived experience and the processuality of doing. All this is radically opposed to the logics that constitute the state.

As an outgrowth of its own journey (*caminar*), the Zapatista experience was able to demonstrate the existence of an other politics, distinct from the politics of the state and its institutions. Several factors converged to make this possible. First was the indispensable critique of the role of the state and vanguardism within their own revolutionary tradition. Second were the betrayals and roadblocks that put an end to years of attempting to dialogue with governmental institutions and seeking the legal recognition of Indigenous rights. Third were the Indigenous communities' organizing forms and the construction of autonomy in the rebellious territories of Chiapas, understood as a step toward liberation from capitalism and reversing the dispossession of our collective power (*potencia*).

The other politics is the opposite of politics from above, which is premised on the people's inability, guaranteeing that the exercise of sovereignty remains limited to experts and public affairs professionals. The other politics is born of shared dignity and based on the collective capacity to do and to organize. Far from the double heteronomy of the state and economy, autonomy is the abundant fruition of politics from below, proof that "we can govern ourselves" so that "the life of the people themselves" may flourish. In brief, autonomy is the expression of the collective capacity to self-govern, according to the forms of life that people feel are their own.

Although autonomy is a situated politics, inscribed in a particular territory and a specific experience, it is not merely a local matter. It is a generalizable political principle, yet not in the abstract, homogenizing way of the state. It does not spread through the principle of the One, as a model to be universalized, but rather as a proliferation of singularities. No autonomy, not even the Zapatistas', can be reproduced. As Subcomandante Galeano writes, "We say that Zapatismo cannot be exported, not even in Chiapas but that each calendar and geography has to continue with its own logic."[102] But the very principle of autonomy can be multiplied, to give way to a world where there is room for many autonomies. At the same time, the Good Government Councils show that various autonomies may indeed coordinate, enriching each other by exchanging different experiences of life, making decisions about issues they have in common, confronting inevitable conflicts that are unlikely to magically disappear.

Autonomy also implies an integral politics, not only because it rejects the separation between the rulers and the ruled and struggles to prevent the reproduction of this dynamic, but also because it is a politics that is harmonized with ethics and reintegrated into daily life. It is about self-governing based on people's own forms of life while also honoring the desire to permanently work at transforming these, to care for Mother Earth and build a full, good life for everyone. This is an understanding of autonomy as "building our own path toward life."[103] In this sense, autonomy is a search for what each group, each community, each people consider to be a good form of life, a dignified and beautiful way of interacting with others and with the world. Politics from below aims to eliminate politics as a separate activity, distinct from life itself.

Despite their uncertain boundaries, one of the main disputes between politics from below and politics from above has to do with how we distinguish between state and non-state political forms. The former aim to (re)produce the dispossession of collective *power-to* and its condensation into a *power over,* while the latter work to preserve this collective power and prevent its capture for the benefit of a separate apparatus.[104] In this sense, more than a politics without the state, autonomy is a politics *against the state.* This is not only because autonomy opposes the state, but also because it requires constantly inventing mechanisms for effectively preventing the capture of collective power.[105]

It is a politics against the state insofar as it restores the collective capacity to govern ourselves and makes power from above useless and unsustainable. This means dismantling it, dissolving it (*destituir*), leaving it without a foundation. That is why the Zapatista teacher Eloisa says, "They're scared we might see that we can govern ourselves." Maybe this dismissive logic was behind the October 2016 proposal of the EZLN and CNI to form a national Indigenous Council of Government. They said their goal was to create a process capable of "dismantling from below the power that is imposed on us by those above."[106] And what allows us to dismantle power from above, if not the capacity to self-organize and self-govern? The same document labels Indigenous peoples' practices like community assemblies, community police, and self-defense forces as "power from below," concluding "This is the power from below that has kept us alive."[107]

This "power from below" is in asymmetric opposition to "power from above"; it does not defeat it by competing for hegemony. Instead, it can only defeat it to the extent that it dismisses it, rendering it without foundation. It is qualitatively different from power from above. It is *power to do* rather than *power over.* It is power from below because it does not seek any above. It is capacity (*potencia*) rather than power. It is the collective capacity to self-govern—the very thing that, from below, can dissolve the power that the state tries to impose from above.

CHAPTER 3

"For Humanity and against Capitalism!"

The Fourth World War, the Hydra, and the Storm to Come

The Zapatistas are building a rebellious and antisystemic autonomy in their territories, and they are committed to national initiatives, from "The First Declaration of the Lacandon Jungle" to the Other Campaign and the formation of the Indigenous Governing Council emanating from the National Indigenous Congress. Yet the local and national dimensions of their struggle only find their full meaning within a larger one, within a scale that encompasses all the peoples of the world and their common enemy: neoliberalism. That is to say, the globalized capitalism that has prevailed since the last quarter of the twentieth century. We must situate all struggles, even the most localized ones, within this planetary horizon. Moreover, the contemporary dynamics of the capitalist system must be understood as part of a war—the Fourth World War—between capitalism and humanity.

Understanding capitalism as war is central to Zapatista word-thought (*palabra-pensamiento*). One of this chapter's main tasks will be to account for it. We will also consider other ways the Zapatistas characterize capitalism's dynamics, such as the metaphors of the Hydra and the storm, while the image of the crack will allow us to imagine the path of anticapitalist resistance.

Zapatista word-thought invites us to fight *for humanity* and *against capitalism*. To understand the strength of their approach, we must explore the various facets of this antagonism in all their depth. And we must also understand how the Zapatistas prevent "humanity" from becoming an empty word, diluted into a lukewarm humanitarianism that accommodates itself to capitalist devastation.

The struggle for humanity and against neoliberalism

From the critique of neoliberalism to anticapitalism

In 1994, the critique of neoliberalism was not yet so present in the Zapatista word. April 10th of that year saw the appearance of Don Durito de la Lacandona—the beetle who was to become one of Subcomandante Marcos's most loyal companions. Durito suggested "studying neoliberalism and its strategy of domination in Latin America," however, neoliberalism is not mentioned in either the first or second "Declaration of the Lacandon Jungle."[1] The first change came in 1995, when "The Third Declaration of the Lacandon Jungle" called for tossing neoliberalism into "the dustbin of history." This is when the Durito cycle truly begins, as he besieges Subcomandante Marcos with his "courses in political economy" and his various pronouncements, such as his affirmation that "neoliberalism is the crisis itself made theory and economic doctrine."[2] Then in 1996, the critique of neoliberalism comes to the fore, especially once the Intercontinental Encounter for Humanity and Against Neoliberalism was convened.

Subcomandante Marcos's June 1997 text, "Seven Loose Pieces of the Global Jigsaw Puzzle," is one of his strongest critiques of neoliberalism.[3] The document identifies neoliberalism's main features: globalization, enabled by a revolution in communications technology; the liberalization of commercial and financial flows; the dominance of financial markets and the loss of state sovereignty (he writes that "globalization is nothing other than the globalization of the logic of financial markets"); the growing strength of large transnational corporations; the exorbitant power of international institutions (the International Monetary Fund, World Bank, World Trade Organization, etc.); privatization and the dismantling of the welfare state; accentuation of social inequalities; overexploitation of labor, combined with the decline of real wages and rising unemployment and precarity; an increase in the number of displaced people, refugees, and migrants; and the integration of organized crime and drug trafficking into the global financial system.

From that moment on, neoliberalism became the fundamental enemy, and the fight against it became the fundamental axis of the Zapatistas' analyses. Subcomandante Marcos wrote, "We know what makes us the same: an enemy, neoliberalism, and a cause, that of humanity."[4] The "Intergalactic Chronicles" also emphasize that "Beyond the national forms that it adopts, neoliberalism constitutes a global offensive against life and against humanity" in such a way that "the universality of the neoliberal strategy must lead to a universality of resistance. We are all facing the same enemy."[5] This is why participants in the Intercontinental Encounter in the summer of 1996 discussed the need for a planetary struggle against this globalized enemy, calling for the creation of "an intercontinental network for humanity and against neoliberalism." That is to say, not a unified and centralized organization (which would be "a new addition to the useless enumeration of the numerous internationals") but a meeting space for articulating many struggles and initiatives together.[6]

Although the Zapatistas' initiative did not immediately give rise to a global network of resistances, one could argue that this proposal materialized into the alter-globalization movement that grew out of the mobilizations against the World Trade Organization summit in Seattle in December 1999, and in the World Social Forum, which met for the first time in Porto Alegre in January 2001. The EZLN did not have a direct role in these initiatives, however, many of those active in these movements have acknowledged the importance of Zapatismo as a precedent and point of reference for their own mobilizations. Whether or not Zapatismo was decisive for the rise of the alter-globalization movement, undeniably the cry of "Enough is enough!" (*Ya Basta!*) on January 1, 1994, was an opening salvo in the struggle against the predominance of neoliberalism, paving the way for others to come.

"The Sixth Declaration of the Lacandon Jungle," released in June 2005, marked a notable turning point. A communiqué issued a year later highlights: "The one responsible for our pain, for the injustices, contempt, dispossession, and attacks that we must live with, is an economic, political, social, and ideological system—the capitalist system." Here, the critique of capitalism *as such* prevails over that of neoliberalism. This was not a radical change in their analysis, since it was already clear that neoliberalism was nothing more than capitalism's specific form as the twentieth century came to a close and the next century began. However, the change in word choice is certainly consequential. First, it helps clarify the ambiguities of various tendencies within the alter-globalization movement, which seemed to limit their criticism to the neoliberal *form* of capitalism. They could not clarify whether they intended to build "alternatives inside capitalism rather than . . . alternatives to capitalism" (the latter is limited to struggling to restore the sovereignty of national states and returning to the Keynesian capitalism that neoliberalism has dismantled).[7] Moving from rejecting neoliberalism to an explicitly anticapitalist stance requires a more radical critique of the status quo. Neoliberalism was the "monolithic thought" (*pensamiento único*) that dominated the nineties, leaving little room for criticism and rendering words like "capitalism" (and, even more so, "anticapitalism") nearly impossible to utter. Yet by the beginning of the new millennium—and especially after the 2008 crisis—critical thinking enjoyed a relative recovery, allowing for more explicit understandings of who the real enemy is. In any case, in 2005, the Zapatista struggle began to identify as anticapitalist, without caveats. Speaking on the anniversary of the uprising in 2015, Subcomandante Moisés updated the slogan that was first launched by the Intercontinental Encounter in 1996: "For humanity and against capitalism!"

Neoliberal capitalism as the Fourth World War

While traditional historiography only recognizes two world wars, the Zapatistas provocatively call neoliberal capitalism the Fourth World War.[8] It is not as strident to characterize the so-called Cold War as a world war, considering how Subcomandante Marcos points out that there were 149 wars between 1945 and 1989 with a total of 23 million deaths (twice as many as during the First World War). Once the Cold War ended with the collapse of the Soviet bloc, the unipolar reorganization of the world did not entail a return to peace. Rather, beneath an increasingly shattered Pax Americana was a growing, globalized chaos that can truly be called a Fourth World War. But how to understand this characterization? Is it a metaphor? A useful exaggeration highlighting the destructive power of capitalism? The obsession of a powerful military commander? (Subcomandante Galeano suggested the latter about his predecessor, Subcomandante Marcos, when he asked, "What else would you expect from a soldier?")[9]

Before taking up these questions, we should review how Subcomandante Marcos defines the Fourth World War: it targets territories, states, national markets, culture, forms of life and—ultimately—humanity itself. If wars always involve "the conquest of territories and their reorganization," then the mass dispossession of territories shows that the Fourth World War is indeed a "new war of conquest."[10] But he argues that the process goes even further, saying "This Fourth World War uses something we like to call 'destruction.' It destroys territories and depopulates them. When it begins to wage war, it has to destroy territory, turn it into a wasteland—not out of destructive zeal, but in order to reconstitute and reorder it."[11] There is always a double process of destruction and reconstruction ("Capitalist war seeks destruction/depopulation and, simultaneously, reconstruction/reorganization"), which allows for the creation of a new geography.[12] Furthermore, since it is a *world* war, it means redrawing the world map in line with the needs of economic powers. These processes may be unleashed through military operations, or in other ways ranging from urban infrastructure projects (by creating chaos in the city, which allows the wealthy to appropriate land and privatize services), to the wholesale elimination of labor ("dumping" millions of workers condemned to unemployment and social exclusion), to structural adjustment measures that work to dispossess territories and natural resources.

The second target is the state and its foundation—the national market—which must be "liquidated by the artillery fire of the new era of global finance."[13] It is a monstrous war in which "the son (neoliberalism) devours the father (national capitalism)." In this war, "Companies and states collapse in minutes, not from the storms of proletarian revolutions, but from the onslaught of financial hurricanes." This war's weapon *par excellence* is the "financial bomb," which includes the effects of free trade agreements, the so-called modernization of the countryside that causes a mass exodus, as well as capital movements that, in a matter of hours, can bring a country to its knees. These bombs, explains Subcomandante Marcos, are much more "rational" than neutron bombs, since they do not destroy infrastructure or labor, but rather manage to integrate both directly into the new world market amid the state's ruin. And although, as we saw in the previous chapter, states do not formally disappear, they lose "the material bases of their national sovereignty," which is why they have no other option than to submit to the whims of the financial markets. Integration into free trade zones accentuates the dominance of the economic over the political. As Marcos writes, "Now, politics is only needed for economic organization, and politicians are business managers. . . . Nations are department stores with governments as managers, and the new regional, economic, and political alliances are closer to a modern shopping mall than to a political federation. The 'unification' that neoliberalism produces is economic, it is the unification of markets to facilitate the circulation of money and goods."

The disappearance of the nation state's very substance—its sovereignty—is one of the main reasons why we can consider neoliberalism to be a world war. This requires "the destruction of history and culture," so as to eliminate anything preventing the generalization of the American Way of Life. Marcos writes, "The North American way of life attacks all the cultures and histories that went into forging their nations. Neoliberalism wages a total war, destroying nations and groups of nations to harmonize them with the North American capitalist model." People's lives do not have to be eliminated if their ways of living can be destroyed. This is why the Fourth World War is "the most complete, the most universal" of world wars: It attacks all nations, all peoples, all cultures.

Some years later, in an epistolary exchange with Luis Villoro, Subcomandante Marcos explained the mechanisms that provoke the "destruction of the social fabric." That is, "the annihilation of all that gives a society cohesion," allowing collective existence to be reorganized, "but now with another logic, other methods, other actors, another objective."[14] In Mexico, Felipe Calderón's "War on Organized Crime" was one of those mechanisms, the real objective of which was to destroy "the social relations that provide the common identity that is the basis of a nation." He did it by "imposing fear, uncertainty, and vulnerability through force of arms."[15] "What social relations can be created or maintained if fear is the dominant organizing principle for a social group? If the sense of the community is shattered by the cry of 'Every man for himself'"?[16] Overall, capitalism's advance requires the destruction of the people's own forms of life, especially those that provide cohesion and a sense of community, so that capital can reorganize territories and remodel entire populations according to its needs.

Finally, this war's target is humanity as a whole. As Marcos writes, "Well, it's a war, a world war, the Fourth one. The worst and the cruelest. The one neoliberalism unleashes against all humanity, everywhere, every which way."[17] By "humanity," we mean not just the group of persons and peoples who make it up, but also what makes us human. Under neoliberalism, "what matters is the law of the market, and the law of the market says that you're worth however much you produce, you're worth however much you buy. Dignity, resistance, and solidarity are all in the way. Everything that prevents the human being from becoming a machine for producing and consuming is declared an enemy and must be destroyed. This is why we say that the enemy of this Fourth World War is the human race. It may not destroy it physically, but it does destroy its humanity."[18] It leads to the disappearance of ethical and self-determined forms of life in which people can recognize themselves, replacing them with ways of being and acting that follow the economy's logic. These range from centering money to the cult of success; from internalizing the quest for efficiency to quantifying everything; from accelerated time and the dictatorship of urgency to thinking of oneself as a business enterprise. In fact, neoliberalism is not active only in the economy, nor does it only attack states; it is an offensive by "the logic of the market to . . . appropriate all aspects of social activity" and "penetrate all aspects of life."[19] One of the characteristics of neoliberal capitalism is precisely the totalizing expansion of economic logic to *all* aspects of life. It therefore seeks to destroy all forms of life that do not conform to it. Which can certainly be defined as a Fourth World War.

From military war to total war

Subcomandante Marcos "didn't understand war just as military war," since in this day and age, war is not limited to the operations of armed forces.[20] The world war that the Zapatistas speak of is not only military, or "only economic." It occurs "everywhere, every which way, all the time."[21] We must understand "war" as encompassing everything that causes the "destruction of nature and humanity," including missiles and media campaigns; chemical invasions in the countryside; patriarchal violence and religious fanaticism; human and organ trafficking; organized crime and forced disappearances; dispossession disguised as "Progress," etc.[22] Subcomandante Marcos calls this "total war," stressing that, since the Cold War, "non-military elements enter into military doctrine."[23] Communications media are an important battlefront, for example, and the enemy can be attacked through economic, political, and diplomatic means. As time went on, the concept of total war became even more important. He writes that, "It's not just a war on all fronts, it's a war that can be anywhere, a totalizing war where the whole world is at stake. 'Total war' now means at any time, in any place, under any circumstances." He refers to total war once again in "Ethics and Politics," as a characteristic of modern warfare in which strictly military force ceases to be the sole determining factor. The goal is no longer just to physically defeat the enemy but to defeat him morally, militarily, as well as through "economic, political, religious, ideological, diplomatic, social, and even ecological" means.[24]

Indeed, the twentieth century marked the transition from conventional war to total war, which extends beyond the military and moves off the battlefield.[25] On the one hand, it involves an entanglement between military resources and non-military means (economic, financial, communication, etc.), since total war implies mobilizing all productive forces, all scientific capabilities, all social energies, and all the subjective means that make it possible to mobilize them. By the same token, the goal is not only to attack the enemy's military strength, but the full range of its mobilizing capacity. Therefore, the distinction between the armed forces and civilian population tends to be erased, resulting in a steady increase in the rate of civilian casualties in armed conflicts. It is a variety of war without spatial or temporal limits, whose operations are within the population, if not completely *against* the population. It is an unlimited war, without end, one that blurs the very distinction between war and peace, that erases the distinction between external (inter-state) war and internal (civil) war. There is a proliferation of undeclared wars with non-state actors, such as the so-called "war on terror," "war on organized crime," and the growing use of counterinsurgency as a means of controlling populations.

So, if militaries themselves long since ceased to conceive of war as a strictly military phenomenon, we should not reduce the Zapatistas' characterization of neoliberalism as the Fourth World War to a mere metaphor. If you happen to consider the "financial bombs" mentioned in "Seven Loose Pieces of the Global Jigsaw Puzzle" as simple metaphors, we note that two years later, Chinese army officers theorized financial activity as a form of "bloodless war" and recommended it be integrated into a strategy of total war.[26] Analyzing how China could beat a militarily superior adversary like the United States, the authors stress that such "non-military weapons" can produce effects as destructive as "military weapons," causing insecurity across the country and "subduing it without spilling a single drop of blood." Finally, they assert the principle of total war itself, in which "it becomes increasingly obsolete to limit war to the military domain," and instead recommend transforming "the entire world into a battlefield."

It is not an exercise in metaphor to see that the aspects of total war described above also characterize contemporary capitalism. Indeed, the analyses of the world's principle military strategists are premised on this operating assumption. Subcomandante Marcos's reflections on the subject are not original because they outline the features of total war, but because they reformulate this concept from an anticapitalist perspective. Doing so involves two arguments that might seem to contradict each other but end up converging in the same analysis. The first argument highlights the importance of (military) war throughout the history of capitalism. He writes, "Capitalism produces for war and because of war. Its advancement and development depend on war, and it is war that articulates its genealogy, its main power line, its backbone."[27] The so-called "primitive accumulation" studied by Marx and discussed by Subcomandante Galeano in the seminar "Critical Thought in the Face of the Capitalist Hydra" includes the violence of colonial conquest, the dispossession

of territories and their plunder through violence, as well as the process of separating producers from their means of production. Yet colonial wars, usually
understood as acts of primitive accumulation, can also be seen as a preview of
total war. They already target the population as a whole and are premised on
unregulated violence, distinct from the rules of conventional warfare. In any
case, the Subcomandante stresses that the use of war and violence does not
only characterize the initial phases of capitalism: "War is not just part of the
origin of the capitalist system, it is part of each and every one of its 'qualitative
leaps.' War is the medicine that capitalism administers to the world, to cure it
of the ills that capitalism has imposed on it." The industrial production of the
means of destruction is fundamental for economic growth and often decisive
for overcoming crises. This was evidenced during the Third World War, which
was an attempt to prolong the war economy of the previous years into a time
of "peace"—without which, Keynesian postwar capitalist growth would have
been unsustainable. In short, capitalism cannot be understood, in any of its
stages, without war.[28]

The second argument is that war had expanded beyond the battlefield.
What is unique about the Zapatista analysis here is how they focus the concept of total war less on conflicts between states (or between states and
unconventional actors), and more on the antagonism between capital and the
populations that it reorganizes according to its interests. They say that "In the
stage of neoliberal globalization, capitalism is a war against all of humanity,
against the entire planet."[29] By transcribing the notion of total war into an anticapitalist key, they emphasize the dramatic destructiveness of capitalism and
the brutality of its antagonisms. As we have already seen, commodifying the
world requires destroying and restructuring territories, eliminating forms of
life based on community ties and capacities for self-organization, and replacing
them with ways of being and subjectivities shaped by the logics of the economy. In addition, ever since the antiterrorism paradigm was imposed as the
new mode of governmentality (especially since the 2001 attacks), all the processes listed above have been brought together and been greatly strengthened
through policing and militarized social control. And while it may not aim to
physically destroy all of humanity, capitalism certainly seeks to annihilate the
bases of resistance, that is, everything that could hinder the commodification
of the world.

What does it mean, from an anticapitalist perspective, to say that neoliberal capitalism makes war against humanity? If this enemy is making war on

all humanity, we should consider our own actions accordingly. (At the same time, we should recognize that the enemy is not a singular actor endowed with a completely unified strategy, since the chaos humanity suffers from is also a product of inter-capitalist competition and rivalry.) In the face of an enemy that could annihilate humanity and that is already systematically destroying all forms of life ill-suited to economic logics, there is only one option: to defend ourselves and prevent such destruction, which ultimately means eliminating capitalism. In a nutshell, understanding capitalism as the Fourth World War presents the following choice: destruction of humanity or destruction of capitalism. This requires us to organize on a relevant scale, which is to say, a planetary one.

Let us be more precise: those who fight for humanity and against capitalism cannot conceive of this war symmetrically, acting in the same way as the enemy. This is why Subcomandante Marcos insists that "our other war" can only be waged ethically. He explains this specifically in reference to the EZLN's choice to take up arms, but his reflections are pertinent to the fight against capitalism as a whole:

> There is a radical insight that stems from including ethics as a determining factor in conflict: the opponent sees that the result of their "triumph" will be their defeat. And I'm not speaking of defeat in terms of "destruction" or "surrender" but rather the negation of their existence as a fighting force . . . The key here is that ours is not a war to destroy our opponent in the classical sense. It's a war to eliminate the grounds for war's realization as well as the possibility for the existence of adversaries (us included). It's a war so that we may cease to be who we are, so that we can be who we should be.[30]

From an anticapitalist perspective, war is not an attempt to physically annihilate the enemy but rather to destroy the conditions that make war possible. Winning means the enemy would no longer have the capacity to be an enemy, as such. It also means dissolving the force that triumphed, instead of glorifying and perpetuating that force indefinitely. The war between capitalism and humanity must be understood in all its asymmetry: while capitalist destruction is the corruption of all forms of ethics by the cold interest and power of money, the struggle for humanity can only be understood as the search for ethics.

Critical thought in the face of the capitalist Hydra

During the seminar "Critical Thought in the Face of the Capitalist Hydra" in May 2015, the EZLN continued its analysis of capitalist war while posing new questions and proposing additional concepts. It was a powerful call for theoretical reflection. In fact, it was somewhat disconcerting for an audience accustomed to sharing experiences of struggle to hear the EZLN insist that practice alone was insufficient and that theoretical renewal was more important than ever. Given that the Zapatistas have always produced original, creative thought, it is especially significant that they decided, during this moment, to call for collective theoretical effort. To be sure, the Zapatistas have a unique understanding of theoretical reflection, insisting that theory can only exist in relation to practice. As Galeano said, "Neither theory without practice nor practice without theory."[31] Practice is the concrete ground from which a fruitful theoretical elaboration can grow (which is why it is also important to determine the practice from which the theoretical gaze looks). Furthermore, theory should not only seek to accumulate knowledge but to transform reality as well. Quoting Galeano once again, "What led us to begin this theoretical reflection is not the need to increase our cultural capital. . . . What's at stake here—and for everyone in their own time, place, and way—is the transformation of reality."[32] This is why the Zapatistas repeatedly pose the question—which is also something of a slap in the face—asking those who elaborate knowledge and theoretical reflection about their degree of commitment, saying "And what about you?" They also invite us to overcome "the persistence of individuality" and consider that "theoretical and analytical work should be collective labor," so that those who are dedicated to it may "decenter yourselves and become powerful in a collective."[33]

There is an urgent need to strengthen theoretical work understood this way. Their insistence was blunt: "We need tools for what we have to do, and those tools are theoretical concepts."[34] We must understand—they said repeatedly—how capitalism is transforming itself and, therefore, how analyses must also be transformed by those who create them and by the struggles that hope to confront it. This is a matter of life and death, because if these transformations are not recognized, rebellions and resistances run the risk of getting lost. Subcomandante Moisés said, "This destruction [of the enemy] is not achieved through thoughts. . . . No, but thoughts can help us understand what we're up against, how it works, what its ways are, its calendar, its geography. To use an expression from the Little School, it can help us understand the ways in which it attacks us."[35] Therefore, "we need critical thought to keep our understanding of the Hydra in constant crisis—that is, in motion."[36]

The capitalist Hydra, devastating but not immortal

Throughout the seminar, the Zapatistas interweaved three main metaphors: the Hydra, the storm, and the crack. The Hydra metaphor is a temporal leap back to Greek mythology, and its use was not without critique during the seminar. It was noted that it is Hercules who defeats the Hydra, an individual embodying heroic virility. But Subcomandante Galeano recalled that Hercules could not have succeeded without the help of his nephew, Iolaus, who saw it was necessary to cauterize the beast's severed head so that new heads would not continue to multiply—but the collaborative aspect of the struggle involving Iolaus is downplayed in most versions of the myth. Moreover, he insisted that "many Herculeses and many Iolauses" are necessary to resist the Hydra and attack it; from the Zapatista perspective the fight against the Hydra can only be collective.[37] Another critique was that the myth presents an exaggerated, totalizing image of the enemy and also suggests that it exists only outside of us, while many participants in the seminar noted that capitalism also makes its way inside of us, penetrating our spaces of struggle and our ways of being. In addition to all this, we might also note the historical ambivalence of the figure of Hercules; he was used by the kings of England in the seventeenth and eighteenth centuries (and was even proposed for the seal of the nascent United States of America) as a symbol of a civilizing power defeating many enemies, such as criminals, pirates, runaway slaves, and even striking workers.[38] Nonetheless, we also know that there is struggle and conflict between contradictory uses of symbols and images.

In the face of these criticisms, we would like to emphasize the relevance of the metaphor of the capitalist Hydra. First, its numerous heads allow us to highlight the multiple dimensions of capitalist domination: it is not only economic but encompasses a wide variety of dimensions. As Galeano says, "This capitalist system is not dominant only in one aspect of social life, but rather has multiple heads, that is, many forms and ways of dominating in different and diverse social spaces. To put it in the terms of the little girl called Defensa Zapatista: 'That stubborn-ass capitalism doesn't take a bite out of you in just one place but in many places.'"[39] This means that struggles against the Hydra must also be multiple, without asserting that some struggles are more important than others ("for example, the gender struggle is secondary and the struggle over political power should be primary").[40] More precisely, the Hydra metaphor allows us to simultaneously visualize the multiple aspects of capitalist domination *and* its unitary and systemic character, since it is a "global world monster," as Comandante Zebedeo had already pointed out in 2003.[41]

A second important characteristic is that the strength of the capitalist Hydra is due in large part to its plasticity, its ability to transform itself, adapting its forms of domination to new conditions and even incorporating rebel criticisms and practices. Subcomandante Galeano says, "It not only reconstructs its destroyed tentacles, but also adapts, mutates, and is capable of regenerating itself completely from any one of its parts."[42] Today's Hydra is not the same as a century ago, or even of twenty years ago, so we need a genealogical study to understand how it has been formed.[43] ("We can find the way to defeat the Hydra if we understand it, if we know what makes it tick, and getting to know it means knowing how it became what it is now.")[44] Further, the theoretical-conceptual effort to understand capitalist domination is never over. "*Compañeros* and *compañeras* . . . things have changed," so that "either we investigate and understand what has changed, or we will have no options to move forward"[45] Further, "We have to seek to change in order to survive. Resistance and rebellion will provide no solution or path if they don't find this change."[46]

Finally, the myth of the Hydra shows us a powerful enemy that causes terrible suffering and enormous devastation. It is "the bloodiest and most cruel monster ever known in reality or fiction since humanity became divided into dominators and dominated."[47] Yet it is not invincible either: "Although we begin from the assumption that the capitalist system is dominant, this is accompanied by the certainty that it is neither omnipresent nor immortal. Resistances exist, whether we know about them or not. The system does not impose its dominion evenly and without disruptions. It encounters resistance from above, yes, but those resistances below are the ones that really threaten it."[48] Despite its almighty appearance, it is possible to get rid of it. All that is needed is to figure out how and to organize accordingly.

In sum, the metaphor of the Hydra helps to accurately define the relationship between capitalist domination and those who combat it. The first keeps expanding, causing devastation of all kinds; it appears so powerful that many conclude that it's not possible to fight against it or that rebellions have no way to succeed. However, the Zapatista rereading of the myth suggests that collective strength and intelligence can confront the monster and extinguish its power. The Hydra metaphor also reiterates that this is a fight to the death. In other words, a war. Therefore, the Zapatistas clarify, "we have decided to challenge the system—not to improve it, not to change it, not to give it a makeover but to destroy it."[49]

The storm, the worst of the worst, and beyond

The metaphor of the storm brings us to the central message of the "Critical Thought in the Face of the Capitalist Hydra" seminar and its *raison d'être*. The Zapatistas explain that, from the treetop that serves as their lookout, they see a terrible storm approaching, which is why they decided to convene a seminar: "A storm is coming and we have orders from the Committee to warn you."[50] More precisely, they say, "We, the Zapatistas, see and hear a catastrophe coming, and we mean that in every sense of the term, a perfect storm." And, seeing that many "people with great knowledge" continue to speak as if "everything continues on more or less the same" and that many forms of struggle continue to reproduce themselves "as if the Hydra had not regenerated its multiple heads," they decided to organize the seminar to determine if this is because of "the syndrome of the night's watch" (which, due to the "selective attention" phenomenon, prevents us from seeing approaching dangers) and whether it can be confirmed that "what is coming is something terrible, even more destructive than before, if that's possible."[51] Perhaps the most important aspect of the image of the storm is that, "If you see signs that something bad might happen, then you should prepare for it."[52] This is the practical conclusion that the Zapatistas draw from the story of Noah's Ark, the story with which they begin the seminar.

Some may say that the image seems too prophetic or, conversely, that the storm is already here. And it is hard to imagine something more terrible than what we are already living, particularly in Mexico. If the EZLN has insisted for a long time that we are facing the Fourth World War, why locate the devastation in the future when it is already a proven, empirical fact? Many will dismiss the Zapatista message as "catastrophism," an obsession with the catastrophes to come that prevents us from seeing the dramas that are already multiplying everywhere. However, we should avoid focusing attention either only on the present or only on the future, as both are important. Worrying about the storm to come in no way implies hiding the extent to which present reality is already *unbearable*. The Zapatistas emphatically highlight this, and they act accordingly, for example, through their unfailing support for the families of the disappeared students of Ayotzinapa, the name of the darkness into which Mexico has sunk. And, while seeing and feeling the present disaster, the Zapatistas also invite us to anticipate *a dramatic worsening of the situation* across the entire planet. There is no choosing between the coming storm and the one that already exists. Those who insist that the storm is already here should not ignore the Zapatista warning that what is coming will likely be much worse. This is not about falling into despair or surrendering to the first messiah or dictator who comes along. Instead, it is a call to prepare so as to maintain the possibility that, in the midst of terribly difficult times, something positive can be born.

We can now move from the metaphor of the storm to its content: the crisis. For the Zapatistas, the storm is but a new stage in the crisis dynamics of the capitalist system. But what kind of crisis? The thesis that the EZLN put forth during the seminar is based on the choice of a particular tool—an "anticapitalist orbital telescope . . . capable of capturing the complete image of the Hydra":

> In this seminar we've borrowed the telescope of Immanuel Waller-stein. . . . [It turns out] that the Wallerstein Orbital Telescope has captured a global image of the World System and has indicated not only that it's a serious mess but also that the fucking capitalist system is in terminal crisis . . . that is, a crisis like never before. The idea that it's *the* terminal crisis, well we Zapatistas don't trust that because we've heard that before, that the fucking system is finally going to die and then it turns out that no, the Hydra regenerates itself and appears with a new face, thirstier for blood and destruction than ever before. In the mountains of the Mexican Southeast, the subterranean telescope (or inverted periscope) *Pozol 6*, revealed the same results: the system is, or will be soon, in a structural crisis.[53]

"Structural crisis" is the substance of the storm, an understanding that stems from the coincidence between the global analyses of Immanuel Wallerstein and those that the Zapatistas' inverted periscope was able to make by looking at their "small world." However, recognizing Wallerstein's contributions does not mean accepting all his conclusions. By questioning whether the current crisis is truly terminal, the Zapatistas distance themselves from one of world-systems theory's fundamental assertions, and they don't assume a bifurcation is inevitable, that "only A or B can result from the crisis." They took a similar position in

2007 during the colloquium commemorating Andrés Aubry. The title of Subcomandante Marcos's interventions ("Neither Center nor Periphery") indicated
they were questioning key concepts of world-systems analysis. Above all, they
rejected the idea that capitalism will end in a terminal collapse, saying "Capitalism's inevitable destiny is not to self-destruct, unless it kills all life on earth. The
apocalyptic prognoses, according to which the system will collapse on its own,
are erroneous. As Indigenous people, we have heard such prophecies for several
centuries. On the contrary: the destruction of the capitalist system will only
take place if one or many movements confront it and defeat it at its core."[54] They
repeated these arguments in 2015, saying there is no preprogrammed collapse
of capitalism, and its end is not predetermined (unless it follows the plotline of
causing the complete destruction of humanity). Therefore, to get rid of capitalism we must fight against it and successfully destroy it. While it is important to
know its weaknesses—the crisis that affects it—we should not expect it to die
from its own diseases. The Zapatistas do not accept arguments about a terminal
crisis, seeing them as excessively deterministic and underestimating the Hydra's
ability to regenerate itself, to open new horizons of accumulation and adapt to
ever-changing conditions.[55]

The issue then is how to understand a structural crisis that is not necessarily
a terminal one. Contrary to a cyclical crisis—which occurs periodically and is
overcome, giving way to a new cycle of accumulation—the dynamic charac-
terizing structural crises is that they tend to become permanent and central
to the mode of accumulation itself. Furthermore, it is a crisis that is not only
economic but intertwines multiple aspects, affecting all the structures of the
capitalist world-system. The Zapatistas assert that today's is "an economic crisis
like never before" that is "intensified by unnatural environmental disasters."[56] It
also includes a political crisis marked by "the loss of legitimacy of 'traditional'
institutions (parties, government, the judicial system, church, army, police,
media, and family) and the lack of any attempt to recover them" as well as other
factors such as the migration crisis (including a predicted increase in the number of migrants by 40 percent) and the violent strategy to dispossess Indigenous
lands and those of peasants in general.[57] Among the factors contributing to a
latent economic crisis, they highlight the phenomenal growth of indebtedness
globally, which amounts to three times the world's gross domestic product. This
is the foundation of finance capital's dominance, which "installs and topples
governments," in accordance with the principle that "whoever lends, rules."[58]
On the other hand, the gross imbalance between the real economy and the

amount of debt is also a point of weakness, leading to collapse during the 2008 crisis—which can certainly repeat itself, with even more acute consequences.

This analysis of the crisis leaves us with many questions, which is why the Zapatistas ended the seminar with a call for "more seedbeds" to continue analyzing the crisis.[59] We can indicate some of these questions. One is about the expansion of financial capital. There are different ways of understanding it, as evidenced when one of the seminar's participants said that financial capital allows the generation of profit "without exploiting the labor force," while another insisted that profit only "comes from the exploitation of labor." Faced with this apparent contradiction, Subcomandante Galeano proposed that, behind the money form, there is a hidden difference between financial profit that does not represent wealth and the profit obtained from work that does. He also suggested that the money that comes from financial activities is "fictitious money," because "it's not backed by labor." Rather, it seeks profit through "the appropriation of future work" and by capturing natural resources to guarantee the growth of public debt.[60]

Another open question (which the Zapatistas presented as such during their speeches) is whether the Hydra has a mother head that would constitute a privileged target, or if it has many vital heads, representing multiple dimensions of capitalist domination. And if there is a privileged target, "Is private ownership over the means of production, dispossession, circulation, and consumption the head without which the system seems incapable of reproducing itself?" In response, "Some say yes, others say no, and others still say 'yes' or 'no' but add 'but there's more to it . . .'"[61] What is expressed here as a question, eight years earlier was an affirmation. The fifth thesis on antisystemic movements asserts that the "central nucleus" of the capitalist system is "private ownership of the means of production and exchange."[62] In moving from making affirmations to posing questions, they invite a debate, making space for diverse understandings. While Marxism's dominant currents say the central nucleus of capitalism is the private property of the means of production, others stress that the system can be reproduced through forms of property that are not necessarily private. Under certain circumstances throughout history, capitalism has proven to be compatible with large doses of state ownership of the means of production, as was the case not only in authoritarian regimes such as Nazism and [Italian] fascism but also in "democratic" ones, such as Italy or France after World War II. Some argue that the Soviet bloc can also be analyzed as a form of state capitalism, in which the predominance of state ownership of the means of production was combined with the preservation of the key elements of capitalist production relations, such as the wage and the separation between workers and those who control the production process. Other Left currents insist that capitalism's most fundamental characteristics are not questions of ownership and property or of wealth distribution. Changing the property regime or equally distributing wealth will not be enough to end capitalism. In these interpretations, what is most essential—the mother head of the Hydra—is rather the social relations inscribed in the wage and the mode of production based on the commodity form and value. In capitalist logic, these are the *raison d'être* of what is produced.[63]

We could go on discussing many more aspects of the crisis. For example, are we talking about the suffering caused by the Hydra's advance, or about the disease that complicates its own reproduction? Are we talking about the crisis that capitalism causes for us or the crisis of capital itself? About our crisis or theirs? On the one hand, there are the triple catastrophes affecting the environment, the social fabric, and ways of being. On the other, there is the latent economic crisis, caused in large part by the excessive expansion of credit and resulting fragility. Obviously, there is no neat division between our crisis and theirs, since much of the devastation we suffer from the Hydra (from climate chaos to the breakdown of political institutions) also hinders its own reproduction. Nonetheless, when we analyze the crisis, it is important to clearly distinguish between aspects of the Hydra's domination that benefit it on the one hand and, on the other, aspects that create problems and can thereby support our struggle against it. Lastly, we should reflect on whether the storm should be understood only as a catastrophe, or if it is also a sign of the Hydra's weakness, making it an opportunity and source of hope for the rest of us.

The wall's cracks and deceptions

The third metaphor is that of the wall and the crack, of "scratching, biting, kicking, hitting with our hands, head, and entire body in order to make in history what we are: a wound."[64] Here again the struggle is presented as a challenge because, like the Hydra metaphor, it presents a stark imbalance between the considerable strength and seemingly unshakable solidity of the enemy on the one hand and, on the other, how laughable the attacks against it seem to be. The 2015 seminar was the first time the EZLN spoke of the crack, using it to describe the Zapatista struggle itself. By describing the struggle as opening a crack in a wall, they expose themselves to the ridicule of those who scorn this way of doing politics, those who say "You will never bring down the wall that way. It is indestructible, eternal, endless." Instead, these people suggest "seeing how you can manage the wall" or "trying to make it friendlier, more just."[65] But the Zapatistas do not despair; they keep on organizing themselves better, in teams, turns, and shifts, because "It doesn't appear in any written texts but rather in the ones that haven't been written and yet have been read for generations, but that's where the Zapatistas have learned that if you stop scratching at the crack, it closes back up. The wall heals itself. That's why you have to keep at it, not only to deepen the crack, but above all, so that it doesn't close."[66] And sometimes, someone walks by and, instead of looking down on them, "They pause, look, understand, stare down at their feet, at their hands, their fists, their shoulders, and their body and then decide, 'This spot is as good as any'. . . . And they go at it."[67] The work of cracking the wall continues:

> The Zapatista also knows that the wall's appearance can be deceiving. Sometimes it's like a great mirror that reproduces the image of destruction and death, as if no other way were possible. Sometimes the wall dresses itself up nicely, and a pleasant landscape appears on its surface. Other times it is hard and grey, as if trying to convince everyone of its impenetrability. . . . But the Zapatista knows it's a lie; they know that the wall was not always there. They know how it was erected and what its function is. They know how deceiving the wall can be. They also know how to destroy it. They are not fazed by the wall's supposed omnipotence and eternity. They know that both are false. But right now, the important thing is the crack, that it not close, that it expand. The Zapatista also knows what exists on the other side of the wall.[68]

The Zapatistas know how important it is to see to the other side of the wall, "so as to imagine everything that can be done tomorrow."[69] The little girl named Defensa Zapatista explains that she knows what is on the other side because, even though she is too short, she was able to raise up her doll so that she could look over and tell her about it. She reports back that "The wall sometimes becomes a mirror, but it's a lie, it just does that so that we think that on the other side it's the same as on this side."[70] And it just so happens that, when it turns into a mirror, the wall becomes watery. This is the moment Defensa Zapatista is waiting for, to enter the wall and maybe even pass through to the other side.

With the metaphor of the crack we have a vision of struggle that is built from small things—things that may seem insignificant but that, through stubborn perseverance, can open a path. And that narrow path can converge with other narrow paths that multiply and join into a common effort. We find a precursor to the crack in the seventh thesis on antisystemic struggles, written in 2007. It says, "Great transformations don't begin above, or with epic, monumental deeds but with movements that are small in size, that seem insignificant to the politician and analyst above."[71] By emphasizing the small, the metaphor of the crack can serve as a counterweight to the Hydra. While the latter invites us to imagine the heroic act of decapitating the monster, the crack invites us to appreciate acts that are only effective through their tenacious, daily, prolonged repetition.

How exactly do the Zapatistas understand the metaphor of the crack? First, theirs is a wall whose appearance and consistency are in flux, in contrast to the typical symbolism of a wall, which would paint capitalism as an unchanging, monolithic mass. Instead we have a fluid and dynamic reality, like the transformations found in the metaphor of the Hydra. The wall's various appearances correspond to aspects of capital's domination, which is sometimes more imposing and sometimes more seductive. The internal consistency of the wall changes as well, implying that anticapitalist strategy should multiply the cracks (the only option for now) while also attacking the internal weakness of the enemy (the structural crisis of capitalism) that could in due course open other paths. Another unique aspect of the crack is the Zapatistas' attention to what lies on the other side of the wall. It shows that the crack is not just some small opening that we can create immediately, in the midst of capitalist domination but also a way to imagine a future that we dream of but that is not yet here, sustaining the effort to go on making cracks in the wall. The Zapatista reading of the crack is not immobilized in the present, instead, it articulates the now of the crack with the tomorrow it allows us to see.

In sum, during "Critical Thought in the Face of the Capitalist Hydra," the Zapatistas structured their analysis around the concept of the structural crisis and three metaphors: the Hydra, the storm, and the crack. The metaphors converge and diverge. The Hydra is an image of the enemy; the storm is the situation it provokes; and cracks are the path of our struggles. Faced with the Hydra, the challenge is to become conscious that we are at war with an enemy who threatens to destroy everything, unless we destroy it first. Faced with the storm, the Zapatistas call on us to prepare, to organize ourselves if we are to survive. Faced with the wall, we are called upon to start building spaces that materialize other possible worlds in the here and now. Thus, the three metaphors complement and correct one another. For example, bringing the image of the crack together with the Hydra or the storm reminds us that it would be mistaken to think that building autonomous spaces is a way to live peacefully, without worrying about the destructive dynamics of capitalism. Instead, the construction of autonomous spaces entails a constant struggle to resist the storm's effects and—to the degree we are able—to attack the Hydra.

For humanity, but what humanity?

According to the Zapatistas, capitalism is, ultimately, "a world war, a war whose only enemy is humanity."[72] This is why, since the 1996 Intercontinental Encounter, the Zapatistas have called for a fight for humanity and against neoliberalism (and now, against capitalism). There is a fundamental dilemma here: either humanity manages to get rid of capitalism, or capitalism will end humanity—either physically, or by destroying the conditions of a truly human life. But how exactly do the Zapatistas understand this thing called "humanity"?

Before we get to the question, it is important to highlight the power of the Zapatistas' call to fight *for humanity and against capitalism*. The relationship between the two elements is decisive. In fact, it only makes sense to fight "for humanity" if we also identify the enemy that hinders this struggle and makes it necessary. Otherwise, the words "human" and "humanity" are the empty rhetoric of a lukewarm humanism, complicit in all oppressions. Today any "humanist" proclamation devoid of a radical critique of capitalist domination is a mystification. It has little credibility, only circulating under the devalued umbrella of "humanitarianism," a gray companion to the advances of the Hydra. On the other hand, it would be dangerous not to clarify what we are fighting *for* when we call for opposing neoliberal globalization. The world is full of religious fundamentalist movements and ultranationalists who also oppose globalization but do so on the basis of an exclusionary identity that rejects any form of difference, leading to xenophobic closures and ethnic confrontations. There are indeed "fanatics [who] say, 'On this islet of the global archipelago, there can only live others who are like me.'"[73] Their critique of neoliberalism is generally focused on denouncing the speculation and greed of bankers—a distorted form of anticapitalism that is often intertwined with an extreme right-wing ideology.

To avoid any confusion with these tendencies, it is necessary to emphasize that the fight against neoliberalism does not aim to restore any identitarian purity but is inherently a fight for all of humanity. It is a fight that does not seek confrontations between peoples, ethnic groups, or religions, but rather seeks to unite all of humanity against our common enemy. In short, it would be useless to propose a struggle for humanity without targeting the globalized capitalism that seeks to annihilate it. But it would be equally dangerous to attack neoliberalism without the perspective of a humanity fighting to save itself, to realize itself through its plurality. "The fight for humanity and against neoliberalism" is the knot that wards off these dangers and, therefore, allows the development of such a powerful perspective.

However, questions about the concept of humanity remain. Two of these will be discussed in the following chapter: the first is the question of universalism, which risks defining "Man" too abstractly and neglecting the differences that are constitutive of humanity; the second is the great division introduced by modernity, which positions man outside and above nature. For the moment we will only ask whether speaking in terms of all of humanity is too "unanimist," erasing social polarities. This issue is even more pressing now that scientists assert that we have entered a new geological period called the "Anthropocene."[74] This means that the human species has gained the capacity to alter its natural environment, not just on a local scale (as it has always done) but on a global scale. In a word, humanity has become as powerful a geological force as volcanoes. Some argue that it is not "the human species" as such that is causing changes to the climate and biosphere but capitalism and its compulsion toward production. They argue that, therefore, this new period should instead be called the "Capitalocene."[75] In this age of the Anthropocene/Capitalocene, talk of "humanity" could lead us to misconstrue the "human species" as being responsible for the ecological catastrophes underway.

Let us return to the Zapatistas' proposals. Who could they be directing their appeals to, if not those affected by globalized capitalism? Clearly there have been changes over the years in the categories of people to whom they have directed their messages. On many occasions, the Zapatista word has been directed to the people of Mexico, especially in the "First Declaration of the Lacandon Jungle," as well as in subsequent declarations. In the years immediately following the uprising, they appeared to favor appeals to "Ms. Civil Society," that social force that organizes itself outside of governments and parties, in which the Zapatistas reiterated their confidence for many years (particularly in their communiqués from 1996).[76] They also seek to connect with all minorities and groups suffering discrimination. For example, Subcomandante Marcos famously identified with all those who find themselves on the wrong side when he declared:

> Marcos is gay in San Francisco, Black in South Africa, Asian in Europe, Chicano in San Isidro, anarchist in Spain, Palestinian in Israel, Indigenous in the streets of San Cristóbal, a *chavo banda* in Neza, a rocker in the CU, Jewish in Germany, ombudsman in *Sedena*, feminist in political parties, communist in the post–Cold War, prisoner in Cintalapa, pacifist in Bosnia, Mapuche in the Andes, teacher in the CNTE, artist without gallery or portfolio, housewife on a Saturday night in any neighborhood in any city in any Mexico, guerrilla in Mexico at the end of the twentieth century, striker in the CTM, filler news reporter in the countryside, *machista* in the feminist movement, woman alone on the subway at 10 p.m., retired person in a sit-in in the *Zócalo*, landless peasant, marginal editor, unemployed worker, doctor without a job, dissatisfied student, dissident in neoliberalism, writer without books or readers, and certainly, Zapatista in the Mexican southeast. Anyway . . . Marcos is all the untolerated, oppressed minorities, resisting, exploding, saying "Enough is enough!" All minorities when they speak up and majorities when they keep quiet and put up with it. All the untolerated looking for a word, their word, which turns the majority into the eternally fragmented, into us. Everything that bothers power and good consciences, that is Marcos.[77]

He especially insists on summoning the excluded, the forgotten, the marginalized. The Zapatistas continued identifying with all those excluded at the opening of the Intercontinental Encounter for Humanity and Against Neoliberalism, seeing them as fellow faceless people who must cover their faces to be seen. They said, "Behind us, you are us. Behind our masks is the face of all excluded women. Of all the forgotten Indigenous. Of all the persecuted homosexuals. Of all the despised youth. Of all the beaten migrants. Of all those imprisoned for their word and their thoughts. Of all the humiliated workers. Of all those dead from neglect. Of all the simple and ordinary men and women who don't count, who aren't seen, who are nameless, who have no tomorrow."[78] They look to the common people, the most ordinary, the smallest, those unseen and unnoticed. Those without name, without face, without home. The nobodies. The "disposable" people that capitalism produces in ever greater quantities—yet another aspect of the neoliberal Fourth World War. As Galeano remarks, "For every obsolete machine there are millions of people who also become obsolete."[79]

But the Zapatista call is not limited to either the floating concept of civil society or to an eclectic cocktail of all possible minorities. Moving beyond them does not mean they forget or deny social differences and the conflicts that arise from them. Although "The First Declaration of the Lacandon Jungle" is addressed to the Mexican people, *El Despertador Mexicano* announced that theirs was "a necessary war on behalf of all the poor, exploited, and wretched of Mexico."[80] In later stages, the Zapatistas reiterated that their fight was located *below*, a rejection of the politics of the state and its institutions and an orientation toward the poor and despised. In the "Critical Thought in the Face of the Capitalist Hydra" seminar, they even recuperate the concept of "class struggle," defined as "this persistent contradiction, oppression-resistance." This mention of class struggle comes up amid reflections on the resistance of the Mapuche people—which is to say, in quite an expanded sense relative to its common usage.[81]

"The Sixth Declaration of the Lacandon Jungle" went on to center exploitation in its explanation of capitalism, and, although it does not explicitly refer to class struggle, their description of social polarization is clearly a reference to the bourgeoisie and proletariat. They write, "In capitalism, there are some people who have money, or capital, and factories and stores and fields and many things, and there are others who have nothing but their strength and knowledge in order to work. In capitalism, those who have money and things give the orders, and those who only have their ability to work obey." "The Sixth Declaration" also spells out the mechanisms that hide exploitation behind seductive commodities, saying, "And it hides everything behind merchandise, so we don't see the exploitation that exists. . . . Or we see an appliance for listening to music . . . but we do not see the worker in the maquiladora who struggled for many hours, putting the cables and the parts of the appliance together, and they barely paid her a pittance." The centrality of exploitation does not, however, prevent them from highlighting other aspects of capitalist domination, such as dispossession ("capitalism also makes its wealth from dispossession, or theft, because they take what they want from others, land, for example, and natural resources"); repression ("in addition to exploiting and dispossessing," capitalism represses "those who rebel"); and contempt for what is different ("capitalism wants everything as it wants, in its own way, and it doesn't like what is different, and it persecutes it and attacks it, or puts it off in a corner and acts as if it doesn't exist"). In short, "The capitalism of global neoliberalism is based on exploitation, dispossession, contempt, and repression."[82]

These dimensions form what the Zapatista word began to call "the four wheels of capitalism."[83] And while "The Sixth Declaration" seemed to maintain the preeminence of exploitation over the other dimensions, the metaphor of the four wheels suggests a more balanced relationship among them. Its strength is in bringing together all those who are affected by capitalism in different ways. There is exploitation at work, and the dispossession that uniquely affects Indigenous peoples and non-Indigenous peasants. It is not an accessory but rather a structural feature, which is especially important during this current moment when so-called "accumulation by dispossession" has become a defining characteristic of the current stage of capitalism.[84] And in addition to the repression of all those who rebel against capitalism, we must also recognize the contempt suffered by minorities, the excluded, and those who are different; it too is a structural feature of a system that produces more and more surplus populations that make up a "garbage humanity" abandoned to social nonexistence.

The image of the four wheels helps bring together quite different struggles, struggles reacting to different aspects of capitalist domination. Indeed, it allows us to reconcile class antagonism with what are usually considered non-class perspectives. It invites us to overcome the traditional opposition (and supposed incompatibility) between the struggles against exploitation and for economic equality, and the struggles against contempt and for the recognition of differences. By helping us overcome these oppositions, the Zapatistas' perspective widens the universe of those suffering the effects of capitalism more and more. In doing so, they show us how multiple resistances can be intertwined, beyond the single sphere of the exploitation of workers. Subcomandante Marcos expresses this clearly in a speech from June 2007:

1. Neoliberal Globalization also produces a phenomenon of resistance that, increasingly and in an ever more radical way, incorporates broad sectors of the population. 2. This resistance is not only from the traditionally exploited sectors. There appear new "actors" saying "no" with greater radicalism than before. For example, disconcerting groups appear: Indigenous people speaking incomprehensible languages (that is, that are useless for exchanging commodities); unemployed youth

mobilizing against the government and demanding respect in their own way; homosexuals, lesbians, and transgender people demanding recognition of their difference; and women refusing to repeat patterns of submission, consumption, and reproduction.[85]

The image of the four wheels allows us to see the multitude of those affected by capitalism in a much more expansive way. A paragraph from "Them and Us" goes further, saying, "What we call the 'four wheels of capitalism'—exploitation, dispossession, repression, and contempt—have been repeated throughout our history, with different names, living up above, while we are always the same ones below. But the current system has reached a state of extreme madness. Its predatory zeal, its absolute disrespect for life, its delight in death and destruction, and its effort to impose apartheid on all those who are different, that is, all those below, is taking humanity to the brink of disappearance as a form of life on the planet."[86] Capitalism's expansion is accompanied by an increase in those affected by it, in those who find themselves, for a variety of reasons, under its domination. Finally, this expansiveness is so powerful that it reaches the extreme of threatening *humanity as a form of life.* That is, the possibility of a life we may consider properly human, which is precisely why there must be a fundamental antagonism between humanity and capitalism.

The social antagonisms created by capitalism are brutal indeed. Disregarding them would lead to naively universal (or "citizen") framings, just as we would be mistaken to focus narrowly on class struggle and disregard the antagonism between humanity and capitalism. The Zapatistas' approach is different from classical conceptions of the working class as the revolutionary subject in two ways. First, historically this class was conceived of as homogeneous, and working-class organizations sought to unify it, to mobilize "the masses." In contrast to this, the Zapatista word conceives of those affected by capitalism in a radically nonhomogeneous way. It repeatedly references the irreducible *heterogeneity* of the dispossessed. This is evident in the long—sometimes seemingly endless—enumerations that give space to the constitutive multiplicity of such diverse *belows.* For example, they ask that we hear the voices of

the student, of the *barrio* dweller, of the teacher, of the housewife, of the employee, of the street vendor, of the disabled, of the typist, of the clerk, of the seamstress, of the delivery man, of the clown, of the gas station attendant, of the telephone operator, the waiter, the waitress, the cook, the mariachi, of the sex worker, the circus performer, the mechanic, the car washer, of the Indigenous, the worker, the peasant, the chauffeur, the fisherman, the taxi driver, the stevedore, the street child, the flight attendant, the pilot, the office worker, the band member, the media worker, the professional, the member of a religious order, the homosexual, the lesbian, the transgender, the artist, the intellectual, the militant, the activist, the sailor, the soldier, the athlete, the bricklayer, the market vendor, the seller of tacos and tortas, the windshield wiper, the car caretaker, the bureaucrat, the man, the woman, the child, the adolescent, the elderly, all who we are.[87]

This conception also helps us expand our understanding of all the groups that are antagonistic to capital. Capitalism itself is expansive in its desire to commodify everything, and this in turn increasingly expands the diverse *belows* that it exploits, dispossesses, despises, and represses, leading to a tendential identification between these *belows* and humanity as a whole. From this basis perhaps we could understand dispossession in a broader way, as encompassing all four wheels of capitalism. It affects the majority of human beings, either as exploited workers, as consumers trapped by the seductions of commodities (and the reality of debt), or as those who are different, excluded or "discarded." Expanded dispossession encompasses the loss or theft of the fruit of their activity, their subsistence knowledge, their lands and territories, their collective capacity to organize, their forms of life, their dignity, their time, the possibility of living as a woman without being harassed or murdered, the possibility of inhabiting places that have not been devastated, polluted, or transformed into lifeless deserts.[88] Finally, capitalism's generalized dispossession even includes the ability to autonomously determine our own lives.[89] It counts more and more people as its victims, to the extent that its breadth *tends* toward all of humanity (without ever encompassing it completely).

Yet this dispossession does not affect everyone equally. Some of its modalities are more brutal; others, softer. And we should not forget the only minority that neoliberalism is careful not to exclude: the society of Power and its faithful servants, who hold both a significant share of capital and power in the conduct of world affairs. However, since capitalism threatens to destroy the conditions of human life, clearly it will end up affecting everyone. But there is no social equality in the face of ecological devastation either; as the movements for climate and environmental justice have made clear, the poorest are the first victims of the (non-natural) disasters caused by climate chaos, as well as by all the different kinds of pollution. Meanwhile elites have an easier time escaping or recovering from them. But as the devastation of the planet becomes ever more acute, it will be increasingly difficult even for privileged groups to save themselves. Once we approach the widespread destruction of the conditions of human life, even millions in the bank will cease to make the slightest difference.

We can conclude from all this that the Zapatistas' conception of humanity is in no way a lowest common denominator or a depoliticized humanism. On the contrary, Zapatista word-thought asserts a stridently *political* notion of humanity, understood through its struggle against that which threatens to destroy it. In fact, it only makes sense to refer to humanity if we understand it as besieged by capitalism's war against it. Furthermore, the Zapatista conception of humanity is both dehomogenized and decentered. They conceive it through the pain, rage, and resistance of the multiple "belows" created by the world of commodities, of the heterogeneous multitude of the dispossessed. It is a humanity understood from below, but from a below that the expansion of capitalist commodification tends to make coextensive with (almost) all of humanity.

In sum, there are two different dynamics that articulate together. On the one hand are the tremendous polarities and inequalities created by capitalism and, on the other, the ongoing ecocide and biocide that demonstrate the increasing antagonism between capitalism and humanity.[90] The two dynamics are distinct, but they intertwine and tend to merge (though never completely). This schema can also help us imagine the transition toward a world liberated from capitalism. If the dynamics of social conflict continue to prevail, this transition would require prioritizing the other dynamic, since emancipation from capitalist barbarism cannot be carried out in the name of a single class or limited set of groups. Instead, this emancipation must benefit all humanity, as the Zapatistas demand when they call on us to fight "for humanity and against capitalism."

✤ ✤ ✤ ✤

Zapatista word-thought synthesizes the dynamics of the capitalist world through several key concepts and images. The Hydra and the storm are its metaphors, while the Fourth World War and the structural crisis are concepts explaining the current stage of capitalism. Above all, the Zapatistas' constant refrain is that we are in a war between capitalism and humanity.

The Hydra illustrates the widespread devastation wrought by an enemy that is fierce and seemingly all-powerful but not invincible. The implication is that there is no escaping direct confrontation, so we need all the collective intelligence and strength we can muster. Meanwhile the metaphor of the crack is an invitation to tenaciously build alternative forms of life, beginning with the smallest things, and repeating them through daily, nearly imperceptible effort. Instead of contradicting each other, these two images of anticapitalist struggle can be combined to great effect. Bringing them together helps free us from the idea that a crack can be a protected refuge, safe from capitalism's efforts to attack and drown them. Building autonomous spaces should not be separated from the antagonistic aspect of the struggle, from the war between the capitalist monster and humanity. This means organizing to defend these spaces, as well as conceiving them as bases from which to launch more committed attacks against the global enemy.

In calling our attention to the coming storm, the Zapatistas encourage us to prepare ourselves for times that will be even more terrible than an already intolerable present. The storm is a product of both the commodification of the world and the structural crisis of capitalism. Capitalism's own dynamics constantly create new obstacles that impede its reproduction ever more, but this is no guarantee that it marches ineluctably towards collapse. Capitalism can surely continue to reproduce itself but not without ever higher human and ecological costs. Perhaps there is no absolute limit to the reproduction of the capitalist system, as long as it succeeds in imposing more brutal forms of hyper-exploitation, of apartheid for the "surplus" populations, of political and social decomposition, of subjective and ecological devastation. What is certain is that if it continues along this path, with all it implies, to overcome the obstacles generated by its own structural crisis, capitalism will lead to *the disappearance of humanity as a form of life*. Here, two different scripts converge: a complete extinction of the human species and an environmental and ontological devastation so acute that it would leave no other option than a deeply degraded, subhuman life. Both scripts are possible, and it is hard to decide which of the two would be the more atrocious.

This is the main reason to prioritize the antagonism between capitalism and humanity—an antagonism that the world of commodities has forced upon us. If we are to fight against the Hydra and weather the coming storm, we must take up the perspective of humanity, since the struggles for its preservation and for dignity are now one and the same. Barring the complete disappearance of the human species, there is likely no other limit to the reproduction of capitalism than the rebellion of humanity against generalized dispossession, in increasingly degraded and dehumanized conditions of survival. This should be a movement of ethical insurgency—supported by the wrath of Mother Earth—to save the possibility of a dignified life on Earth. Herein lies the relevance of the fight for humanity and against capitalism.

CHAPTER 4

"We Want a World Where Many Worlds Fit"
Indigenous Struggle and Planetary Resistance

The Zapatistas' struggle is for life and against capitalism. It is also a struggle for national liberation, with hopes of refounding Mexico. And finally, their uprising and subsequent struggle to build autonomy throughout their territory in Chiapas is undeniably Indigenous. While these three dimensions each operate across distinct spatial scales, they are by no means incompatible. The Zapatista struggle cannot be reduced to any one of these, nor is it simply their sum. Rather, it is a tapestry that transforms each of the elements it weaves together.

The Zapatistas are particularly creative in interweaving Indigenous demands and a territorial project on the local level with national and planetary perspectives, which forces us to rethink both the Indigenous dimension of their struggle and what is commonly called "universalism"—that which is shared by all humans. This in turn forces us to re-analyze—now from a broader perspective—how Zapatista word-thought understands the concept of "humanity." It offers novel articulations of difference and universality, particularity and shared humanity, the individual and collective, as well as people and nature. In doing so, Zapatista word-thought forces us to question the foundations of Western modernity, a task that is critical if we are to escape the grasp of the capitalist Hydra.

Our efforts here are guided by the Zapatista call to dream and to build "a world where many worlds fit." In fact, this chapter is an attempt to understand this call and to explore its profound implications.

The Zapatista Experience

A political understanding of Indigenous struggle

Indigenous uprising and national liberation

Some commentators have questioned whether the Zapatista struggle is truly Indigenous. They argue that the EZLN did not make demands for Indigenous recognition during their initial uprising, only adding them later as they improvised a new discourse and found that this ethnic dimension attracted considerable support. Even though these critics acknowledge that the EZLN's support bases are almost completely Indigenous, they regard them as the puppets of *mestizo* leaders who use these communities to drape their revolutionary ideology in more attractive garb.[1] In fact, since the very first days of 1994, a central strategy of the federal government's propaganda has been to cast doubt on the Indigenous character of the Zapatista uprising. Former President Carlos Salinas de Gortari himself repeatedly argued that the word "Indigenous" does not appear in the "First Declaration of the Selva Lacandona."[2] No, the word does not appear, but it requires a large dose of bad faith to deny the Indigenous character of a document whose first words are "We are the product of 500 years of struggle" and that, further along, denounces "an undeclared genocidal war against our peoples."[3] After these first words, speaking of five hundred years of resistance to colonial domination, there follow phases of a history common to all Mexicans, making it clear that the "First Declaration" does not emphasize the Indigenous dimension because the uprising's principal objectives were national in scope. The beginning of the EZLN's first public document is therefore a subtle weaving together of Indigenous and national perspectives that creates a framework where the latter clearly predominates. In fact, responding to the propaganda directed against them, on January 6, 1994, the EZLN affirmed that its struggle was both Indigenous and national. (They also took the opportunity to clarify that there were no foreigners in their ranks and to deny any contact with Guatemalan and Salvadoran guerrilla organizations.) They said, "The government says this isn't an Indigenous uprising, but we say that if thousands of Indigenous rise up in struggle, then it is indeed an Indigenous uprising."[4] They continue, emphasizing that the great majority of their troops and officers are Indigenous, with the exception of a few non-Indigenous people who had joined them, such as Subcomandante Marcos. Finally, they affirm that "The political leadership of our struggle is completely Indigenous. 100% of the members of the Clandestine Revolutionary Indigenous Committees . . . are of Tsotsil, Tseltal, Ch'ol, Tojolabal, and other ethnicities."

Malicious jabs aside, it is clear that the EZLN is an Indigenous organization. While the *mestizo* Subcomandante Marcos was its spokesperson and the head of its military until 2014, he was relieved by Subcomandante Moisés, a Tseltal Indigenous person. The Indigenous Clandestine Revolutionary Committee, the EZLN's political leadership, is composed exclusively of Indigenous people. But the EZLN's ethnic composition is by no means homogenous. On the contrary, its members are from distinct Mayan peoples speaking different languages, such as Tseltal, Tsotsil, Tojolobal, Ch'ol, and Mam, as well as a few Zoques (a non-Mayan Indigenous people) and *mestizos*. Its polyethnic character has obliged the EZLN to recognize its internal differences and work to articulate them within a concrete, collective project. So for example, alongside general historical and cultural differences, the diversity of languages alone necessitates either a string of translations or the use of Spanish as a *lingua franca*. Therefore, while the category of "Indigenous" brings together many different peoples vis-a-vis *mestizos*, the Zapatistas' Indigeneity is itself diverse. And this is even more so within the National Indigenous Congress, which brings the Zapatista rebels' struggle together with those of other Indigenous peoples from across Mexico.

The EZLN has assumed a perspective of struggle shared by many peoples of the American continent on the occasion of the fifth centenary of the colonization. Remember that most of the ten thousand Indigenous people who marched in San Cristóbal de las Casas on October 12, 1992, and tore down the statue of Diego de Mazariegos—the conquistador who founded the city—were (secretly) EZLN members. Then, a month after the 1994 uprising, the EZLN wrote to the "500 Years of Indigenous Resistance" Council in the state of Guerrero, "We're very happy to know that our Amuzgo, Mixteco, Nahuatl, and Tlapaneco Indigenous brothers are aware of our struggle for dignity and for the freedom of the Indigenous and of all Mexicans."[5] They then formulated their initial demand for Indigenous autonomy on March 1 of the same year, during the Cathedral Dialogues in San Cristóbal, writing, "As Indigenous people, let us organize ourselves and govern ourselves autonomously. . . . Justice shall be administered by Indigenous peoples, ourselves, according to our customs and traditions." They also demanded respect for Indigenous people and their cultures, writing, "Our rights and dignity as Indigenous peoples shall be respected, with regard to our cultures and traditions. . . . We Indigenous people no longer want to be the object of discrimination and contempt." There were also more specific demands, guaranteeing the rights to land, housing, health, education, and information.[6]

As mentioned previously, the outlook of the January 1st uprising was primarily a national one. Its call was directed to all Mexicans, leaving the Indigenous dimension in second place. In a long series of interviews, Subcomandante Marcos explained that, during preparations leading up to 1994, "[The CCRI insisted that] I had to be very clear that this was not an Indigenous war but a national one. They said, 'We don't want people who aren't Indigenous to feel excluded. Our call has to be broad, for everyone.' And they were even a bit suspicious when my remarks went too far toward the Indigenous side. They said to me, 'You're talking about Indigeneity a lot. They're going to think this is a local movement, an ethnic one.'"[7] So here we have Indigenous people who are so wary of being locked into ethnicity that they chastise their *mestizo* spokesperson for emphasizing it too much!

Later they made a more explicit connection between the Indigenous and national dimensions of their struggle. First, they succeeded in making the Indigenous question a national question.[8] This was especially evident when they chose to make "Indigenous rights and culture" the theme of the first round of dialogue in San Andrés—and thereby the first step in transforming the Mexican state. The slogan of the National Indigenous Congress, "Never again a Mexico without us," also shows how Indigenous peoples' demands are understood within a framework that implies a transformation of the entire nation. Solving Indigenous peoples' problems means changing Mexico itself. As Marcos writes, "The Indigenous question is a national one, not only because there are Indigenous people throughout the Mexican territory or because they are an essential part of the history of this country but also because they seek unity through difference with all others who make up today's Mexico. By recognizing this difference in the supreme law of the land and including it in an emancipatory national project—one for sovereignty and independence—we can thereby create justice and make it possible to defend the homeland from being liquidated in a fire sale."[9] Because of its national dimension, the Indigenous question has to be connected with other issues, like those proposed for the subsequent rounds of dialogue at San Andrés. However, the government's inaction forced the EZLN to spend years focusing its political efforts on demanding the fulfillment of the San Andrés Accords on Indigenous Rights and Culture. Yet while Indigenous demands seemed to override all else between 1996 and 2001, we should remember that they were the Zapatistas' way of struggling for the entire nation. Alongside constitutional recognition of Indigenous rights, the Zapatistas' central demand during the March for Indigenous Dignity was for "Mexico [not to] permit the sun to rise without this flag having a dignified place for us who are the color of the earth."[10] Clearly, the Zapatista struggle has always braided together Indigenous and national strands, albeit with different accents and relationships according to different moments.

Avoiding ethnicism in Indigenous struggle

The composition, perspective, and practices of the Zapatista struggle are undoubtedly Indigenous, but this struggle does not want to be solely Indigenous. It would be a grave mistake to think that Indigenous struggle can only combine with others by ceasing to be Indigenous, or inversely, that a broad political project cannot be truly Indigenous. Unfortunately, many scholars assert these oppositions: between the Indigenous and the national or between an ethnic perspective and a general political project. The practice of Indigenous peoples—especially that of the Zapatistas—refutes them.

Here I attempt to characterize the Zapatista struggle as ethnic but not ethnicist. The word "ethnic" refers to how the struggle is understood in terms of self-recognition as Indigenous peoples, as original peoples. It would be helpful to investigate in depth Indigenous conceptions of Indigeneity. It is likely that we would learn that for Indigenous peoples, Indigeneity is not a question of physical or biological traits, but of distinct cultures and the historical experience of resisting and surviving the devastation of their worlds.[11] The word "ethnicist" refers to a perspective that only considers ethnic criteria, making them absolute, so that ethnic identity is asserted in opposition to all others.

The Zapatista struggle is Indigenous but not solely Indigenous. They have always called for a national struggle that is not premised on an unbridgeable divide between Indigenous and non-Indigenous peoples. For example, in a letter quoted earlier, the EZLN confirms the receipt of a message from Guerrero's "500 Years of Indigenous Resistance" Council, not only in the name of "all Indigenous peoples of Mexico," but also in the name of "all Mexicans, Indigenous and non-Indigenous," and in the name of "all honorable people who walk the good path."[12] By joining together Indigenous and non-Indigenous peoples, they avoid ethnicism—that is, asserting ethnic particularity against those who do not share it. (Ethnicism might, for example, call for a struggle against the oppression of Indigenous peoples, designating all non-Indigenous peoples as enemies.) On January 3, 1996, in their inaugural address to the National Indigenous Forum, and in the presence of the advisors to the San Andrés dialogues, the EZLN stated: "We are Indigenous. We have suffered centuries of discrimination, persecution, indifference, and death. Often the executioner has had fair skin, but other times death and deceit have had dark skin and spoken our same tongue. The true path also carries the word of men and women with fair skin and a different tongue. In the world that we Zapatistas want, there is room for all skin colors, all tongues, and all paths."[13]

The first sentence establishes Indigeneity as who we are, conceiving the struggle historically, with all the humiliations this identity implies. However, they immediately relativize the ethnic aspect of this assertion. If there are Indigenous people who place themselves on the side of oppression and non-Indigenous people working to eliminate it, then the struggle's true dividing line is not between Indigenous and non-Indigenous peoples. We should be able to cross the boundaries of ethnicity, without denying it or minimizing its importance. The EZLN makes this explicit in the same speech, saying, "We cannot combat the racism of the powerful using a mirror that reflects back the same thing, but reversed: The same irrationality and the same intolerance but now against the mestizos. We cannot combat racism against Indigenous peoples using racism against mestizos." This is why it is important to avoid essentializing ethnicity. Rather, we should look for ways to relativize it by using other, nonethnic criteria. This is why the Zapatistas could say on Columbus Day in 1994 that, "There are those with fair skin who know the pain of the other.[14] Our struggle includes them. And there are those with dark skin and white arrogance. Our fight is also against them. Our struggle, armed with hope, is not against the mestizo, it is against the race of money. It is not against a skin color but against money's color. It is not against a foreign language but against money's language."[15]

Their 2001 march was designated "The March of the Color of the Earth" and "The March of Indigenous Dignity." But the Zapatistas ceaselessly repeated that, for it to be an Indigenous peoples' march, it had to also be one of non-Indigenous peoples. They affirmed that the color of the earth aspires to be "a color with all the colors that clothe the earth," except for "the color of money."[16] Upholding Indigenous dignity means reversing the historic discrimination of colonial relations, and this can only be done through just relations with the non-Indigenous. This relational aspect is important for understanding dignity, which is nothing other than a bridge uniting the Indigenous and the non-Indigenous:

> When we speak of Indigenous dignity, we are speaking of what we are as Indigenous peoples, and of what the other is who is not like us.

Indigenous dignity is not dominating the other who is not Indigenous, subjecting him, destroying him, humiliating him, ignoring him, forgetting him. Indigenous dignity is a bridge which needs an other side to extend to, an other to see and to be seen by. When we speak of the March of Indigenous Dignity, we speak of the Indigenous who see ourselves as Indigenous, without shame, without embarrassment, without sadness, without the death of what we are. When we speak of the March of Indigenous Dignity, we are also speaking of the Indigenous who are being seen—which is to say respected—by the non-Indigenous. When we speak of the March of Indigenous Dignity, we are also saying that we Indigenous peoples see and look at the non-Indigenous, which is to say that we are respecting them. The March of Indigenous Dignity cannot be just of the Indigenous. The March for Indigenous Dignity must be the March of the Indigenous and of the non-Indigenous.[17]

This means upholding Indigeneity, but without idealizing or essentializing it. And, above all, without locking it within a strictly ethnic perspective that would imply rejecting the non-Indigenous. This allows us to escape the two extreme positions that unfortunately monopolize debate in the contemporary world: either dismissing ethnic demands in the name of the universal, or essentializing them in the name of a particular identity. The path signaled by Zapatista thought on Indigenous struggle is neither the one nor the other: it affirms Indigeneity without isolating it.

Indigenous struggle and anticapitalism

Struggle is another criterion to consider. As the EZLN said when celebrating 503 years of Indigenous resistance, "Skin color does not make someone Indigenous. It comes from their dignity and always struggling to be better. All of us who struggle are brothers, no matter what our skin color or the language we learn as we walk."[18] Here the primary criterion is undoubtedly struggle. Indigenous dignity is not an essence. It does not derive from ethnic belonging. It must be mastered and defended through resistance against domination.[19] Being Indigenous matters and, above all, struggling matters. This is what makes it possible to join forces with other, non-Indigenous struggles. Moreover, the enemy is not defined by the color of their skin but rather by the color of money. The enemy is neoliberalism or, to be clearer, capitalism.

The Zapatista Experience

The Zapatista struggle is both Indigenous and anticapitalist. For some this may sound contradictory (if not impossible), given that for these critics Indigeneity must remain limited to demands specific to original peoples, while anticapitalist struggle means reproducing the same old proposals for revolutionary universalism that always deny the importance of the ethnic question. However, the path of the Zapatistas avoids these characterizations and brings together Indigenous struggle and an anticapitalist perspective in a mutually empowering way. That is, the anticapitalist perspective is what prevents Indigenous struggle from falling into the isolation of ethnicism. Meanwhile, the Indigenous element revitalizes the anticapitalist approach through an incisive critique of its basic concepts and practices. Moreover, because Indigenous peoples are on the front lines of struggles against accumulation by dispossession, they have very concrete reasons for understanding their struggle from an anticapitalist perspective.

There are concrete examples that can help us understand the Zapatista conception of Indigenous struggle. A conversation between Australian Aboriginal filmmakers and the Morelia Good Government Council is illustrative.[20] The filmmakers focused their presentation on the customs and rituals of their people, and then the members of the Council began asking their visitors how they organized their struggle against their government. Since they apparently did not see their action as struggle, the discussion ended with a sense of misunderstanding and incomprehension between those with a cultural understanding of ethnicity and those who conceive of it in relation to political struggle. This episode shows how support bases serving a temporary position on the Good Government Council do not limit their self-identified Indigeneity to cultural identity, nor do they separate it from a radical struggle for social and political transformation. It shows how the Zapatista struggle distances itself from the dominant uses of ethnicity that tend not only to isolate it but to reduce it to its cultural dimension. This is part of today's prevailing culturalism, which depoliticizes all claims and demands. On the contrary, the Zapatista perspective on Indigeneity is not absolutist and is openly political, or rather, anticapitalist.

More about ourselves, more about others

Another example comes from autonomous education. Instead of closing itself off within ethnicism, autonomous education is understood as "a permanent dialogue between different cultures." In this sense it is a deeply intercultural practice that does not need to fetishize itself (meanwhile, many state institutions that take up this title are intercultural in name only).[21] As a member of a municipal council of La Garrucha explains, rooting education in the community does not mean idealizing traditional values or rejecting broader outlooks. "Our education comes from the community, and the community is the school. We understand that, yes, there are things from our culture that are good to use, but there are other things that we must change. Not everything in our culture is good, but we see that we need to keep the best and bring it together with the best of other cultures. And that way we can learn from the whole world."[22] Likewise, an organizer (*encargado*) from the education committee of a new village in the autonomous municipality of Francisco Villa affirms that "The way we see it, the *compañeros* want everything to be part of the school, and above all they want the school to improve the community, to move us forward, to not forget who we are as Tseltales, so that the children respect and learn from the Mayas, and how our ancestors lived on the *fincas*. They want to know how *compañeros* in other states and other countries are going about their struggles."[23] It is rare to see such a clear-sighted awareness of how incomplete one's own culture is, showing how this is precisely the starting point for effective intercultural practice.

The Zapatista Autonomous Rebellious Secondary School (ESRAZ in Spanish) in Oventik is another example. It began in 2000, and its coordinators were eager to relate education to community life and strengthen oral and written Tsotsil. But they flatly refused to enclose their project in the specifics of Mayan identity, and instead defined it as "a school of the peoples of the world." They used the many dimensions of Zapatista struggle to create an educational project that combines a critical appreciation for Indigenous culture, the wish to belong to a reconstructed nation, and openness to the struggles of the world's peoples.[24] The vigor of their emancipatory project allows them to both affirm and subvert identity and belonging. This sort of rebellious interculturality allows them to both intensify the recuperation of their own culture and open themselves to the other worlds that exist within this one.[25]

The political practice and educational experience of the Zapatistas are guided by an uncommon logic: seeking together to learn more about themselves and more about others. There is in fact no contradiction between these aspirations. It is only the blindness associated with rigid categories that leads us to think that cultural affirmation means rejecting the other, or that opening toward the world means leaving behind cultural traditions. On the contrary, the practices we are discussing here aim to strengthen the connection to one's own culture while also learning from all the others that make up humanity. However, this is only possible under one condition: the boundary between self and other cannot be essentialized; it must instead remain flexible, movable. Once we recognize our cultures as incomplete, identity can become non-identity. It disconnects from any fixed being and makes possible becoming other.

Beyond identity?

National and ethnic particularity is usually discussed using the concept of identity, an idea that—while not abounding in the Zapatista word—is still present. For example in "Ethics and Politics," an Indigenous "identity" is affirmed while speaking of "a collective national identity" on its way to being destroyed by capital's wars.[26] Subcomandante Marcos also remarks on the work of Luis Villoro, who defines collective identity as "those characteristics in which an individual recognizes themself as belonging to a community."[27] Villoro then clarifies that identity is not an unchanging inheritance but built over time and, as such, changing. Subcomandante Marcos adds the idea of a "multitudinous identity that does not nullify, humiliate, or conquer."[28] This means we can have various identities at once and, above all, those with different identities can be in community with one another.

This conception of identity is notably different from the prevailing one. The clamor to defend "our identity" characterizes ethnicist struggles, aggressive nationalisms, and the extreme xenophobic Right. Their conception of identity is exclusive and exclusionary, hateful of the other, of difference. Additionally, the very word "identity" points toward the identical, a fixed (essential) and single (exclusionary) identity—raising doubts as to whether to use the concept at all. It is possible to give it another meaning, as the authors of "Ethics and Politics" do, but this means swimming against the stream of the prevailing use of the term.

Apart from the words used, it is more important to explore which of the formulations mentioned above are found in Zapatista thought. The answer is clear: the Zapatistas reclaim and defend "what we are" as Indigenous peoples, especially against "the dispossession of what we are as Indigenous peoples."[29] It is entirely legitimate to affirm that we are against what denies us and attempts to destroy us. And if this is to be called "identity," then so be it, but we should also recognize another current within Zapatista word-thought. Although it seeks to defend "what we are" against that which denies it, the meaning of this changes in the light of declarations such as "Behind us, we are you," as they asserted at the inauguration of the Intercontinental Encounter in 1996.[30] In saying this, they ask the world's struggles to identify with the Zapatistas', thereby breaking down the distinction between "us" and "you." "Our" identity is broken the moment it identifies with a multiplicity of "yous" who recognize themselves in the Zapatista struggle. Non-identity prevails, and this goes beyond with the greatest possible force the exclusive attachment to "what we are."

Moreover, if Zapatista word-thought invites us to defend "what we are" against that which denies it, this does not mean freezing it to prevent any change. Instead, they make this invitation so that we ourselves can change "what we are" as we like. Zapatista struggles seek to defend themselves against capitalist destruction but also to change everything, ourselves included. In this sense the inauguration of the 1996 Intercontinental Encounter also affirmed that "You see that we're the rebellious mirror that seeks to become glass and break itself. You see that we are what we are so that we may cease to be what we are and become the you that we are." In this way they try to defend "what we are" but also fight "to cease to be what we are." The difference between the mirror and the glass, as shown in "The Story of Mirrors," is that "The mirror shows me what I am, and the glass what I can be."[31] Beyond what I am (or what we are), the Zapatistas privilege what I can be (and what we can be). Furthermore, we should note that the verb "to be" is the expression of Power par excellence, proclaiming—as did the God of the Old Testament—"I am who I am, the eternal return."[32]

If it is important to defend "what we are" against that which denies it, this is because it also allows struggle for what we have yet to become. In "The Story of Searching," they say that "to live is to search, to search for ourselves" since "everyone we come across is still to find themselves."[33] Thus *we are not*, but we struggle to find—that is to say, to keep searching for—what we still are not. In this way, Zapatista word-thought breaks the identification of "us" with "what we are" and privileges a possible "us" that is not yet and that struggles to exist. This means recognizing the non-identity of the self, recognizing the presence of the other in the self. This is what the story "The Others That We Are" shows: "In every man, in every woman, there is an other. The other is hidden, guarded. Waiting, it waits. It is there. Sometimes it's a scratch, imperceptible without but defining within. Other times it's an earthquake that breaks the dull everyday. Sometimes it's skin, a caress, or a rough rubbing that scratches with tender fury the outside skin and reveals the other skin, the skin of the other, the other that we are. But it is always pain that forces out the other that we are without being it yet."[34]

Zapatista word-thought takes up the logic of identity and non-identity together. Sometimes one prevails over the other, but both are always present and articulated together.[35] They affirm identity, that which defends "what we are" against threats. But its meaning changes when the "we" seeks to join many "yous" and also because we must "cease to be what we are" and struggle to become what we are not yet. In this way, that which Indigenous peoples call their own can be strengthened, together with their many experiences of "becoming-other," while also allowing modernity's traditions to be subverted by the original peoples' ways of being and living. It is by no means simply a theoretical debate to speak of identity and non-identity. It is a profound effort to overcome the categories that contain and divide, making it possible for Indigenous struggles to interlace with many other anticapitalist struggles.

After the late "Marcos" bid farewell to Old Antonio and Durito, who had accompanied him for years, Subcomandante Galeano acquired a new narrative accomplice, even more emblematic of the rejection of closed conceptions of identity.[36] Since its first appearance in November 2013, the cat-dog has critiqued fanaticism, that is to say, the exclusionary attitudes of those who do not tolerate difference (including both religious and lay fanaticism).[37] Trying to both bark and meow, it is "neither cat nor dog" but "cat-dog," thereby challenging absolute identification and exclusive categories. Here, the Zapatista word favors difference and not identity, writing "Difference is a sign that all is not lost, that we still have a lot to see and to hear." When asked "Is it a problem of identity?" the cat-dog responds, "One doesn't choose who they are but rather who they could be. And life is no more than that complicated transition, achieved or truncated, from one thing to the other." They privilege the inconclusive over self-identity, becoming-other over being. It is highly suggestive that Subcomandante Galeano, whose name symbolizes the stage of Zapatista struggle beginning in 2012–2013, chose a hybrid creature to accompany him on his path, one who threatens fixed and exclusive identities while privileging difference, who recognizes both the other as well as the other in one's self.

Many worlds and a planetary community

Intertwining the Indigenous, the national, and the planetary
We have seen how the Zapatista struggle brings together Indigenous demands with a national perspective. Now we will look at how it articulates

national struggle with a planetary horizon. The equilibrium between the two has changed throughout various stages of the Zapatista trajectory. Barely present during the first year of the uprising, the international aspect of Zapatismo first peaked in 1996 with their preparation for and coordination of the Intercontinental Encounter for Humanity and Against Neoliberalism. Afterwards, they periodically reaffirmed this international dimension, particularly through "The Sixth Declaration" (even though its impulse was oriented more toward the Other Campaign than toward the Zezta International). Remember that, at the beginning of 2013, the reformulation of the Sixth in "Us and Them" affirms—in no uncertain terms—a *planetary* terrain of anticapitalist struggle, requesting that we leave behind overly rigid demarcations between the national and the international.[38] They made good on this suggestion via the World Festival of Resistance and Rebellion, which took place in December 2014 and January 2015, as well as other international events mentioned previously. It is worth mentioning that the planetary is distinct from the international (a term that is barely present in the Zapatista word). This is because "planetary" does not refer to the framework of the nation-state but to the earth in its totality.[39] So too does the qualifier "intergalactic," which was humorously invoked through the Encounter in 1996.

Despite holding the two in various equilibriums, the Zapatistas have made a constant effort to articulate the national and the planetary (including the Indigenous and the planetary, just as the World Festival of Resistance and Rebellion tried to inspire). It is critical to establish this connection, especially in the time of global capitalism. The transnationalization of capital and the commodification of everything work to homogenize and standardize ways of life. Yet this process also generates new divisions and separations. Subcomandante Marcos coined the term "fragmented globalization" to describe this, writing, "Homogeneity is very far from being the characteristic defining the turn of the century and new millennium. The world is an archipelago, a puzzle whose pieces change into other pieces, and the only thing that is really globalized is the proliferation of heterogeneity."[40] One of many expressions of this is the dizzying rise of social inequality, the process of fragmentation many states have undergone, as well as all the walls and barriers erected to impede the ever-greater flows of migrants (a reality so impactful that it compelled the EZLN to organize a campaign called "Confronting the Walls of Capital: Resistance, Rebellion, Solidarity, and Support from Below and to the Left").[41] In this context it is more important than ever to connect national demands with planetary perspectives.

In fact, in a world of fragmented globalization, efforts to reclaim the nation could very well feed xenophobic insanity and the passion for walls, as we see in many countries—the United States first among them. This is what leads to the ethnic and nationalist fundamentalisms mentioned in the previous chapter. It is a deadly serious phenomenon, and to drive it away we must connect the national with the planetary.

This link is what differentiates Zapatista patriotism from identitarian isolation and xenophobia. We have already looked to the Intercontinental Encounter of 1996 for examples of this, as it was an antecedent to and inspiration for the alter globalization movement that took hold in 1999. During this meeting, the Zapatistas invited participants to "build an International of hope." They also reclaimed dignity as "that nation without nationality, that rainbow that is also a bridge, that murmur of the heart that cares not for the blood that enlivens it, that rebellious irreverence that mocks borders, customs, and wars."[42] Zapatista nationalism is clearly also a critique of identitarian xenophobia. Take this portrait of Old Antonio for example:

> Instead of developing a passionate xenophobia, Old Antonio took from the world everything good that it made available, without concern for the land where it was born. Referring to good people from other nations, Old Antonio used the term "internationals," and he used the word "foreigners" only for those estranged from the heart. It didn't matter if they were of his color, language, and race. "Sometimes there are even foreigners of the same blood," Old Antonio would say, to explain to me the absurd nonsense of passports.[43] The Zapatistas unite hope for a country without nationality with a denunciation of foreigners who share their supposed nationality. Nestled between the two is the space that the Zapatistas allow for their understanding of the nation.

Old Antonio's words encapsulate the lived experience of thousands of Zapatista support bases who, thanks to the uprising, have come into contact with supporters from all over the world, creating what is commonly referred to as "international Zapatismo."[44] Solidarity networks formed in countries throughout the Americas and Europe, and many people—whether they were part of these networks or not—traveled to Chiapas to participate in the many encounters organized by the EZLN. Sometimes their participation was as observers in the civilian peace encampments created on the heels of the February 1995 attack. Others have participated in the solidarity project of distributing Zapatista coffee or in other such projects. Many have taken language classes at CELMRAZ (the Zapatista Autonomous Rebellious Center for Spanish and Mayan Languages) in Oventik, or they were students at the Zapatista Little School. Throughout it all, Zapatista support bases have lived together and exchanged with people from many horizons, and they have done so in a spirit of hospitality, openness, and collective struggle. Zapatismo's international dimension is not only expressed through massive encounters or their efforts to weave together planetary networks of resistance and rebellion; beyond all this, it has also influenced everyday life in the autonomous Zapatista territories, however modestly.

Finally, Zapatismo is simultaneously an Indigenous uprising for autonomy and to recover dignity, a national liberation struggle to transform Mexico, and a rebellion for humanity and against capitalism. These three spatial scales—rootedness in a concrete territory, the national level, and the planetary one—are tightly bound, so tightly linked that *none of them can be understood outside their relationships with the others*. The articulation of these three scales is what makes it possible to avoid the dangers that arise when any one of them is isolated: essentialist and exclusive ethnicism, intolerant nationalism and xenophobia (linked to the fragmented globalization of neoliberal capitalism), and abstract universalism that ends up denying the differences among actual human beings.

Indeed, the relationship between these distinct scales might be understood as a spiral.[45] "The Thirteenth Stele," which announced the birth of the Zapatista Caracoles, suggests that the conch's spiral is a way to understand the comings and goings between the interior—what is most one's own—and the other, that which is distant and yet seeks to approach the heart.

> They say that they say that they said that the conch represents entering into the heart—that is what the very first ones said about knowledge. And they say that they say that they said that the conch also represents leaving the heart in order to walk the world, which is how the first ones spoke about life. Also, they say that they say that they said that they used a conch to call together the collective, so that the word would go from one to the other, giving birth to an agreement. And they also say that they say that they said that the conch was an aid, so that the ear could hear even the most distant word.[46]

The Zapatista Experience

The following quote is an even clearer expression of the Zapatistas' way of relating the interiority of the heart with others who are out there in the world. It evokes a very Zapatista way of reflecting collectively, which is a constant spiraling coming and going, intertwining into a single path that—up until now—we have only discussed as distinct spatial scales:

> For many hours these beings, with their dark-brown hearts, have traced with their ideas a great spiral. Starting from the international, their gaze and their thought have turned deep within, passing successively through the national, the regional, and the local, until arriving at what they themselves call "*El Votán*, the guardian and heart of the people"— the Zapatista peoples. And from the outermost curve of the spiral they think words like "globalization," "war of domination," "resistance," "economy," "city," "countryside," "the political situation."... At the end of the path from the outside to the inside, in the center of the spiral, there only remain the initials: "EZLN." Afterwards, there are proposals and these are drawn in thought and in the heart—windows and doors that only they see (among other things, because they still don't exist). The disparate and dispersed word begins to make a common and collective path. Someone asks "Is there an agreement?" "There is," answers the now-collective voice. The spiral again begins to trace a path, but now in reverse, from inside toward the outside. The draft also follows the inverse path until on the old blackboard there only remains a phrase that is delirium for many, but for these men and women is a reason to struggle: "a world where many worlds fit."[47]

We are all equal because we are all different

This articulation between the ethnic, the national, and the planetary poses a challenge, since it joins together perspectives that are generally considered incompatible. This is not necessarily so, but it certainly is within dominant, modernist forms of thought—those that have shaped the Western capitalist world. In fact, within the framework inherited from the eighteenth century Enlightenment, to affirm the universal—that which is common to all men— is to either deny concrete particularities or consider them irrelevant. This is not merely a theoretical problem: it is what leads dominant forms of Marxism to reproduce modern universalism by ignoring or deriding ethnic struggles,

170

particularly Indigenous ones.[48] This is because class is considered to be the single, fundamental axis of conflict, and also because emancipation is considered the realization of universal values (to wit, those of "European universalism"). It is clear then that, to elaborate Zapatista word-thought, they had to articulate Indigenous struggle with a revolutionary perspective, which required a deep critique of their own tradition and everything within it that stems from the foundations of modernity.

What is the problem with the classic universalism of the Enlightenment? It has been criticized for basing itself in an abstract idea of Man, erasing concrete differences among real beings, starting with gendered differences. It affirmed the equality of all humans, but this equality was mostly juridical and therefore abstract, asserted without even recognizing the heterogeneity that could undercut it.[49] Another critique is that universalism is nothing but the universalization of a few specific—and in this case Western—values. According to this critique, the Modernist universalism that arose in Europe in the eighteenth century was the same "European universalism" that became so central to the capitalist world-system and has accompanied its imperial expansion.[50] In other words, it is the friendly face of Western domination and has gone hand in hand with colonialism and the racist ideology that accompanies it. Then we must ask: Can there be a planetary perspective that does not reproduce the failures of abstract European universalism? Can one be built based on the distinctiveness of places, the singularity of experiences, and the particularities of real men and women, without leading to another universalization of particular values?

Doing this requires thinking of the particular and the universal as two clearly distinct poles that can only be brought together through the hard work of establishing bridges between concrete differences. Or we may be better off dropping the universal altogether and instead thinking about the common on a planetary scale.[51] These logics are manifest within the Zapatista experience, in the way it understands Indigenous struggle and in its articulation of the three scales mentioned above. We also find it in the illuminating words of Major Ana Maria at the inauguration of the 1996 Intercontinental Encounter, when she said, "Welcome to this corner of the world, where we are all equal because we are all different."[52] Here, the paradoxical "because" breaks with the idea of equality and human unity defined *despite* differences among individuals, peoples, or sexes. Instead, it upholds an understanding of equality and unity as lived through differences, lived from their full recognition. Her remark, which synthesizes a lived experience, provides a foundation on which to build an other universalism, one that is now concrete, that takes on all the differences and par-ticularities of human experience. It is therefore a process that advances through the difficult effort to reconcile the particular and the common, the importance of situated forms of life and concern for all of humanity.

In doing this, we walk a fine line between destroying diversity through homogenization and essentializing differences through particularism. But it is a path that allows us to escape the false dichotomy between a universalism that denies particularities and an identitarianism that denies universality. There are two premises underlying this effort to bring equality and difference together, to join particularity with a planetary commons: on the one hand is an open conception of particularity, as with the Zapatistas' conception of Indigeneity, and on the other is a concrete approach to the universal. This allows us to avoid two opposing attitudes that predominate in today's world and that mutually reinforce each other's respective limitations: While some deny particularities (as to make universal assertions), others enclose themselves within them (and completely deny the universal).

This logic finds its fullest expression in the Zapatistas' repeated call to build "a world where many worlds fit."[53] Such an emblematic expression deserves to be understood in its full scope. We should go beyond reducing it to a simple cel-ebration of difference. Rather, it should be understood as a radical affirmation of the principle of multiplicity, at every possible scale. In the "Fourth Declara-tion of the Lacandon Jungle," this affirmation refers above all to Mexico and the desire to construct a country where "all the peoples and all their languages have a place," one where there is a place for the singularities of all peoples, especially Indigenous peoples. During the Intercontinental Encounter in 1996, the many worlds that Major Ana Maria mentions are "the thousands of little worlds across the five continents." Elsewhere, it might refer more specifically to the differences among struggles and rebellions that join together in any national or planetary network.

We might also relate the affirmation of many worlds to the practice of autonomy as a politics of multiplicity, understood based on situated experi-ences, rooted in a specific territory and a particular history. This is how we might understand the words of the "Fourth Declaration," which speak not of small differences but of a genuine multiplicity of worlds. It reads: "Many worlds make themselves. Many worlds make us . . . We make true worlds."[54] Experiences that are built in a singular space and—as is true of autonomies—through a specific collective configuration are properly called "worlds" because they imply ways of living and of relating to the environment that are appropriate to each place and that result from freely chosen trajectories. In contrast to a politics conceived from above—which tends toward the One—the logic of autonomy leads to affirming a plurality of worlds. It demands we take seriously the constitutive multiplicity of human (as well as non-human) reality.

Calling for "a world where many worlds fit" is a combative claim. It is affirmed against the homogenization of the world of the commodity and the generalization of quantification to all aspects of life. It asserts that a true multiplicity of worlds cannot flourish under the rule of capital. On the contrary, a world where many worlds fit would only become fully possible with the elimination of the capitalist Hydra. Yet the disappearance of the Hydra is not enough, as we must also stop thinking of post-capitalist emancipation as the realization of the universalism of the One. If it is to allow for the flowering of a multiplicity of worlds, there is not just one way to understand the exit from the capitalist world. Furthermore, the struggle for a multiplicity of worlds begins now: by confronting the tyranny of capital, we are already breaking with the fatalism that only one world is possible. We are already breaking with the One of the world as it is. As Subcomandante Galeano writes, "Across the whole planet are born and grown rebellions that refuse to accept the limits of diagrams, rules, laws, and norms. There are not just two genders, nor seven colors, nor four cardinal points on the compass, nor one world."[55]

At the same time, to speak of "a world where many worlds fit" does not mean simply acknowledging the multiplicity of human experiences, as if it were a matter of mere coexistence. Rather, the affirmation that there are "many worlds" is articulated with "one world" where they all fit. Moreover, we should not understand this "one world" simply as a container, as some neutral space that just so happens to have enough space for all of them. If the affirmation of "many worlds" is to have a radical meaning, then the "one world" that establishes something common among them must be radical as well. First, this "one world" could refer to our common home, the planet Earth. While the earth's inhabitants each experience it through their particular places, the devastation resulting from capitalist productivism has also made it into more and more of a shared challenge for us all. In this context, to care for "the world" and repair it as much as possible is the most obvious thing that the multiple worlds that live within it have in common. Another meaning is that something common can emerge among the different worlds that come together, and this commonality emerges from their heterogeneity instead of from their uniformity, through differences and not just through identity. It is a commonality that accumulates substance through the multiplicity of experiences, not from the postulate of the unity of the human. The many worlds that fit in the world do not remain isolated, nor do they aspire to autarky. Rather they seek each other out, exchange, cooperate, and face the inevitable tensions and conflicts in the best way possible. They seek the interpenetration of their memories and geographies, in processes where shared concerns, (partial) translatability of experiences, and the disturbing splendor of the discrepancies are all equally important.

Clearly "a world where many worlds fit" also contributes to a new understanding of the universal. During the March of the Color of the Earth, Subcomandante Marcos even combined the phrase with the words used by Major Ana Maria in 1996, speaking of the need to establish bridges between Indigenous and non-Indigenous peoples. He said, "Only in this way can we build a house—which is what they used to call 'the world'—where we can all fit, all of us who are equal because we are different."[56] By calling the space that houses many worlds a "home," he shows that it is clearly not just a neutral space, but a place that is inhabited and where life is made in common. Importantly, we see an overlap (at least a partial one) between "a world where many worlds fit" and "we are equal because we are different." In fact, the assertion that many worlds exist and the recognition that we are different are but two statements of the same multiplicity. To affirm that many worlds fit in the same world and that those who are different are equal both highlight what is shared. And each case features a tight link between the two sides of its statement, between the multiplicity and the shared. This is how we may join the Zapatistas in rejecting the two extreme postures. On the one hand, we should avoid affirming differences without worrying about what is shared (leading to absolutizing, isolating, and opposing them). On the other hand, we should avoid asserting the One without considering differences (which would amount to negating them). It is rather a matter of recognizing what is shared *in and through* differences.

To express this difficult balance, we might be better off renouncing the concept of "universalism," which in fact hardly appears in Zapatista word-thought. Some have proposed speaking of *pluriversalism,* but this neologism completely abandons the "uni" in favor of the "pluri," which seems to substitute a homogenizing unity for a proliferation of pure differences. To speak of uni*pluri*versalism or of pl*uni*versalism, uniting the "pluri" with the "uni" might better express the conjunction of the shared and the singularities. Another option, if we wanted to conserve the notion of universalism (which has its advantages in a period marked by the multiplication of excluding identities), would be to contrast the universalism of the One and its premise of homogeneity with a "universalism of the multiple" that is built through and in the differences. The latter is a form of universalism that goes so far as to deny the One and instead attempts to construct the common—that which makes differences equal without negating them as differences, without imposing any abstract, homogenizing unification. If we decide to renounce the term "universalism" altogether, we might think of this "one world" that harbors a multiplicity of worlds as a *community of differences,* not a community based on sharing the same essence or characteristic. Rather, it is an *inessential* community, without conditions for belonging. A community that emerges from a heterogeneity of experiences and is built by searching for what is shared. That is, it is based on a notion of the common that is in no way a homogeneous One or an abstract unity. In inviting us to dream of and give birth to "a world where many worlds fit," the Zapatistas seek to recognize the multiplicity of worlds and reconcile this with the search for human community.

Humanity as a planetary community

We can develop these ideas more by once again considering the notion of humanity. In the previous chapter, we saw that this term features prominently within the Zapatistas' word-action, placing itself (and placing us) within the war between capitalism and humanity. Indeed, anticapitalist struggle is constantly calling upon all of humanity to confront attempts to destroy it. During their journey, the Zapatistas have always seen the effort to construct autonomies in the rebellious territories as complementary to the broader, planetary struggle to mobilize humanity against the capitalist Hydra. Across them all, "humanity" is part of what binds together this "one world" where many worlds can fit.

Yet there are plenty of reasons to abandon the very notion of humanity. In the first place, it seems to postulate a kind of depoliticized "unanimity," since it includes all human beings as if they were united within one big family. Secondly, within European universalism, humanity has generally been conceived based on an abstract idea of Man. Finally, classical humanism conceives of this Man as separate from nature (and superior to it). Contrary to all this, Zapatista word-thought allows us to understand the notion of humanity differently, distancing itself from these troublesome conceptions. We have already seen how they reject unanimist conceptions and instead decenter humanity, perceiving it from below and—above all—as engaged in a battle against those who would destroy it. In fact, the notion of humanity only makes sense if we recognize this war and the enemy it must face to save itself.

We can now move to the second aspect of the critique of the notion of humanity. As part of European universalism, classical humanism understands "Man" as an abstract idea. It is an idea that disregards the duality between men and women and is even more dismissive of the other genders that also exist (something that, on the contrary, is very present in the Zapatista word, as it is careful to address all men, all women, and all non-binary people).[57] The notion of humanity, on the contrary, postulates the unity of the human race, ignoring the concrete differences among the peoples of the world. We cannot overlook the contrast between the abstract character of this understanding and real-world attitudes that assert vast differences between full humanity and those confined to a sub-humanity that is subject to contempt and racism. There is, then, no shortage of reasons to declare war on this Man, a Western hegemonic construction, at once abstract and conceived using specifically European values. It is possible, however, to declare war on this Man and at the same time rescue the notion of humanity. In fact, if our thinking is based in particular, concrete situations and affirms a multiplicity of worlds, we can break with abstract universalism, and humanity can be conceived on the basis of its differences. "Humanity" is therefore part of this "common" that must be elaborated in the weft of its constitutive heterogeneity.

The Zapatistas insist on reclaiming humanity, and they have done so in a way that avoids the pitfalls mentioned above. For them, humanity is a horizon of struggle. In the words of Comandante David, it is a "planetary community" that allows differences to meet, to listen to one another as equals, and to nurture one another.[58] The commonality of such a community is that we are inhabiting the same planet, as well as our shared responsibility to safeguard it from ongoing devastation. Perhaps this commonality can also be built through a patient labor, up until now barely undertaken, to find isomorphisms and correspondences between the fundamental values of different cultures—with dignity being one of the top contenders to start with. We limit ourselves here to just one suggestion, drawing on one of the meanings the word *humanitas* had for the ancient Romans. For them, *humanitas* was not the sum of the human beings who inhabit the earth, but rather a sentiment, a virtue. It was the attitude that makes someone decide to welcome a stranger as if they were their brother (or sister).[59] It is the basis of hospitality, and it is more than that. It is what makes it possible to ward off the fear of the unknown, that which is different, and it does this by assuming a closeness to the one who seems the least close. It can do this because it asserts a sense of community that may potentially embrace any human being. Perhaps today, more than ever, we need this *sense of planetary community* as a precondition for encounters among all our unique experiences.

A third element is still missing: the relationship between the human and the not human, which we will return to at the end of the chapter, but we can outline some aspects of it here. The Zapatistas' assertions show how two different perspectives can indeed coincide. We can reject a unanimist conception of humanity and declare war on Man (abstract Man, that is) while at the same time understanding humanity as a horizon of struggle amid a war against what would negate it. We can advance an understanding of humanity that rejects the universalism of the One and that refuses to homogenize concrete beings into an abstract totality, an understanding that asserts a community of differences. That is the sort of humanity we find in Zapatista word-action: *a planetary community of differences.*

Leaving capitalism, leaving modernity

Zapatista word-thought then proceeds to take another step forward. If the many worlds that exist are to continue expanding, if there is to be equality among them, then we must break down this hegemonic Western thought that masquerades as universalism. Its supposed universalism is not the expression of some European "essence" but a historical creation forged in the heart of Europe through domination and exclusion. Specifically, it is a system of representations and values called "modernity" that emerged alongside the capitalist world-system dominated by Europe and later the United States. However, the current crisis of capitalism has thrown modernity into crisis, as illustrated by the rise of postmodernity since the late seventies. This is a symptom of the crisis of late capitalism, not a framework for how to overcome it.[60] Postmodernism itself is immersed in this crisis and sinks into it. Zapatista word-thought stands in stark contrast to postmodernism and is even directly opposed to it at times. For this reason the fight has to be on two fronts, breaking down the foundations of modernity without falling into the morass of postmodernity. This is the path of Zapatista word-thought.

Modernity has three pillars. The first is its concept of Universal History, forged in the second half of the eighteenth century as the linear march of

Progress, a unified movement of constant, all-encompassing improvement. The second is possessive and competitive individualism, shaped by capitalist ways of being. Collectivity is essential for overcoming these obstacles, but we will see later that the affirmation of collectivity alone is insufficient; the diametric opposition between the individual and collective, created by modern thought, has to be broken. Finally, the third pillar is the separation between Man and nature, with the former being outside and superior to the latter. Working from this vantage point, he (Man) uses science to know nature and relentlessly exploits it using industrial technology. This is another reason to overcome modernity, to create a different relation between humans and Mother Earth.

Overcoming the opposition between the individual and the collective

The importance of the collective in Zapatista thought comes as no surprise, as it is rooted in the life of Indigenous communities. As Subcomandante Marcos explained, the Indigenous communities of the Lacandon Jungle "began organizing for survival in the only way they could survive: together, collectively. The only way people could continue onward was by joining with others. So the *compañeros'* words always feature the word 'together,' the word 'we,' the word 'united,' the word 'collective.' This is fundamental to—and I'd even say the very core of—Zapatista discourse."[61] This collectivity is not part of some Indigenous essence or Mayan identity, rather concrete living conditions make it essential to organize collectively. Neither should we reproduce the stereotype of a homogenous community living outside history, without hierarchy, in harmony and permanent consensus. The Zapatistas are careful to point out that this so-called "sense of community" is not exclusive to Indigenous peoples and can continue to be found in the popular cultures that have not been shattered by capitalism's competitive individualism.[62] Zapatista word-thought does not just refer to community as it is lived by Indigenous peoples and in Mexico's popular neighborhoods; they also call on people to overcome the limitations of individual rebellion by forming collectives of all kinds. In fact, we all need to overcome our competitive and egocentric attitudes in order to create the collective power needed to fight capitalism and bring about new worlds.

While collectivity is "the core" of Zapatista theory and practice, it does not mean that we should do away with any concern for individuals. Subcomandante Marcos demonstrated as much when he presented his evaluation of the March of the Color of the Earth to Indigenous communities meeting in Oventik. He chose not to address them as collectives but as all the individualities that constitute them, saying, "I present myself to each of you, the committees that lead us. . . . Each of you gave me the responsibility of leading the people out and returning them safely. . . . You gave us the order to carry the Zapatista name with dignity, and we did so. . . . You told us to bring our demand for the recognition of our rights and culture to those above and we did so . . . I pass the baton back to you, *compañero, compañera*."[63] The importance of collectivity in Indigenous communities is not negated by this, but it shows that it is compatible with a sense of singularity, thereby allowing the Subcomandante to address each member of the EZLN.

Similarly, in the stories that are so emblematic of Subcomandantes Marcos and Galeano, instead of speaking of the Zapatista communities generally, they bring unique individuals to life, such as Old Antonio, beloved and mischievous children such as Olivio and Toñita, and most recently Defensa Zapatista and Pedro.[64] We began hearing from ordinary members of the EZLN in the first communiques from January 1994, when Javier surprised the Subcomandante by suggesting that, instead of inviting brutalized supporters to the Lacandon Jungle, they invite the police who beat them. Or Ángel, "a Tseltal whose greatest honor is having read Womack's entire book on Zapata. (And whenever someone doubts his achievement, he says 'It took three years. It was a pain, but I finished.'")[65] Or Susana, a Tsotsil woman accused by her male comrades of instigating the EZLN's first uprising, which is to say that she gathered proposals for the Women's Revolutionary Law in dozens of communities. After its publication one man made the lamentable remark that "the good thing is that my wife doesn't know Spanish," and a woman shot back saying, "Well you're screwed because we're going to translate it into every Indigenous language."[66] Later on, the literary characters who embody Zapatista ways of being became more prominent, such as "investigation commissioner" Elías Contreras and more recently the young girl Defensa Zapatista, with her unique, assertive style that is also emblematic of the new generations of Zapatistas. In these stories she shows her ethic of collectivity by caring for all the individuals around her, even the weird and mundane ones who would be forgotten in a competitive world. For example, "Defensa Zapatista takes on as her objective something to carry out collectively and does not conceive of herself as a leader or a boss; in fact she has selected the position that shines the least—defense. . . . Her job is to seek out and find who wants to join, who will play as a team. . . . And when she values positions like ball boy as equally important, when she includes the little pig and the cat-dog who runs crooked, and makes the desire to play the only requirement—this is her way of saying 'Let's be in the struggle' . . . I can think of nothing more Zapatista than what this little girl's efforts symbolize."[67]

We must not forget that resistance is built from individual decisions. As Subcomandante Marcos put it, "In any part of the world, at any time, an ordinary man or woman rebels and ends up tearing off their clothes sewn from conformity, clothes that cynicism has dyed gray. Any man, any woman, of whatever color or tongue, says (and says to themself) 'Enough!' . . . Any man, any woman can be brave enough to resist power and take the path of dignity and hope. Any man, any woman can decide to live and to struggle for their part in history."[68] As we have seen, again and again, the EZLN has demanded that we overcome the limitations of individual rebellion and organize with others, but this does not negate the fact that collective rebellion is made up of individuals looking to transform themselves, to break with the reigning conformity and find their own ways of living. This helps us see the collective struggle from the perspective of singularities, unlike the old collectivist rhetoric of "mass struggle," which proclaimed the end of the individual.

It is critical to turn here to the ways capitalism mystifies individualism. For Subcomandante Marcos, "Those above say the individual is the most important, that you have to worry about yourself and not others, that being cynical and egotistical are virtues, that goodness and solidarity are defects to be rectified, that any thinking that's collective or communal is a sign of totalitarianism, that the only freedoms are individual."[69] Yet at the same time, "If we look up at the future promised by those above, we see we aren't what we are. We're a number, not a history. . . . In that future we're not ourselves, we don't attain individuality and live our own history, with its virtues and defects, desires and frustrations, victories and defeats, dreams and nightmares. No, we're just a number." So individualism is a false promise, which is why the Subcomandante says that "the fallacy par excellence of modernity" is "individual liberty."[70] Despite its individualist ideology, the capitalist system tends to deny us individuality and instead offers a falsified, quantified identity. So while the commodification of life teaches people to be "numbers who accumulate numbers," thereby impoverishing and homogenizing their life experiences, only anticapitalist struggle can fully affirm individualities. Only by battling the capitalist Hydra can we "be individuals and live our own history," one with "dignity as its main pillar." Subcomandante Marcos contrasts people living as numbers in the world above with the story of Pedro, a Zapatista child born in exile, far from his village occupied by the federal army. He laughs at his decision to address a group of academics regarding "an Indigenous child, instead of speaking of world revolution." Yet this is a way of understanding the Zapatistas: "rebels who refuse to be numbers."[71]

These analyses suggest we should struggle both *against individualism* (to defend or recuperate a sense of collectivity) and *for the flourishing of individualities* (that are currently denied through homogenizing commodification and quantitative ways of being). Zapatista word-thought calls on us to abandon unified and homogenous versions of collectivity (be they community, nation, or the proletariat as "masses"). In bringing together a rejection of individualism and recognition of individuality, their understanding of collectivity affirms the singularities and differences that make it up. Subcomandante Marcos's remarks are full of important, fulsome, and sometimes interminable enumerations, which, as mentioned in the previous chapter, allows him to give space to the wide multiplicity that constitutes those "below." His lists express a logic of de-homogenization, opening up categories and exposing the multiplicity within them. So, it is inadequate to speak of "Indigenous" struggle and important to de-homogenize the category, observing that "Mexico 'below' is Mazahua, Amuzgo, Tlapaneco, Najuatlaca, Cora, Huichol, Yaqui, Mayo, Tarahumara, Mixteco, Zapoteco, Maya, Chontal, Seri, Triqui, Kumiai, Cucapá, Paipai, Cochimí, Kiliwa, Tequistlateco, Pame, Chichimeca, Otomí, Mazateco, Matlatzinco, Ocuilteco, Popoloca, Ixtateco, Chocho-Popoloca, Cuicateco, Chatino, Chinanteco, Huave, Pápago, Pima, Tepehuano, Guarijio, Huasteco, Chuj, Jacalteco, Mixe, Zoque, Totonaco, Kikapú, Purépecha, O'odham, Tsotsil, Tseltal, Tojolabal, Ch'ol, Mam."[72]

While this is indeed a struggle to strengthen collectivity, such a collective—be it a community, ethnicity, nation, or class—is not homogenous. It could only be made so through extreme violence, of the sort that has extended beyond symbolic violence to include many forms of genocide and extermination throughout history. In the story "Always and Never against Sometimes," we find yet another example of the Zapatista critique of unifying and uniform logics. In this story "Always" and "Never" are the reigning empires, and they will not tolerate "Once" or "Once Again," who form the family "Sometimes." The moral is clear: "The 'always' and the 'nevers' are imposed from above," through universal laws and homogenizing globality, while the particularizing logics of below "are the 'nuisances' time and again which, sometimes, is another way of saying 'those who are different,' or, from time to time, 'the rebels.'"[73]

We must chart a path that overcomes the false opposition between the individual and the collective if we are to reject individualism but not individualities and construct collectivity. Subcomandante Marcos suggests this in "Ethics and Politics":

> Don Luis, in your missive you discuss the theme of the individual and the collective. It's countered by an age-old argument. . . . The collective, as they say, erases and subjugates individuality. And so, in a crude theoretic leap, they begin singing the praises of a system where, as they say, any individual can become what they will, for good or for bad, because freedom is guaranteed. . . . We say that the fundamental desires of all human beings are life, liberty, and truth. And maybe we can even speak of a progression: better life, more freedom, more knowledge. Is it possible for an individual to fully achieve these aspirations and their respective progressions within a collective? We believe so. In any case, we're sure they can't achieve them without one.[74]

Those who look down from above contrast the individual and the collective. From there, they affirm that the collective necessarily negates individuality, meaning the individual must assert itself *against* collectivity. But it should be evident that this is a false dilemma, considering that individuals can neither survive nor grow outside the collective dimension of their lives. Collectives can not only avoid subjugating individuals, but also allow them to achieve their full aspirations.

We are clearly not trying to assert collectivity against individuals (or individuals against the collective). Instead, we reject modernity's supposed contradiction between the individual and collective. Modernity asserts the freedom of the individual by rejecting the ties that connect him with his collective reality (this is why the philosophers of the seventeenth and eighteenth centuries invented the myth of the "state of nature" preceding the social contract, imagining that individuals can exist without society and are of greater value than it). Or it affirms collectivity by rejecting the particularities of the individuals that are part of it (consider the homogenizing state, the struggle of the unified party and masses, or the quantifying effects of commodification). As we see in Zapatista word-thought, overcoming this dichotomy requires reconciling the virtues of collective organization with the recognition of individual singularities. It requires an appreciation of the heterogeneity that constitutes collectivity.

We therefore need another way of understanding collectivity and another way of understanding the individual. On one hand (as discussed above), part of this work is to comprehend collectivities through their heterogeneity, refusing the perspective of the One and instead asserting the multiplicity of worlds and the ability to build commonality through difference. On the other hand, there can be no individual self-fulfillment outside of life's concrete reality, which is composed of many collectivities. An individual's life only exists thanks to relations with other humans. Rather than impeding the realization of their individuality, these relations are what make it possible. If we understand this, we can go a step further and posit a *relational* conception of the human person. People are the product of many interpersonal relations, first with their parents and all those who help raise and socialize them, fully incorporating them into their culture. Above all, these relations are not simply added to a pre-existing "I," but instead, they constitute the "I" and are literally part of it.[75] In this sense, an "I" is not simply an "I"—it is also a "we." This idea destroys the supposed dichotomy between the individual and the collective, since we can only hold them in opposition by disregarding each human's fundamental relationality, by forgetting that we are interlaced together as "we beings." In this way, Zapatista word-thought invites us to rid ourselves of the false opposition between the individual and collective and, in doing so, to overcome one of modernity's defining characteristics: positing an individual apart from their transindividual existence, without the interpersonal and collective dimensions so essential to their being.

Belonging to the earth, appropriating the sciences

As we have seen, for the Zapatistas the earth is more than simply ground to be plowed. Mother Earth encompasses the full variety of spaces and living beings that inhabit it. Indeed, it is a force (*potencia*) understood to be maternal, the source of all life. As Subcomandante Moisés explained, "Mother Earth is what gives us life."[76] Unlike Western modernity's conception of "nature," Mother Earth is not a thing apart from human beings since, as with parentage, they have a vital, sensuous relation with her. Moreover, because it is the source of all life, Mother Earth is understood as a force that our survival depends on. The slogan "The Earth doesn't belong to us, we belong to it" is all the more significant when we contrast it with the famous slogan from the Zapatistas of the early twentieth century: "The land [earth] belongs to those who work it." The former principal puts a limit on the latter: the right to work the land does not entail full ownership over it but is instead subordinated to our *belonging to* Mother Earth and our responsibility to care for it.

How are these principles manifest in the Zapatistas' practice? As mentioned earlier, agroecology is a set of practices unlike those of agroindustrial productivism, as agroecology seeks a better equilibrium with Mother Earth. Agroecology includes polyculture, the use of native seeds, organic production, preventing deforestation, the regulation of hunting and fishing, the preservation of rivers, and the maintenance of natural resources. Most importantly, this is all practiced within a way of life where community and territory are closely connected. As Guadalupe, an education promoter in the Oventik zone says, respect for Mother Earth is fundamental: "Now we respect the Mother Earth that gives us life."[77] We also see it in their many rituals, especially when they ask Mother Earth's permission before planting the *milpa*: "We maintain our ways of observing religious and civil celebrations. We maintain and strengthen our care for native seeds and for our ways of feeding ourselves from the products that there are in our communities, because they're healthy and organic. We maintain and strengthen our ways of caring for Mother Earth, praying to her, and respecting the earth and everything that there is in this nature of ours."[78] We should also note that, within Mayan peoples' traditional understandings, there is a strong continuity between humans and all the other beings that are part of Mother Earth. On the one hand, humans, animals, plants, hills, and rivers are all endowed with (*dotado de*) *ch'ulel*, the animating force that gives humans their vital energies, will, and consciousness, but it is not unique to them. On the other hand, some of the animating forces that determine a human's personality may be those of animals, rivers, or natural phenomena like the wind, rain, and lightning.[79]

These practices and ways of understanding the relation between humans and the universe are a radical departure from those of modernity, which is based on the complete exteriority of Man and nature. It postulates an "exceptionalism," that allows Man to place himself outside that which, beginning in the seventeenth century, comes to be called "nature" in its modern sense. And it goes without saying that "outside" also means "above"—a position that authorizes both his ability to understand this object using science and his right to exploit its resources. Just as Descartes proclaims in his famous formulation, from this moment onward Western Man aspires to use his scientific and technical knowledge to make himself "the master and possessor of nature." Breaking with modernity therefore requires breaking with this separation between Man and nature, and there are various ways to proceed in this endeavor. The Zapatista way is to reintegrate human beings into what we might call "nature," what they more accurately call Mother Earth. In fact, if we continue speaking of "nature," even to argue for a new relationship with it, we run the risk of maintaining it as an entity of which man is not a part, thereby reproducing the exteriority of man and nature characteristic of modernity. It is critical that human beings are understood as part of Mother Earth, that we embrace all the implications of *belonging to* it ("it doesn't belong to us, we belong to it"). This does away with Descartes's dreamworld of humans as "master and possessor," and they cease to be the center of that world. Capital-M "Man" is no more.

This brings us to the third aspect of the reformulation of the notion of humanity. In addition to the aspects already analyzed, we must now consider the assumption that Man is outside nature and distinct from animals. The Zapatistas seek to break from the abstract conception of capital-M "Man," with its exceptionalism and superiority vis-a-vis the rest of the world. It means understanding humans as animals that—despite their particular features— share more characteristics with non-human animals than classical theorists acknowledge. More broadly, breaking with capital-M "Man" means reintegrat- ing humans into the full ensemble of interactions found in the world of life, that which Indigenous peoples call Mother Earth and others refer to by other names. Lowercase-m "man" accepts that he *belongs to* something greater than himself, that he no longer occupies the supreme, central position Western modernity placed him in. Moreover, in our effort to *decenter* our gaze, we cannot even assert that Mother Earth is the center of creation. If we take on the *intergalactic* per- spective suggested by the Zapatistas, this decentering is greater still: instead of occupying the center, the Earth is part of a much greater assortment of galaxies that form the universe.

Nonetheless, there are further considerations that counterbalance all this. For the Zapatistas, the radical critique of modernity's foundations does not imply it should be completely liquidated. Consider the relationship the Zapatistas have forged with the sciences through large events in 2016 and 2017 called "The Zapatistas and ConSciences for Humanity." They convoked them on the premise that science, as well as art, are indispensable for the world we want to build.[80] The result was long, remarkable encounters where speeches by the EZLN were interspersed between seminars from scientists from very diverse disciplines, from ecology and evolutionary biology to mathematics and astrophysics. They were presented to a lay audience, including a group of two hundred "students" coming from the five Caracoles. Many of the Zapatistas' supporters were perplexed by the event (and the way it was carried out), given their tendency to critique science, or even reject it outright as an expression of Western modernity and the capitalist world system. Instead, the EZLN's interventions were a fierce defense of scientific knowledge. They discarded postmodern critiques of science as absolute relativism, given that postmodernism considers all scientific production to be nothing but discourses that are either completely dependent on subjective factors or can be reduced to their social conditions of production.[81] On the other hand, there are also critiques of science that are not the least bit postmodern. For example, they recognize that scientific truth is produced within a highly polarized field, where scientists enjoy relative autonomy while also suffering under capitalism's antagonisms. This affects the kind of knowledge produced, but the results do not necessarily cease to be scientific truths, which are truths subject to controversy.[82] All this goes to show that we can indeed defend scientific knowledge against postmodern relativism without falling into an objectivist or dehistoricized understanding of science.

Beyond engaging in these debates, the most important aspect of ConSciences is its extraordinary process of popular appropriation of the sciences. This initiative has been propelled by a younger generation of Zapatistas, asserting their need to discover knowledge.[83] The scientists' speeches were directed toward them, and these youth have been charged with processing this knowledge, sharing it with their communities, and finding ways to integrate it into autonomous education and community practice. Above all, the ConSciences gatherings have disturbed the stereotype that Indigenous peoples are confined within the bounds of traditional knowledge (including Zapatismo's own traditional knowledge, as presented by Old Antonio). The events seemed to proclaim, "Don't confine us to tradition! We also want to know how scientific knowledge can help us build the worlds we seek."

This is why the Zapatistas defended the importance and validity of scientific knowledge in general, while insisting on the importance of critique and rejecting the way scientific practice gets corralled into the service of capitalist productivism. A delegation of Zapatista students offered brilliant concluding remarks to ConScience's first meeting, saying "Yes, we need science to save humanity and the planet. And we believe another science is possible—a science not for destruction but for life."[84] They emphasized the need to build "an autonomous science," "a science in constant relation to our peoples" because "the knowledges of our peoples are just as valuable as science, but we need science too." They ended by promoting "all the sciences, for all men and women."

These Zapatistas clearly understand science to be a battlefield, divided between those at the service of capitalism who contribute to the destruction of humanity and the planet, against those making a decisive effort to save it. But we must understand that, to achieve this, science cannot remain the exclusive purview of scientists. Yes, their research should retain its autonomy, and it is also vitally important that it respond to popular concerns and connect with popular mobilization. Moreover, the Zapatista students denounced one of the most grievous aspects of science: its bid to claim a monopoly on legitimate knowledge, thereby devaluing all other ways of knowing. The Zapatistas advocated instead for interaction between (and the mutual transformation of) scientific and popular knowledges.

The ConSciences process is undoubtedly an unprecedented initiative. Worldwide, what other popular struggle has dedicated such effort to organizing scientific forums of this magnitude? Despite the inevitable difficulties and controversies, it has opened an unexpected path that offers both a radical critique of modernity and a selective reappropriation of some of its most emblematic achievements. This charts the course toward scientific knowledge that might help us care for and cure this world that we so desperately need—so that many worlds can fit within it.

One of the Zapatistas' greatest contributions is their ability to bring together struggles at various scales. They are simultaneously an Indigenous uprising building autonomy, a national liberation struggle, and part of a planetary war to save humanity from capitalist destruction. These three perspectives are neither opposed nor incompatible. Instead, they must be understood in relation to one another. It is this interconnection that allows each to avoid the risks that it carries when held in isolation. A quick glance across today's world shows that the lens of ethnicity can easily become essentialist and exclusive, that the defense of the nation can foment intolerant identitarian chauvinism, that universalism can promote a homogenizing negation of difference.

Conversely, as we see in the Zapatistas' word-action, the struggle to build Indigenous autonomy is always also a struggle for a dignified place within Mexico, as well as part of the global war pitting humanity against the capitalist Hydra. Nor does the struggle for national liberation isolate them from the other peoples of the world. Instead, it is part of a planetary struggle to form networks of resistance and rebellion. Figuring out how exactly to assert particular demands and ways of being without playing into identitarian passions and xenophobic hatred is a difficult task, but the Zapatistas have a clear principle for navigating it all: identitarian claims are dangerous because they tend to isolate the particularities that define them. Instead, we can affirm "what we are" without encasing ourselves in an identity, thereby allowing fraternity with struggles waged by people who are not "what we are," but who are attacked through the same war and who share similar dreams. This avoids the tired confrontation between the two positions that dominate the world stage: either reject all demands particular to a certain ethnicity (or whatever other grouping) in the name of the universal, or make these demands absolute and thereby foster identitarian, racist, and xenophobic fanaticism. The Zapatista experience points toward another path that affirms particularity without isolating or absolutizing it. Yet this path can only be pursued by bringing together various scales, including an understanding of the planetary community that goes beyond the historical limits of universalism.

The Zapatistas' contribution here is to call on us to create "a world where many worlds fit." This is premised on a true multiplicity of worlds, which is directly related to the affirmation of a politics of autonomy and a recognition of what these many worlds can *share* and, in doing so, create a planetary community. None of this can be premised on the One. Just as a politics from below is premised on collectives able to act together while respecting their differences, the task here is to understand commonality *from* and *in* its constitutive heterogeneity. Instead of erasing particularity and adopting the universalism of the One, Zapatista thought-action suggests that it is possible to claim both a multiplicity of worlds and a planetary community of differences.

Zapatista word-thought generally calls this planetary community of difference "humanity." Their use of the word is clearly distinct from that of universalism and abstract humanism. The Zapatistas' struggle for humanity is a declaration of war on that which destroys it: capitalist productivism and the reifications of the market. For the Zapatistas, humanity is not a homogenous, abstract totality, but a community of difference. As Major Ana María said, "We are all the same because we are all different." We should also distance our understanding of humanity from its modernist conception, which puts "Man" at the center of the world and separates "Him" from nature. In calling on us to fight for humanity and against capitalism, the Zapatistas focus our attention on this planetary community of differences that encompasses all of us. But this is not an *exclusive* form of belonging, as we also belong to Mother Earth. Understanding ourselves as humanity can and should include recognition of an even larger community of all beings that inhabit the Earth. To the extent that the distinct scales of belonging are not conceived in an essentialized way and therefore not exclusive, there is no longer incompatibility between the affirmation of a community of life anchored in its territory, that of humanity as a planetary community of differences, and that of the community of all the beings who inhabit the Earth.

The Zapatista struggle is undoubtedly Indigenous. The Indigenous communities of Chiapas have built it through their rebellious determination and ability to resist. Their strength is rooted in suffering through five hundred long years of colonial oppression and the longing to recuperate a dignity that was wounded but never destroyed. This requires overturning the consequences of five centuries of domination, including genocide, exploitation, and dispossession, as well as humiliation, racism, the destruction of Indigenous cultures, and the imposition of the conquerors' ways of thinking and of being first through feudal and ecclesiastical mentalities and then through capitalist modernity. Undoing this colonial domination clearly requires *decolonizing* our ways of thinking and of being. As we have seen in this chapter, the Zapatistas have made significant contributions to the collective struggle to break with the foundations of Western capitalist modernity.

The Zapatistas have contributed to our work of decolonizing ourselves, yet they have done so without referring to the decolonial and postcolonial discourses that are currently in fashion. Moreover, it is worth pointing out some particularities of the Zapatista way of understanding this task without isolating the issue of coloniality, without absolutizing the dichotomy imposed by this form of domination.[85] They do not essentialize "the West" as an enemy from which all ills emerge, something we should entirely reject. (Consider, for example, their attitude toward the sciences.) Indeed, it would run completely counter to the Zapatista perspective to assert an absolute opposition between the West and the not-West, given how they build bridges between all those below in struggle, no matter what continent they find themselves on. Within Zapatista word-thought, Indigenous peoples struggle to continue being "what we are," which must be understood within the struggle for a different world—one made of many worlds, which we share as a planetary community of differences. Finally, the task of decolonizing ourselves cannot be thought of outside of its relation to the anticapitalist struggle to save all of humanity from the gathering storm, which is why the Zapatistas seek to articulate struggles at various scales and across various registers. In this way, the effort to free ourselves from modernity—the thinking of the hegemonic West—appears as an indispensable dimension of the struggle against the capitalist Hydra.

CHAPTER 5

"Our Struggle is for History and against Oblivion"
An Other Grammar of Historical Times

History is omnipresent in the Zapatista word. Within it, memory and dignity are equally important and closely tied.[1] Indeed, the Zapatista uprising has been defined as a struggle for memory and against oblivion: "The war that began on January 1, 1994, was and is a war to make us heard, a war for words, a war against oblivion, a war for memory."[2] The uprising had a symbolic objective as well as a military one: "On the last night of the year 1993, we left here, from the Tsotsil mountains of the Mexican Southeast to take the city of San Cristóbal and to take our place in the history of Mexico."[3] The Zapatista struggle is an Indigenous insurrection, a national liberation struggle, and a planetary anti-capitalist rebellion. And the Zapatista struggle has another important dimension beyond these three: its reclamation of history, its roots in a deep time charged with memory.

As a *rebellion of history*, the Zapatista struggle has been enormously creative. Beyond its critique of the eighteenth century conception of history as Progress—which has gone on to comprise the foundation of both Marxism and the hegemonic thought of capitalist modernity—the Zapatista gaze has also identified new conceptions of time and history that are being circulated during the neoliberal stage of capitalism in order to confront and break with them. In doing so, they draw on the experience of Indigenous peoples, which involves a very different perception of time and memory. In the confrontation between these vastly different conceptions of history—the tradition of Indigenous communities, history as Progress in modernity and orthodox Marxism, and the perpetual present of neoliberalism—the Zapatista rebellion has opened pathways toward a new conception of historical time that is capable of articulating pasts, presents, and futures in a different way. This is essential if we are to walk toward a world in which many worlds fit.

National history and dispute over memory

National history and Indigenous struggle

At the time of the uprising, the history that the Zapatistas claimed was, above all, national history. This focus allowed the EZLN to define its own position and condemn their adversaries in a language known to all Mexicans. It ensured a broad social reception for Zapatismo and located the Chiapas rebels within national history, something the official discourse then attempted to refute. In this way, the Zapatistas conjured a widely shared national imaginary, demonstrating that a nation is nothing other than "a shared history."[4] At the same time, this national imaginary was in dispute with power, demanding a critical reinterpretation, far from the official versions of that "ridiculous history . . . taught in school."[5]

The references to national history that prevailed during the first years of the uprising had their roots in the earlier political formation of the first members of the EZLN. Thinking back to his first readings of *El Despertador Mexicano*, Subcomandante Moisés remembers "that it talked about Mexican history." Subcomandante Marcos explains that his name is that of a dead comrade "who is the one who gave me history classes, a person with encyclopedic knowledge of the history of Mexico."[6] The origins of the EZLN, its Marxist-Leninist provenance and its insistence on *national* liberation, explain why the nation's history continued to be the dominant framework in the communiqués of the first years. Rather than a "people's history," it sought to recuperate national history *for* the people. Thus national history prevailed over any historical perspective of Indigenous peoples during this time. Subcomandante Marcos acknowledged that the significance of five hundred years of resistance—so important to Indigenous peoples—was not appreciated by the EZLN until 1992.[7] The mobilization in San Cristóbal de Las Casas that toppled the statue of the conqueror Diego de Mazariegos on October 12, 1992, was a decisive moment in this regard. However, even after recognizing the importance of the memory of five hundred years of resistance, the EZLN continued to emphasize a national perspective over an Indigenous one.

As noted above, the opening sentence of "The First Declaration of the

Lacandon Jungle" exemplifies this relationship. Their assertion that the Zapatista uprising is a rebellion of memory—"We are the product of 500 years of struggle"—is a distinctly Indigenous perspective on history. However, after this reference, the thread of time is interrupted. Three centuries of colonialism are skipped over, and the narrative resumes with Independence and the subsequent trajectory of the nation.[8] As mentioned previously, while preparing for the uprising, the consensus was to direct the message to all Mexicans and avoid any implication that it was addressed only to Indigenous people. For this reason, although generic references abound to both "exploitation and persecution," as well as the resistance of Indigenous peoples, there is scarce mention of precise facts in the history of Indigenous peoples.[9] The period before the Spanish Conquest is rarely mentioned, and even then, only in a very general way.[10] Not much space was given to the history of Chiapas, not even to the great Indigenous rebellion of 1712 that extended over all of the Highlands and the northern zone.[11] That is the degree to which they avoided mentioning any local, regional, or ethnic history, instead centering the entire nation. While the Indigenous dimension of the Zapatista word is quite important, it was shown through stories like those of Old Antonio rather than historical references. In sum, at the time of the uprising and in the years immediately following it, the history that the entire Mexican nation holds in common prevailed over the Indigenous perspective of five hundred years of exploitation and resistance.

The Zapatistas' discourse evolved as time went on. There was a first inflection point between 1997 and 2001, as they mobilized for the constitutional recognition of Indigenous rights. During this time, their struggle for memory was to demand that Indigenous peoples have "a dignified place" in the national narrative.[12] It was not only a matter of "settling the score with history" and its injustices; the fate of the nation was at stake, as the Zapatistas called on them to recognize that Indigenous people were indispensable to the nation and its future. "Today, with the Indigenous heart that is the dignified root of the Mexican nation . . . with the Indigenous people, a new and better country is necessary and possible. Without them, there is no future as a nation."[13] The right relationship between the two perspectives is one in which national history envelops ancestral history, but the Indigenous peoples find in their ancestral history the dignity that makes them the root, heart of the nation, its foundation, and vitality. The references to national history we find during this period are often more critical, as when Subcomandante Marcos in Milpa Alta, during the March of the Color of the Earth, says "We are here because we are trying to correct a mistake. . . . The history of this country is a history of mistakes. But, until now, it is they who make the mistakes, while we *are* the mistake, and the ones who pay for it."[14] Beginning with the 1996 International Encounter, the historical references also extend to the American continent, summoning the dreams of Bolívar, Che, and those who confronted dictatorships, especially in Argentina and Chile.[15] This then opens toward the memory of people's struggles everywhere.

Finally, references to national history became less frequent, though did not disappear completely, around 2001–2003 when dialogue with the state ceased. After that, the construction of autonomy proceeded outside of any constitutional framework. The renaming of the political-cultural centers of the five Zapatista zones is emblematic of this moment. In the early years, they were called "Aguascalientes," alluding to national history, while from 2003 onward, the "Caracoles" refer to the conch shell used in Indigenous traditions as a musical instrument and to call the community to assemble. The snail (caracol) is also a symbol of another way of acting, moving, and thinking about time, in contrast to the demands of efficiency, productivity, and acceleration characteristic of the capitalist world.[16]

The present, repetition of the past?

When they appeal to history in their political action, the Zapatistas often draw parallels between past and present events. Today and yesterday seem to respond to each other, as in a mirror. This happens with both negative events, such as the Conquest ("Today, the Conquistadors' persecution of the Indigenous people is repeated. . . . The modern invaders of our lands now occupy the government"); as well as positive ones like Independence ("We are the same ones who fought against the Spanish conquest, those who fought with Hidalgo, Morelos, and Guerrero").[17] The Mexican Revolution especially lends itself to this logic. In October 1997, when 1,111 Zapatista delegates traveled to the country's capital, a communiqué stated, "The newspapers that went on sale today say that the Zapatistas are about to arrive in Mexico City and that they met with the Villistas. The date is hard to make out, it could be either 1914 or 1997." And the EZLN's open letter "To Emiliano Zapata" concluded, "That was in 1914. Now, in 1997, history has not changed."[18] The parallels can turn sinister, as in February 1995 when a military operation against the communities and the General Command of the EZLN revived the specter of Chinameca, where Zapata was betrayed and assassinated. On this occasion, Subcomandante Marcos's mood turned dark, and he proposed to the government a meeting with the following agenda: "Date: April 10, 1995, in the afternoon. Place: Hacienda de Chinameca, Morelos. The only agenda item: History of Mexico."[19]

References to the Mexican Revolution grant today's struggle the same dignity as historical events, and much of the EZLN's political identity rests upon the claim that the Zapatistas of today are the same as those of yesterday.[20] This reverberation between the past and present became particularly intense during the final stretch of the March of the Color of the Earth that retraced the footsteps of Emiliano Zapata. On March 6, 2001, in Cuernavaca, Subcomandante Marcos read a letter to the people of Morelos, which he claimed General Zapata had entrusted to him, urging them to "accompany [the EZLN] in their endeavor, which is the same one that the Liberation Army of the South fought for."[21] In the following days, the EZLN comandantes were in Cuautla and Anenecuilco, where they were received by Diego and Ana María Zapata, Emiliano's children. They then went to Chinameca and Tlaltizapán, where the Zapatista delegation ratified the *Plan de Ayala*.[22] Finally, on March 10, one day before entering Mexico City, they stayed in Xochimilco, as Zapata and Villa did in December 1914. Upon arriving they said, "We thank the people of Xochimilco, not only for giving us shelter and sharing their food but also for protecting us on the eve of entering Mexico City. . . . Many years before, these dignified lands sustained the two greatest representatives of the Mexican Revolution, General Francisco Villa, head of the Northern Division, and General Emiliano Zapata, head of the Liberation Army of the South. In this way, the revolution from below was nourished by those from below, those who are the color of the earth."[23]

While the past and the present can be joined together to great effect, it risks implying a static conception of history. In various communiqués, history is presented as more of the same, with expressions such as "Don't doubt that the nightmare repeats itself" or "History, tired of walking, repeats itself."[24] We can read this insistence on a repetitive history in two complementary ways. On the one hand, because oppression and social inequality endure, historical events confer legitimacy on current actions. The greater the resonance between the one and the other, the stronger the parallel. However, in several interviews (and therefore in a less formal register), they explicitly recognize historical transformations, and even differences with some of their most beloved personages. For example, the Zapatista commanders point out that the agrarian rules implemented by the EZLN differ from those of Emiliano Zapata, since they seek a more collective distribution than *ejidal* property allows, and for his part, Subcomandante Marcos critically analyzes the failures of the 1914 Convention in Aguascalientes, suggesting how the 1994 National Democratic Convention could be more successful.[25] Depending on the context, one or the other analysis prevails: either recognizing differences and incessant change, or emphasizing continued domination and the repetition of the past, looking to history to dignify present struggles.

On the other hand, the idea that history repeats itself could be related to traditional societies' conception of time. Although not exactly cyclical or static, it is a conception of time that is more attentive to what returns than to what proceeds, which was the dominant conception in the ancient Mesoamerican world, before the Spanish conquest. According to a Nahua saying, cited by Bernardino de Sahagún in the *Florentine Codex*, "What was done long ago and is no longer done, will be done again, will be so again."[26] While this concept continues in today's Indigenous communities, time is not so much a circle as a snail (*caracol*), whose spiral never passes through the exact same point again, bringing the events of the past closer to those of the present. In this nonlinear perception of time, the distant past, present, and events yet to come can overlap and even be confused with one another.[27] In Zapatista word-thought, this conception is manifest in a fusion of historical time and mythical time: Emiliano Zapata is fused with Votán, heart of the people in the ancient Tzeltal calendar, attributing to him not only the ability to survive his own death, but five centuries of previous existence. He becomes "Votán Zapata, the smoldering fire who lived our death 501 years."[28] Thus, when Subcomandante Marcos narrates the life of Zapata to Old Antonio, the latter replies with the story of Ik'al and Votán, of whom Zapata would be no more than a particular apparition.[29] "Votán Zapata" is incarnated in successive historical figures—"Name without a name, Votán Zapata saw as Miguel, walked as José María, was Vincente, was named Benito, flew as Pajarito, rode as Emiliano, shouted as Francisco, dressed as Pedro."[30] These embodiments are all a clear expression of mythical time in which Votán returns.

Is there a contradiction between this concept of history—centered on the repetition of the past—and the hope that animates the Zapatista uprising, that imagines the possibility of a different future? Further, is this the same as power's discourse, that the world always reproduces itself in the same way, which is why the imposition of domination and the failure of rebellion are inevitable? In fact, for a movement that seeks social transformation and emancipation, it would be a strange self-limitation to lock itself in circular or static time. For this reason, the idea of a history that repeats itself must be combined with other perceptions of time. In fact, if it is possible to learn "historical lessons" from the past, it is precisely to prevent history from repeating itself.[31] The Zapatista struggle clearly points toward a way out of the repetitions of the past. When it comes to the assassination of Zapata, one must "do everything possible so that history does not repeat itself." A few days after the betrayal of February 1995, Subcomandante Marcos reassured himself, writing "Guadalupe Tepeyac was not Chinameca."[32]

In his opening remarks at the Intercontinental Continental Encounter in July 1996, Subcomandante Marcos outlined a history of the continent, recalling the dreams that shaped it, from Bolívar to Flores Magón and Che Guevara. These figures gave historical legitimacy to the event since each of those dreams "is repeated here" in La Realidad. But, on this same occasion, the Subcomandante challenged the idea of a history that does not change, making it clear that the vision of these heroes is only partially reproduced. Its repetition is "the same but different," and today's dream is both "rupture and continuity" with theirs.[33] Finally, he goes on to affirm "We are and are not the same" and concludes, "We are the stubborn history that repeats itself so as not to repeat once again, looking back to be able to walk forward." A message addressed to Mexico City during the March of the Color of the Earth clarifies how the Zapatista comandantes follow the footsteps of the general of the Liberation Army of the South. It reads, "So we will walk the same path of history, but we will not repeat it. Yes, we are from before, but we are new."[34] This overcomes the contradiction between a history that repeats itself and the desire for emancipation. They recognize in history a mixture of the known and the unprecedented, which at times makes it sound like gibberish. But political struggle clarifies the possibilities for transformation that lie within history.

Living memory, contested memory

Zapatista word-thought establishes a very close relationship between memory and history: it aims to bring them closer, to unite them, rather than differentiate them. Memory and history relate through basic material realities like land and home that give stability to human existence. They can be conceived as firm ground to walk on. For example, "The historical ground that sustains us matters; it prevents us from falling into oblivion."[35] The omnipresence of the dead and the ancestors gives memory and history a spatial location. Memory for the Zapatistas is a way of speaking of a present invaded by thousands of specters whose wounds are still open, who demand justice and call for resistance.[36] It is a way of conjuring a past in which, given present conditions, the dead cannot let the living rest, nor rest themselves. Memory is the presence of a living past charged with multiple grievances—from the massacres of the Conquest and the imposition of the colonial order to forced labor on the *fincas* and the racism and injustice that persist today. The oppression suffered on the *fincas* by the parents of those who joined the EZLN is the *lived* experience that synthesizes enduring colonial domination.[37] While Zapatista memory is one of pain, it is also one of dignity and resistance that summons the present struggle.

Another important aspect is that, for the Zapatistas, memory has the capacity to encompass the past, present, and future—a fully historical vision ("memory and its insistence on founding and casting humanity in past, present, and future").[38] Zapatista memory is a past configured in the present but also a project of transformation that looks to the future. They write that the greatest gods told themselves that "Memory is good . . . because it is a mirror that helps to understand the present and promises the future."[39] Thus, the Zapatista word strongly identifies history and memory, and even seems to use the two terms synonymously. They are associated not because history is reduced to rote recollection of the past (as tends to occur in postmodern neoliberalism) but rather because the meaning of memory is broadened as much as possible. The following communiqué is very eloquent on the matter:

> Our elders taught us that to celebrate memory is also to celebrate tomorrow. They told us that memory is not turning our face and heart to the past, it is not a sterile recollection that speaks with laughter or tears. . . . Memory always points toward tomorrow, and that paradox allows the nightmares to not be repeated in that morning. It allows the joys, which are also in the archive of collective memory, to be created anew. The first ones say that above all memory is a powerful inoculation against death and a necessary nourishment for life. For this reason, whoever preserves and protects memory, preserves and protects life; and whoever does not have memory has died. . . . Those who were and remain on the bottom . . . did not leave us a new world, complete and finished, but rather some clues and hints for uniting dispersed fragments—to

piece together yesterday's puzzle, to slice open the wall, frame a window, and build a door. Because it is well known that doors were once windows that were once slits, that were once and remain memory. Maybe that is why those above are afraid—because those who have memory have a door to their future.[40]

There is also a dispute between two conceptions of memory, one example of which is the often-mentioned march on October 12, 1992, when thousands of Indigenous people, a good number of them members of the EZLN, toppled the statue of Diego de Mazariegos. Two antagonistic memories clashed that day: that of the *coleto* elite from colonial San Cristóbal de Las Casas who, just fourteen years before defiantly erected a statue of the conquistador who had subjugated the Indigenous peoples of the region; and, on the other hand, the memory of those resistant and rebellious peoples who confronted colonial imposition.[41]

For Zapatista word-thought, statues represent the very essence of official memory: "Durito says that Power creates statues not to write history but to assert its own eternal omnipotence. To tell the story of Power, says Durito, it is enough to describe the statues that exist in the world's time and space. . . . Durito says that a statue is a TRUTH (like that—in capital letters) that hides under stone its own arbitrariness and inability to signify anything. . . . A statue is no more than the affirmation of the dominator and the marginalization of the dominated."[42] The statue expresses power's reliance on a "museumified" past, as well as its pretension to eternity. But sometimes statues are toppled; or a bird—like Zapatismo, which "is just one among many thousands that fly" . . . "follows the law of the birds, and shits on the statues."[43]

The dispute over memory can also revolve around the very same figures and events. While we emphasize the similarities between today's Zapatistas and yesterday's, we must not forget that the Mexican state also tries to appropriate the places, symbols, and figures of Zapata's legacy (Salinas de Gortari even named his son Emiliano). Subcomandante Marcos referred to this conflict when the March of the Color of the Earth visited Chinameca:

My General Zapata . . . has to decide if he is going to be there in the museum or here in the street and the countryside. . . . The issue is whether Emiliano Zapata becomes what you all are, people who struggle every hour and every day, as you are—as a youth, as a child, as an adult, as an elder, in your job—to transform an intolerable situation, one that must change . . . Zapata did not die here on April 10. He changed his face. And now what's in dispute is if his face belongs to the museum, a statue that doesn't speak, that doesn't feel; or if it is the face of all of you, the inhabitants of Chinameca, the inhabitants of Morelos, and the inhabitants of the country.[44]

In the land of Zapata and his many statues, the dispute is more intense between the dead memory of the museum and the living memory incarnated in the people and their present struggles. How do the two memories, the official one and that of the Zapatistas, differ? Could it be that they represent two ways of utilizing the past, ways that are politically antagonistic yet symmetrical in their search for legitimation? Either way, the differences are considerable. In the case of Zapata, the official memory becomes ever more vacuous, not only because it gets reduced to statues and museums but because—since President Salinas's reform of Article 27 of the Constitution—government policies have methodically reversed the achievements of the *campesino* struggles at the beginning of the twentieth century, especially those of the Zapatistas. This was evident in 2010, when the Calderón administration was unable to offer the least acknowledgement of the centennial of the Mexican Revolution.

In contrast, the memory of Emiliano Zapata is alive among the Zapatista communities of Chiapas. They celebrate him every year on the day of his assassination, and many a communiqué has been issued on this occasion.[45] More importantly, Zapata is considered "the commander in chief of the EZLN." Each EZLN member carries him in their name, transforming Zapata from a heroic singularity into a collective embodiment. Comandante Mister declared that "We the Zapatistas have these ideas of struggle in our hearts, and we are proud to carry on the name of our unforgettable General."[46] In Zapatista territory, his figure is not petrified in towering statues, but disseminated in popular images associated with everyday life, like murals on slabs of wood, photographs, or embroidery. It is a sign that his presence is alive, as are the events of the Mexican Revolution, especially in autonomous education. Above all, instead of conjuring meaningless or misleading images, the present struggle for communal land and autonomy shares the same fundamental inspiration as Zapata's. Herein lies the difference between the emptiness of official commemorations and the living memory of the communities. The latter is a decisive source of energy for present action: from the example of past rebellions to the rage born of the ancestors' suffering, to the desire to honor the unfulfilled dreams of previous generations.

The importance of memory and history is not only expressed in the EZLN communiqués but also permeates the experience of autonomy in the rebel territories, where there is a true thirst for history. It emerges, for example, when the Good Government Council of Oventik ends a letter with "Long live memory and let oblivion die!"[47] It is reflected, above all, in autonomous education, taught as a history of the Mayan peoples, and at the same time of Mexico, and all the peoples of the world. A history that is understood as struggle and for struggle; a living history whose task is to denounce social domination. Laying bare forms of exploitation and oppression, especially during the colonial era and then in the *fincas*, awakens rage and ignites the present struggle. Remembering past resistances and rebellions allows us to see that domination could never completely overcome dignified rage, and that today's rebels must take up the unfinished task of their ancestors. In this way, the past is charged with the intensity of the present. However, the historical perspective must also be a detailed, critical one, as to diagnose the present situation and understand past forms of domination. In the mirror of history, the reflections of past and present provoke strong emotions, but distinguishing their differences requires analytical intelligence. Both are necessary for action. This is how living memory and the present, pierced with the wounds of the past, can face one another, recognizing each other in order to differentiate themselves. In this way, they clear the way for desires that have not yet been fulfilled, neither in the past nor in the present.

History against the perpetual present

Fighting for history and against oblivion is closely related to long-term Indigenous resistance to colonial rule, which is fundamentally predicated on forgetting. Commenting on the photo of an insurgent killed in the fighting in Ocosingo, Subcomandante Marcos attributes to him these dignified words: "I am Álvaro, I am Indigenous, I am a soldier, I took up arms against oblivion."[48] Here, oblivion encapsulates the condition imposed on Indigenous peoples. Faced with the erasure that characterizes their oppression and marginalization, the rebels take up memory as a weapon, to claim their legitimate place in the conscience of the nation. Indigenous peoples are therefore both those most closely linked to memory and those who suffer the most from oblivion. They are lost memory, denied roots, "the forgotten heart of the nation (*patria*)," a heart that can still be found, because by "speaking from its Indian heart, the *patria* keeps its dignity and memory."[49] Thus, the Zapatista struggle is a rebellion against oblivion and for memory.

Neoliberalism, triumph of the perpetual present

Besides the struggle for memory and against oblivion that began with colonization, Zapatista thought identifies another struggle between history and oblivion. This perspective was outlined during the preparations for the 1996 Intercontinental Encounter, and then fully developed in communiqués issued in 1998. "The San Andrés Negotiations: Between oblivion from above and memory from below" is largely focused on analyzing the government's non-compliance with the San Andrés Accords but also clarifies that oblivion is not only related to colonial domination suffered by the Indigenous people. Rather, in the globalization of the capitalist economy, all human beings suffer from the obliteration of memory, whose principal causes "are the multiple forces of the Market." Consequently, "The great fight of the end of the 20th Century"—and now of the beginning of the twenty-first—pits "the Market against History."[50] Thus, the struggle against oblivion suggests a more general analysis of historical time. It is worth citing at length the part of this text that clearly relates oblivion to the outsized influence of the present in the current neoliberal world:

On one side is the Market, the new sacred cow. Money and its conception of time deny yesterday and tomorrow. On the other side is History (always forgotten by Power). Memory and its insistence on founding and casting humanity in past, present, and future. In the world of "modernity," the cult of the present is a weapon and a shield. "Today" is the new altar upon which principles, loyalties, convictions, shame, dignity, memories, and truths are sacrificed. For the technocrats under whose rule our country suffers, the past is no longer a referent to incorporate and build from. For these professionals of oblivion, the future cannot be anything more than a temporary extension of the present. History is destroyed by denying it a horizon that goes beyond the neoliberal "here and now." There is no "before" or "after" today. The search for eternity is finally satisfied: the world of money is not only the best of all possible worlds, it is the only one necessary.[51]

In the neoliberal world, that is, in the autocratic realm of the commodity, "Today is the new tyrant" who, to better ensure its dominance, makes the past disappear into oblivion and erases any prospect of an alternative future.[52] Thus a perpetual present is imposed, made up of glittery and illusory novelties, that in an ever-accelerated way only substitute the same for the same. In the idolatry of the almighty "today," oblivion is born, and history denied.

In a single blow, neoliberal domination seeks to destroy historical consciousness and close all future horizons. There is no future other than the repetition of present domination. The powerful believe and make others believe in their eternity. As Marcos said, "Power looks at itself in the mirror and discovers it is eternal and omnipotent."[53] This analysis was developed extensively in 1996, giving rise to multiple variations: from a Shakespearean script that casts Salinas de Gortari as Macbeth and the January 1 rebels as a walking jungle that crushes his illusory omnipotence; to biblical allusions where power speaks the words of the Judeo-Christian divinity: "I am who I am, the eternal return."[54] But there is no more effective myth to sustain power than this notion of "the end of history," perfectly staged in the ruins of the Berlin Wall as "a symbol of its omnipotence and eternity."[55] The end of history turns the neoliberal present into eternity; it also allows the powerful "to sell a version of a future that is impossible without them in power."[56] The deification of "Today," the triumph of oblivion, and the illusion of an everlasting present are expressions of the same thing: the time of the global market. Under its rule, there is no past to discover or future to look forward to—only the trap of a perpetual present.

Zapatista word-thought considers this "perpetual present" to be a form of temporality imposed by neoliberal capitalism. Two phenomena converge here. On the one hand, the reign of "today, today, and nothing but today" is the idealization of immediacy and instantaneity. We see this, for example, in the rapid rhythms of channel surfing and Internet searches, or in the compulsion to constantly check our cell phones and respond to every message without delay. We live under the dictatorship of urgency, in which everything must be finished as soon as possible. These phenomena heighten the "tyranny of the clock" and tendency towards acceleration that have characterized modernity since its inception. Other examples of speed-up include maximizing time efficiency, "just-in-time" production, rapid stock turnover, the speed of capital's movement, and the speculative gains of high-frequency trading that, through computerized algorithms, allow buying and selling the same security several times in a single second. All of this is simply an intensification of the capitalist logic of productivity and profit. However, there is also a qualitative leap wherein speed-up ceases to apply only to economic activity and permeates all aspects of life, including subjectivity itself.

There is also a second, more radical break with modernity's conception of time, which asserts a Universal History assumed to always move toward Progress. It is a unified process of improvement, constant and all-encompassing. Such a scheme could be assumed with absolute certainty, guaranteed by the laws of history. The faith in a radiant future was unwavering, despite the momentary setbacks of history. However, in neoliberal and postmodern times this vision of history has totally collapsed. The idea of Progress has become untenable, even while the rhetoric of development and modernization continue to run their course, especially via messaging from electoral campaigns and government propaganda. In any case, the knot modernity used to bind hope and certainty is definitely unhitched. Today, when young people wonder about their future, the accumulation of more and more difficulties and uncertainties causes great anxiety. The future is sealed off, it seems unimaginable.

Finally, the perpetual present combines two closures: on the one hand, by negating a historical perspective open toward the future; on the other hand, through an accelerated temporality privileging the immediate and the urgent. In this way, the tyrannical time of the commodity has destroyed the time of history. The hands of the clock, ever-marking "now," have become the "today" of a perpetual present, but it is still only a tendency to forget the past, to lack any perspective on the future. Neither has been fully realized. In fact, other orientations to the future remain and even proliferate. Still, it is crucially important to identify and critique the perpetual present. In making this critique, Zapatista word-thought highlights the most recent transformations of the capitalist Hydra, its particular forms of domination. This is how we can design alternative configurations to defeat it.

History, bridge between past and future

Because neoliberalism's perpetual present denies history, history becomes ever more necessary. And while capitalist logic would enclose us within the narrow limits of the present, Zapatista word-thought aims for a simultaneous recovery of the past and the future. The bridge between past and future is expressed in a paradoxical formula that proposes "walking backward" or "looking backward to be able to walk forward," which evokes Alice traveling to the other side of the mirror, or Durito taking a lesson from crabs, and Old Antonio looking for his way.[57] Looking back to be able to move forward highlights the usefulness of knowing the past to expand our perspectives and expectations for the future. For example, Marcos recounts a conversation with Old Antonio, writing, "'But why did you tell me that, when you don't know what's next, you have to look back? Isn't it to find your way back?' I asked. 'No,' answers Old Antonio. 'Not to find the way back. . . . When you turn to look back, you realize where you left off. That way you can see the path that didn't serve you well. . . . Now that we know it didn't work, we won't walk it again, because it led us where we did not want to go. So we make another one, to take us where we want to go.'"[58] Old Antonio explains that, when we are confused about which way to go, it is useful to look at the path already taken. Thus he defends the need for historical knowledge, for relating to past struggles by recognizing their value while opening them to critique. He points out past mistakes and yet still considers the path useful because, by taking us where we did not want to go, it showed us what does not work. Knowledge of the past allows us to distance ourselves from it and leave it behind. This is the only way to not repeat it, to avoid falling victim to it again.

Zapatista word-thought also values the past, a feature that is undoubtedly related to the Indigenous dimension of the struggle. It is the past of Mexico's first inhabitants, and it lives on in the cultures of Indigenous peoples. Marcos says, "the past is the key to the future. In our past we have ideas that can serve us in building a future where everyone fits, without crushing one another in the way we are crushed today by those who live above us. We will find the future of the nation by looking to the past, to those who first inhabited us, those who first thought us, those who first made us."[59] The crucial alliance between past and future is a way of demanding the integration of Indigenous peoples into the Mexican nation, not only as their right but as a necessity for the nation. As the EZLN writes, "The noble Mexican nation rests on our bones. If they destroy us, the entire country would collapse and begin to wander, aimless and unrooted. Prisoner of shadows, Mexico denies its tomorrow by denying its yesterday."[60]

Rather than only concerning Indigenous peoples, the link between past and future is addressed to everyone, insofar as it is a critique of the temporality dominant in the neoliberal world. The tyranny of the perpetual present is based on forgetting the past and negating the future. History, on the contrary—in its struggle against the market—must strive to reestablish both the memory of the past and the possibility of the future. Neoliberalism's "today" seeks to convince everyone that there is "neither a before nor an after." Rejecting this reigning temporality requires historical consciousness and a memory of the past, so that we may overcome the fallacy that the present is eternal and instead reopen an orientation to the future other than its repetition. Faced with domination's lie that things were always just like this, the fact of knowing that historically there existed worlds different from ours destroys the illusion of the perpetual present, revealing a radically other past, and the promise of a future no less different. Therefore, the strategic alliance between past and future proposed by Zapatista word-thought results directly from the need to fight against capitalism's perpetual present. Rebellion confronts an eternal present of oblivion and despair, and must reverse the sinister grammar of historical times. That is why the Zapatista struggle characterizes itself as an Indigenous rebellion that "challenges the present disenchantment by putting one foot in the past and another in the future."[61] And while it arose from an Indigenous rebellion, the alliance of the past and the future is fruitful for all who confront the domination of the capitalist Hydra and its perpetual present.

There is considerable power in bringing the past and future together. It allows us to claim the positive value of the past ("The past is the key to the future") while avoiding the danger of being locked into its repetition. History understood as repetition is, after all, an important weapon of the powerful, with which they try to discourage the non-conformists, saying "Rebels of the world! Unite in your defeats! You can claim no victories in your days gone by.... Recycle the old, imitate me. I am the same as always, with a touch-up here and there. I am the past renovated, the same nightmare, now with the added bonus of being globalized.... Don't try the new, repeat the old."[62] This risk of being locked in the past and in cycles of repetition was expressed even more clearly during the March of the Color of the Earth:

> The powerful want to ensnare the current Indigenous struggle in nostalgia . . . to enclose it in the past, like when they say that "The past has come to claim outstanding debts." . . . As if paying off some accounts would wipe away that past, and then the "today, today, today" which Fox has used as an electoral platform and as a governing program could reign without any problem.[63] The same "today" that neoliberalism has

turned into a new religious creed. . . . The Mexican Indigenous struggle has not come to turn back the clock. It is not a question of going back to the past and exclaiming with a voice full of emotion, that "the past was always better." I think that [neoliberals] would have tolerated and even applauded that. No, we the Indian peoples have come to re-wind the clock. With our struggle we read the future that was sown yesterday, that is cultivated today, and that can only be harvested if we struggle, that is, if we dream. . . . In short, we Indigenous people are not part of yesterday, we are part of tomorrow.[64]

The Indigenous world must avoid the trap of locking itself into an idealized and frozen past; otherwise, it will end up in museums and folkloric exhibits.[65] Zapatista word-thought insists that the past (and therefore also a present strongly linked to the past) can have a highly positive value; but it does not give up a claim on the future. Or, to put it the other way around, Zapatista word-thought shares modernity's desire for the future but not at the cost of rejecting the past and erasing it completely. In the Zapatistas' proposals, past and future cease to be the irreconcilable enemies they were under the reign of modernity. Instead, there is a unique—though not entirely unprecedented—alliance between them.[66] It is not about returning to the past, but traversing the past to project into the future. This is how Zapatista thought-action challenges the perpetual present of neoliberal domination.

A different conception of historical time

In chapter 4 we saw how Zapatista word-thought breaks with the foundations of modernity, but we have not yet considered their rupture with the modern conception of history: history as Progress, or the process of the One Unified Subject marching toward an Ever-Better Future. In the second half of the eighteenth century, this vision represented a radical novelty compared to traditional conceptions that privileged repetition and tethered what could be expected tomorrow to the experiences of yesterday.[67] In the modern conception of history, this link is broken. Tomorrow has to be new; the future must be completely separated from the past. The future (no longer the past) is the magnetic pole of this vision of history. The present is valued only to the extent that it breaks with the past, which is seen as archaic. While its most glorious moments can serve to sustain national mythologies, the past is seen primarily as dead. Everything related to it must be eliminated, so as not to hinder the march of Progress.

Zapatista word-thought distances itself from these approaches that are characteristic of modernity, while opposing the rule of the perpetual present imposed by neoliberal capitalism. Their word-thought simultaneously confronts two conceptions of history that correspond to two successive configurations of the capitalist system: one based on the myth of Progress; and, in the midst of its ruins, another that encloses us in a perpetual present. Forced into a fight on two fronts, Zapatista word-action outlines a new grammar of historical time that challenges both the grammar of modernity and of neoliberal postmodernity.

Reclaiming the anachronistic in the face of Progress

Ever since the first years of the uprising, there has been a critique of Progress in the Zapatista word, albeit sometimes implicitly. For example, when they denounced the new war of conquest against the Indigenous peoples, we read "Today, the persecution of the rebellious natives by the conquerors repeats itself. The modern invaders of our lands now inhabit the highest reaches of government. . . . Brutality and contempt are concealed in the word 'Progress.'"[68] In recent years, this critique has become more explicit. For example, during the seminar "Critical Thought in the Face of the Capitalist Hydra," Subcomandante Galeano opened his first speech with a reference to Walter Benjamin's comment on Paul Klee's painting *Angelus Novus*. For Benjamin, the Angel of History sees "one single catastrophe that keeps piling wreckage upon wreckage in the storm that we call Progress."[69] The storm with which Galeano begins the seminar is another name for the devastating advance of capitalist commodification. It helps us bring together, in the same constellation, Zapatista word-thought and Walter Benjamin's attempt to elaborate history against the grain, a history that breaks with the scheme of Progress and its foundation in a notion of homogeneous, empty time.[70]

The analyses presented by the EZLN in the "Critical Thought in the Face of the Capitalist Hydra" refute the classic vision of Progress, a vision whose promises are all shattered: The war against humanity intensifies; the nightmare grows more and more terrible; the coming storm announces the "destruction of nature and humanity."[71] More than an unfulfilled promise, Progress is a deception, an illusion. From the beginning, it has been an enticing disguise for the devastation caused by the advance of capitalism, its war on humanity, and the plunder of many peoples, especially native populations. Subcomandante Galeano identifies "the dispossession disguised as 'Progress'" as part of the war against humanity: "Those at the top call this process of dispossession 'PROGRESS,' and it is one of the synonyms of 'modernity.'"[72] Speaking of the wall of capitalist domination, he also says, "Most of the time, the wall is a great marquee that repeatedly flashes P-R-O-G-R-E-S-S."[73] And in 2018 he said, "In reality, the 'development' and 'progress' that the system offers hides that it is only concerned with its own development and progress; and, most importantly, hide that such development and progress are at the cost of death and destruction of entire populations and territories."[74]

The Zapatistas' perspective is far removed from the vision that, even from historical materialism, praised capitalism's development of the productive forces as a beneficial advance, a necessary stage in the march of history. What the Zapatista vision sees in "Progress" is war, dispossession, pain, and devastation—that is, what Marx referred to as the "frightful vicissitudes" caused by capitalist production.[75] At the end of his life, Marx could see it this way because of his interest in the Russian rural communes, and in quite a similar way, Zapatista word-thought assumes the point of view of Indigenous peoples and their traditions of community life. As Moisés and Galeano write, "For us—the Zapatista original peoples—the storm, the war, has continued for centuries. They came to our lands with the hoax of their domineering civilization and religion. Back then, the sword and the cross bled our people. With the passage of time, the sword was modernized and the cross was dethroned by the religion of capital, but it continued demanding our blood as an offering to the new god: money."[76]

We have spoken of a war on two fronts, which Subcomandante Galeano's remarks in a seminar dedicated to the "Walls of Capital," in April 2017, help us see more clearly. He began unexpectedly, placing an hourglass on the table and recalling that, during the San Andrés dialogues, the government's delegation was "in despair because Zapatismo had to consult with the communities on even the smallest agreement."[77] This is a clash of two temporalities: the capitalist one that is obsessed with speed and the imperative of efficiency, and the other of Indigenous peoples who have preserved a rhythm rooted in the life of rural communities. (Here I should note that the Zapatistas have made the snail into a symbol of a temporality that resists the dominant accelerationism, because the snail "makes us understand that we walk slowly but, yes, we advance. We prefer to walk rather than run because we are going very far.")[78]

Subcomandante Galeano went on to say that, because of this, the Zapatistas are seen as backward and anachronistic: "They have told us that, in the digital age, we Zapatistas are like those clocks that work with springs and gears, which must be wound by hand. 'Anachronistic,' they said. 'The past that comes to settle accounts,' they declared.' 'Historical backwardness,' they murmured. 'An unfinished task of modernity,' they threatened."[79] But provocatively, instead of trying to refute these critiques, he chose to accept what he called as "our archaic way (which, more than pre-modern, is prehistoric)," and affirmed that the Zapatistas "are more like an hourglass." The Zapatistas refuse to compete in the race for modernity. They are not looking for the most advanced, the latest novelty. On the contrary, they accept anachronism. They value what is associated with the past, that is, what modernity despises as a sign of archaic backwardness.

These are fundamental ruptures with the framework of modernity, but the Zapatistas do not stop there. Subcomandante Galeano adds a different element, explaining that the hourglass contains "the secret of the Zapatista method" because it allows us to "see the time that has elapsed" as well as "the time to come." This is the opposite of neoliberal time, which demands that we only "pay attention to that brief moment in which a grain of sand reaches the narrow passage, to then fall and join the moments that accumulate in what we call 'past.'" The sense of time that dominates today demands that each human being "live in the moment, live in a present that can be slimmed down even more with the latest technology. Do not think about the time that has already become yesterday, because in the vertigo of modernity, 'a second ago' is the same as 'a century ago.' Above all, do not look up at what comes next." Thus, what begins as a critique of modernity ends up denouncing neoliberalism's perpetual present and reclaiming both the past and future that allow us to confront it.

Now we can return to the relationship between Zapatista thought and that of Benjamin. There are good reasons to associate them and equally good reasons to differentiate. Benjamin's "Theses on the Concept of History" sought to liberate historical materialism from the bourgeois vision of history centered on the idea of Progress and based on historicism's homogeneous, empty time. Benjamin sought to break the continuity of this time with his notion of the revolutionary event as a messianic eruption. He glorified "a present which is not a transition, but in which time take a stand and has come to a standstill."[80] However, now the main enemy is no longer the linear vision of history shared by bourgeois ideology and traditional Marxism. Today it is somewhat dangerous to follow Benjamin in making the present the key to a reconceptualization of history, given the perpetual present of the market, the ephemeral instant that has become "the new tyrant," disappearing the past into oblivion and denying the prospect of a distinct future. (Although we should note that Benjamin's messianic present, which breaks the continuity of domination as to open toward another future, has nothing to do with the perpetual present of neoliberalism.) Furthermore, while the Parisian revolutionaries shooting at clocks in 1830 represented for Benjamin a consciousness that they were about to "make the continuum of history explode" (Thesis XV), for Subcomandante Marcos, it is intellectuals in the service of power who "take aim at the clock of history in order to stop time, and thus ensure that there will be no tomorrows other than the one they are presiding over."[81] So, although there are important affinities between Benjamin's thought and the Zapatistas', they are separated by a radical change of context: the dominant forms of historical temporality are not the same, so they do not fight against the same enemy. The Zapatista critique of the modern conception of history shares many features with Benjamin's, but the Zapatistas have had to go one step further to confront a form of temporality that the German philosopher could not foresee: the kingdom of the perpetual present that is spreading amid the ruins of Progress.

Walking by asking questions, because what is missing is yet to come

The idea of a bridge between past and future is key to a new conception of historical time. It creates an arrangement that was unthinkable within previous conceptions of history. The bridge between past and future stands in stark opposition to neoliberalism's perpetual present and, in fact, emerged as a weapon of struggle against it. It departs from the modern conception of history, which values the future only to the extent that it breaks with the past. And it also differs from more traditional conceptions of time, in which the present and future must simply reproduce the past. Zapatista word-thought moves between three pre-existing times: the reiterative time of Indigenous peoples, the unilineal and progressive time of modernity, and the perpetual present of neoliberalism. It surpasses them all in search of unprecedented representations of historical time. From Indigenous time, it takes up the positive assessment of the past, but without allowing itself to be locked into a circular repetition. This is why the Zapatistas insist that Indigenous peoples are contemporary and their longing is for the future. From modernity they recover the hope of a different and better future, while refusing to do so by rejecting the past. Here they also dispel the illusions of Progress, whose true face is Capital's war on humanity. Finally, as with the neoliberal time that prevails today, they too are incredulous about Progress, but they strive to revitalize hope and reconstruct a conception of history that completely upends the grammar of the perpetual present.[82]

Above all, reopening the future is especially important. It swims against the stream of the perpetual present, which confines us to the temporality of immediacy, without any possibility of a hopeful future. The task, therefore, is to restore the future; but not just any future. There are in fact certain futures that proliferate under the reign of the perpetual present, such as the future of financial speculation, concerned with the indicators of tomorrow's markets and the next microsecond's profits. There is the future of the dizzying overgrowth of credit, premised on some degree of confidence that the borrowed money will return. There is the future, of imminent climate catastrophe, that increasingly occupies the airwaves. What the Zapatistas seek to restore is a true future, one with hope, making it a future that is truly different from the present. But it is not easy to reopen the future as the storm approaches. And there is something even more difficult: reopening the future without returning to modernity. This implies inventing an *other* future, an unprecedented form of future.

This is where we find the most decisive contributions of Zapatista word-action. How do they allow us to sketch out a future of hope that is distinct from modernity and its unsustainable idea of Progress? The Zapatistas' invitation to walk by asking questions (*caminar preguntando*) is extraordinarily helpful in this pursuit.[83] It means that the path is not set in advance but is made by walking. It means that it will not be a straight, predetermined line (like that of Progress), that there is no certainty guiding the path's trajectory. On the contrary, the path is made from questions and doubts, both those that we may have before starting to walk and those arising with each step, constantly modifying our initial intentions. When you walk with questions, it is unlikely that the path will end up straight, arriving exactly where you imagined. Walking by asking questions means the process of walking is what gives the path its direction.

Walking by asking questions discards Progress's certainties, its inevitable laws of history, its predetermined future. This was the future in modernity: a future known in advance, not in all its details but at least in its major trends. The broad tendencies were certain, and this is why they could be foreseen and directed through the mechanism of planning. This science of the future was espoused by the experts in charge of setting state policy, just as it was embraced by all the vanguards who—based on the absolute certainties derived from history's laws—aimed to guide the masses toward their felicitous consummation. Contrary to all this, walking by asking questions means that no one holds certainties, nor can they invoke a foreknowledge of the future, which makes this principle a powerful antidote to vanguardism.

At the same time, walking by asking questions is not an aimless stroll, but rather an attempt to blaze a path. Understood in the context of collective struggle, it is not just about escaping from immediate oppression, because for that, any path would do. If questions arise, it is because one is looking for where to make the path. As Old Antonio said above, the path that "led us where we did not want to go" and nevertheless "served us because that is how we discovered it didn't work" is the path that allows us to see what was not done well and thereby allows us "to make another path to take us where we want to go." While in Old Antonio's account, the right path is not laid out in advance, there is an awareness of where he wants to go. ("You started out looking for a path that does not exist. You had to make it.") There is no certainty about it, but the desire to reach something moves us to set out along the path. A force moves us *toward* what does not yet exist, and this is the force of an anticipatory aspiration.

Another principle that is omnipresent in the Zapatista word, at least since 2005, is "what is missing is yet to come" (*falta lo que falta*). It reminds us that—despite the struggle's advances, especially in the construction of autonomy—we must focus on the unfinished part and be attentive to what is to come.[84] What has been done only finds its full meaning in relation to what is still missing. Therefore, "walking by asking questions"—blazing a trail without the guidance of certainty—must be understood together with "what is missing is yet to come"—which reminds us of the path that remains to be made. "What is missing is yet to come" suggests that the struggle should not consider the present situation without the anticipation of what is not yet.

The Zapatista thought-word assumes a certain form of anticipation—understood as concern for what is not yet. At the same time, "walking by asking questions" discards any idea of planning. Here is the key to reopen the future without restoring that of modernity: to conceive a form of anticipation that does not reproduce modern planning. For that, anticipatory impulse must not enclose the process it generates with predefined limits. In other words, the desire for what does not yet exist will not take us exactly where we imagined. However, such anticipation is indispensable to start walking—on the condition that it does not become a rigid scheme that prevents the process of walking by asking questions.

Thus the future is understood as open: just one possible future, and an uncertain one at that. This future, fragile and indeterminate, does not easily lend itself to mass mobilizations—unlike modernity's future, known in advance and guaranteed by the laws of history. But that future, the one embodied in the promise of Progress, was a dangerous illusion that can no longer be sustained in the epoch of the perpetual present. The *other future* outlined in the Zapatistas' proposals must be invented by walking. It is nothing more than an uncertain and very improbable possibility.[85] At least it truly is a future, perhaps more so than modernity's future, which was a planned future, trapped in the cage of a linear and inescapable history. The fragile future that is yearning to be reborn is an indeterminate future-to-come (*por-venir*) that may perhaps come about through the process of struggling for a dignified life for all.

One more point. Zapatista word-thought refuses to assimilate history into the single and straight line of Progress. But does this mean we should follow postmodern thought in declaring that any idea of linear history should be rejected, thereby exploding it into scattered, isolated fragments? We find a clue in the importance of the path in the Zapatista word. Are these paths not lines as well? We must therefore differentiate between various types of lines. Walking by asking questions draws a line of a very different variety than those of modernity. A highway—in its quest for the most direct way to connect points A and B—is an example of a modernist line. The modern line tries to move toward its objective as quickly as possible, never looking back to the path already traveled. In contrast, the path of walking by asking questions is a trajectory, seeking its way in the process of making it. It is a trajectory driven by an anticipatory desire that does not know its point of arrival in advance. Moreover, there is uncertainty at every moment about where to step next. The path of walking by asking questions is a trajectory (or line) made while looking back, made by integrating questions arising from the experience of walking. It is not straight, but rather sinuous—a trajectory that may even spiral along like a snail (*avanzar caracoleando*), always careful to incorporate the past in order to better project itself into the future.[86] Furthermore, taking into account the Zapatistas' insistence that there are multiple "modes" of struggle, the path of walking by asking questions cannot be one. Against the Eurocentric scheme of Progress-based history, there cannot be only one trajectory for all humanity. There must be many paths, as to reach a world where many worlds fit. In sum, Zapatista word-thought suggests that history should be seen neither as a single and straight line of Progress, nor as the complete absence of a line we find with postmodernity, erasing any notion of a historical process. Walking by asking questions invites us to see history as a tangle of turbulent lines, divergent and discordant, which can, however, open the way toward what we desire, what is not yet.

As a war for memory and history, the Zapatista struggle is rooted in deep time, deeply lived. For Indigenous peoples, it implicates the foundational violence of conquest by an overwhelming Other who destroys their world, initiating today's enduring colonial domination. Under various historical forms, the continuity of colonialism entailed exploitation, dispossession, contempt, and repression, crystallizing into one of its most brutal forms: oppression on the *fincas*, which was suffered by the parents of many Zapatistas, as well as by some of the oldest Zapatista rebels themselves. Theirs is also the deep time of traditional forms of life, which continue to transform and manifest in the present of Indigenous communities. This is what the vindication of the past refers to, to such a degree that the Zapatistas assume themselves to be anachronistic. Yet the fundamental struggle here is to defend a form of life based on community against the advance of commodification, characteristic of capital's war against humanity, spreading destruction everywhere it goes. However, respect for a form of life rooted in tradition does not mean idealizing the past or being confined to the reproduction of what came before. The construction of Zapatista autonomy simultaneously reclaims traditional community and endeavors to transform it, as we see with women's struggle against the "bad traditions" of gender oppression. The struggle of men and women to change their lives within the community framework underlies the image of the bridge that unites vindication of the past and hope for a different future.

The singular proposals of Zapatista word-thought regarding time and history emerge from life in the rebellious Indigenous communities. And they are also related to the other dimensions articulated through the Zapatista struggle, which is at once an Indigenous uprising, a national liberation struggle, and a call for planetary anticapitalist resistance. For this reason, they are compelled to confront neoliberal capitalism's version of time and history, which the Zapatistas rightly identify as the perpetual present. Confronting this hidden but essential aspect of contemporary domination, they made a strategic move to break down the mental barrier that resigns so many people to thinking there is nothing other than the eternal now. It is a move that takes up the past and future in a single gesture—something that seems to be in tune with a mode of attachment to life in the community that is also transformative.

Breaking with the perpetual present requires, first, reopening the future. The audacity of January 1, 1994, was a very concrete contribution to this process. At that point, there were two possible options: either to restore the future of modernity, which frames history as the linear march of Progress, or to invent another modality of the future. There are plenty of reasons why the first path had to be discarded. Completely assuming the Indigenous dimension of the struggle entails an "anachronistic" attachment to the past, contrary to the logic of modernity, which has been the most powerful vector of contempt against Indigenous peoples, and the destruction of their forms of life. Furthermore, the belief in Progress is unsustainable when there is a gathering storm that threatens to annihilate humanity. Finally, the classic form of Revolution from which Zapatista word-thought has distanced itself was based precisely on the principles of modernity. The vanguardism that the EZLN has emphatically rejected was also based on the scheme of linear historical time, conferring on those who claimed to be experts in the laws of history the ability to guide the masses, certain that they knew how to accelerate history's march toward a glorious future, guaranteed in advance. The very concept of Revolution was forged within the framework of the modern conception of history, only acquiring its current meaning at the end of the eighteenth century, whereas previously it only referred, for example, to the movement of the planets. Perhaps the Zapatistas' reluctance to resort to the word "revolution" is not only due to the state-centric strategy associated with it but also because it has been part of a conception of history that can no longer be sustained.

In sum, the Zapatistas' experience and reflection have led them to a novel conception of historical time, which is informed by the following: vindicating a community rooted in tradition, while rejecting the simple repetition of the past; inheriting the modernist ideas of historical materialism but recognizing the impossibility of reproducing them; and unveiling and confronting the new figure of the perpetual present. What emerges from this process is neither a closed circle, a straight line, or an immobile point. It is not one image, but many. It can be a bridge (or a fold) joining past and future, a spiral, a mountain path or, rather, a network of many paths twisting and turning, that are blazed with a machete of questions. They advance toward the future, moved by the desire for what is not yet but without abandoning all of the past. On the contrary, they can move in a spiral, turning toward the past to better project themselves forward. They clear uncertain paths, knowing only that they do not know where they will go. Uncertain, fragile, improbable paths. Paths that do not result from a single trajectory but from multiple trajectories: many paths are needed to build a world where many worlds fit. To refound a credible and desirable emancipatory project, it is necessary to break with the modern conception of history, without reproducing the closed circle of tradition or enclosing oneself in the perpetual neoliberal present. Far from the standards of European universalism, such a project might be relevant for the many worlds that yearn to escape annihilation and find their place in a grander world.

Final Thoughts

The Zapatista uprising happened in a moment of deep disillusion, when the triumph of neoliberal capitalism and confinement in the perpetual present seemed most absolute, when there was not even a spark of hope left. The cry of "Enough is enough!" (¡*Ya Basta!*) on January 1st, 1994, defied the possible and gave lie to the end of history. It reopened a crack, daring to dream another reality and struggling to build it. The only way to widen this crack was through the determination and audacity of thousands of men and women who, on New Year's Eve, risked their lives to say "Enough!" to five hundred years of colonial oppression, "Enough!" to decade after decade of party-state dictatorship, "Enough!" to the neoliberal present-made-eternity.

The Zapatistas realized that all previous models were in ruins. They had to search for a new path, creating one where none existed. They did it through doubts and questions, using indefinition as a compass ("Zapatismo is not, it doesn't exist"). At the same time, the Zapatista path demonstrated an uncommon capacity for resistance, against all the attacks against them—military, paramilitary, counterinsurgent, from the media, etc. Thanks to their capacity for self-transformation and their constant political inventiveness, they found a way to overcome the mistakes and the exhaustion that inevitably come with struggling under such adverse conditions. They helped transform all of Mexico, especially the final collapse of the PRI party-state system. They reopened the Indigenous question, keeping it at the center of the national agenda for years. While the hopes raised by the signing of the San Andrés Accords ended in disappointment, the shock waves from the Zapatista uprising changed the perception of the Indigenous peoples as well as their own self-perception, aiding in the ongoing struggle to recuperate their historically negated dignity. The Zapatistas also helped pave the way for the cycle of international mobilizations against neoliberalism, and for the efforts—the first in a long time—to weave together networks of resistance at a planetary level. Little by little, the Zapatistas found their own distinctive path. They traveled from their initial lack of definition toward necessary definition, but not closed or dogmatic ones. Together with the initial "no" (the rebellion of "Enough is enough!"), they added a constructive "yes," the resistance that allows us to build what we dream of.

In fact, the construction of autonomy in the rebellious territories of Chiapas has become an ever more important dimension of the Zapatista experience. It is yet another uprising, which tens of thousands of men and women continue to participate in with the same daring as on January 1, 1994—although it is through their tenacious, everyday, constructive efforts rather than through the danger of the insurrectionary moment. Here they are armed with health and education, the arts and sciences, the administration of justice and self-government. In fact, tens of thousands of men and women have gone about governing themselves, separating and subtracting themselves from the structures of the Mexican state. They do so to defend a mode of life with community organization at its heart, instead of resigning themselves to its destruction through commodification— the way capitalism wages war on humanity. They do so—not to preserve some immutable form of the community—but to be able to revitalize and modify it in the ways they themselves decide. They do so to build a collective reality that is different from their own traditions and distanced from the logics of the Economy. It is a collective reality whose course they chart for themselves, through their own mistakes and without a predetermined model. They have thereby convincingly shown that it is possible to self-govern, based on one's own form of life, without surrendering to the heteronomy of the state. This does not result in any easily reproducible model, but nonetheless it is a living source of inspiration that has contributed to the contagion of autonomy. Thus with the construction of autonomy in the rebellious territories of Chiapas, the initial Zapatista crack has widened, even though Subcomandante Moisés himself calls it "our small slice of freedom," suggesting that what is missing is still yet to come.

Autonomy is a territorialized construction within the interstices of the world-system. We can see it as a liberated space, or rather one in the process of liberating itself, a space able to claim and defend a small parcel of freedom that, at least in part, escapes systemic determinations. But autonomy is not under- stood to be a self-sufficient or self-centered space; it cannot be an end in itself.

Final Thoughts

In the Zapatistas' thought-action, the territorialized construction of Indigenous autonomy and resistance must be articulated with the struggle for national liberation and the effort to weave together planetary networks of rebellion and resistance. More precisely, we must understand the construction of autonomy as part of the world war between humanity and capitalism.

From an anticapitalist point of view, this war requires a collective effort to reconstruct a credible and desirable vision of emancipation. The Zapatistas' contributions here have been far-reaching. They are not just theoretical contributions, as they are rooted in the concrete practices of rebellion and resistance, especially when it comes to autonomy building. The Zapatista crack cannot be reduced to the limits of the territorial construction of autonomy, since its inspirations can spread to other scales of the struggle and be shared in other geographies. It is in this double dimension ("neither theory without practice, nor practice without theory") that Zapatista word-thought-action finds its full force.

We might also ask what made these contributions possible? Undoubtedly, the encounter of different traditions has been important, insofar as the Zapatista "mode" made it possible for them to listen to and transform each other. The critical encounter was between an Indigenous tradition of resistance forged during five hundred years of colonial domination and a Latin American emancipatory tradition directly linked modern European thought, in its Marxist variant. To be more precise, the main ingredients in the Zapatista "cocktail" are as follows: a tradition of Indigenous struggle strongly rooted in communal organization and the sense of collectivity that derives from it; an emancipatory tradition inherited from Marxism, but forced by the desolate history of the twentieth century to almost completely rethink itself; and an effort to critique contemporary capitalist domination, understood not only in its constant features but also (and above all) in its current specificity, as brought about by neoliberal transnationalization and financialization. This configuration—which forces the critique into a multifront battle—may help explain the creativity of Zapatista word-thought.

Zapatista word-action highlights the need for a radical anticapitalist struggle that understands there can be no solution to humanity's problems until it has liberated itself from the capitalist Hydra. This is no easy task, and the problems multiply when we consider that this struggle must also avoid reproducing many of the approaches underlying the twentieth century's revolutions. They were revolutions that dashed the hopes of so many of the world's peoples, ending up as criminal tragedies in quite a few cases. Asserting a vision of emancipation that is both credible and desirable requires emancipating ourselves from the state-centered, modernist, productivist—not to mention Eurocentric and patriarchal—schemas that contributed in no small measure to the descent of the twentieth century's revolutions.

Zapatista word-action proposes a liberatory path that does not pass through the state, the party, or any other modality of unified organization, based as they are on homogeneity and hegemony. As such, these organizational forms reproduce the vanguardist logic of politics from above. The Zapatistas try, by contrast, to elaborate an other conception of politics that starts from below and builds itself *from and within* a multiplicity of experiences, ways of seeing, and modes of acting. It is a politics that requires acting together amid differences, and to that end, strengthening the art of listening, the disposition to learn, and the sense of proportionality.[1] Above all, this politics breaks with the centrality of the state. We know from both history and theory that the dynamics of any state structure tend toward consolidation, appropriating the collective capacity to act and accentuating the disassociation between governors and governed. But there is another possible path that does not pass through the state: autonomy(ies). The politics of autonomy(ies) is a situated politics, a politics of multiplicity that is built from the particularities of forms of life rooted in concrete, specific territories. The politics of autonomy(ies) is based on the shared capacities of all; it is understood as an expression of the collective capacity (*potencia*) to do. At the same time, autonomies do not seek enclosure in self-sufficient and self-centered cells. On the contrary, they seek to encounter, dialogue, and coordinate with others, just as the Good Government Councils have done, for example. The possibility thereby arises for different kinds of confederation between autonomous entities at every possible scale—nothing less than the materialization of a world where many worlds fit.

Such a renovated anticapitalist perspective must also avoid productivism: celebrating the development of the productive forces and trying to run ever faster in the direction history points toward (that is to say, in the direction of Progress), even when it only accelerates the destruction of life on the planet. Moving against the grain, the Zapatistas reclaim the anachronistic. They refuse to project themselves toward the future at the cost of devaluing what is associated with the past, beginning with community and the ways of being that accompany it. This is precisely what capitalism is bent on destroying, always, in all corners of the globe. Renouncing the modernist-productivist perspective projecting itself into the future, traveling at full speed on the locomotive of history, the Zapatistas instead share Walter Benjamin's perspective that revolution is humanity activating the emergency brake. We must exit that mad train that carries all of humanity toward destruction and the abyss. Only then can we even conceive of the dream of a bountiful, dignified life for all, rooted in a sense of proportion and respect for Mother Earth.

Emancipatory approaches must also rid themselves of their former Eurocentric biases. They must abandon abstract (European) universalism and instead think from and through heterogeneity, looking for what is shared. In this way they can affirm a multiplicity of worlds and recognize a planetary community of differences. This requires undoing the hegemony of modern-western thought, a philosophy that has accompanied the global rise of capitalism. It also requires decolonizing ourselves while taking care not to isolate this perspective from the anticapitalist dimension of the struggle. And it requires leaving behind modernity's basic "myths," especially the myths of Progress, of individual freedom, and of man as master of nature. The western self—understood not as an essence or a "race" but as a way of being shaped by the hegemonic thought of modernity—is a mutilated being. He lives a linear time that demands that he discard the past in order to move forward. His freedom is bought at the cost of negating the relational and transindividual dimensions of his being. Moreover, in order to become "Man," he has separated himself from nature, he has separated himself from the world. He is a being not anchored in time, without community, without a world. Here is where we find enormous value in the encounter with the Indigenous world because, despite centuries of subjection to colonial imposition, it has managed to keep alive certain modes of being and living, that are somewhat foreign to those of modernity. In particular, it has kept alive the experience of community, an other perception of time, and an other relation with the nonhuman world and Mother Earth.

This is how Zapatista word-action has been able to deepen the critique of modernity and reformulate an emancipatory project on new foundations. Its otherly grammar of historical time allows us to imagine fruitful alliances between past and future, connections that were previously impossible to conceive of. By understanding people's personality to be constituted through their relations, they overcome the supposed incompatibility between the recognition of individuality and the sense of the collective. By understanding humans belong to Mother Earth instead of owning it, they reconcile the need to fight for humanity with belonging to the wider community of all earth dwellers.

The Zapatista Experience

The Zapatista path is forged through a triple rupture. It is a rupture with the many forms of contemporary domination and with prior ways of understanding the rupture itself. Reformulating an emancipatory vision that is credible *and* desirable requires emancipating ourselves from prior emancipatory schemas. For this, a decisive support can be found in Indigenous peoples' traditions of resistance and forms of life; while bearing in mind that they make self-determined efforts to break with certain aspects of their own traditions. This triple rupture contains three dynamics that, as they intertwine, work to reinforce each other. This is how the Zapatista word-thought-action opens a singular path. Fortunately, while it is a singular path, it is one that forms constellations with other traditions and other experiences.

The Zapatistas have helped rescue hope when it seemed all but dead. And it takes more than a simple declaration to restore hope. Wishing for hope is not enough. We can confidently say that the Zapatistas have revived hope because they have taken concrete steps and made the theoretical and practical contributions necessary to sustain it. They have done so in many ways, especially by daring to plunge headlong into the improbable on January 1, 1994, and through everything it gave rise to. They have done so, to great effect, by building autonomy in the rebellious Zapatista territories and through the demonstration it provides. They have done so through many hints, teasing out a credible and desirable emancipatory project, which offers a vision and hope to the struggle to save humanity and the planet from destruction by the forces of money and the market.

🌿 🌿 🌿 🌿

We end by once again turning our attention to the thousands of men and women, insurgents, militia members, and support bases who make up the EZLN. Nothing discussed in this book would have been possible without their courage on the final night of 1993 and their long, clandestine preparation beforehand. Nothing would have been possible without their tenacity as they invented and built autonomy. Nothing would have been possible without their stubbornness, both in preserving their communities' forms of life and transforming them in their own ways. Nothing would have been possible without their mode of being, rooted in the very soil where they walk step by step, collectively. This, for me, continues to be the most beautiful and mysterious part of the Zapatista adventure.

Bibliographic Notes

Communiqués and Documents of the EZLN

EZLN. *Critical Thought in the Face of the Capitalist Hydra, I.* Durham, NC: PaperBoat Press, 2016.

_____. *EZLN, Documentos y comunicados.* 5 volumes. México City: Ediciones Era, 1994–2003.

_____. *"Freedom According to the Zapatistas."* First-grade textbooks: *Autonomous Government I, Autonomous Government II, Autonomous Resistance, Participation of Women in Autonomous* Government. Milwaukee, WI: Autonomous University of Social Movements, 2013. ausm.community/escuelita.

_____. *La fuerza del silencio. 21.12.12. El EZLN anuncia pasos siguientes.* México City: Editorial Eón, 2013.

_____. *La rebelión de la memoria. Textos del subcomandante Marcos y del EZLN sobre la historia.* Edited by Jérôme Baschet. 2nd edition. San Cristóbal de Las Casas, Mexico: Cideci-Unitierra, 2010.

_____. *Seis Declaraciones de la Selva Lacandona y otros documentos.* México City: Editorial Eón, 2016.

EZLN and Andrés Aubry. *Planeta tierra: Primer coloquio Internacional In memoriam Andrés Aubry: Movimientos Antisistémicos."* San Cristóbal de Las Casas, Mexico: Cideci-Universidad de la Tierra, 2009.

Galeano, Subcomandante Insurgente. *Habrá una vez...,* México, 2017.

Marcos, Subcomandante Insurgente. *En algún lugar de la Selva Lacandona. Aventuras y desventuras de Don Durito.* México City: Editorial Eón, 2008.

_____. *Escritos sobre la guerra y la economía política.* Edited by Sergio Rodríguez Lascano. México, Pensamiento Crítico, 2017.

_____. *El Viejo Antonio.* 3rd edition. México City: Editorial Eón, 2010.

🌿 🌿 🌿 🌿

All of the EZLN's communiqués can be consulted on: enlacezapatista .ezln.org.mx.

The journal *Rebeldía* (between 2002 and 2011) is another key source.

Other books relevant to specific moments in the Zapatista trajectory

Le Bot, Yvon and Subcomandante Marcos. *El sueño zapatista: entrevistas con el subcomandante Marcos, el mayor Moises y el comandante Tacho, del Ejército Zapatista de Liberación Nacional.* Barcelona: Plaza y Janés, 1997.

EZLN. *Crónicas intergalácticas. EZLN. Primer encuentro intercontinental por la humanidad y contra el neoliberalismo.* Chiapas, México: Planeta Tierra, 1997.

Muñoz Ramírez, Gloria. *The Fire and the Word: A History of the Zapatista Movement.* Translated by Laura Carlsen and Alejandro Reyes Arias. San Francisco: City Lights Books, 2008.

Some additional studies (apart from those that are mentioned in relation to each chapter).

The majority of the bibliography is mentioned in the notes for each chapter.

On the meeting in Vicam convened by the National Indigenous Congress and the EZLN, see Joani Hocquenghem, *La cita de Vícam: Primer Encuentro de los Pueblos Indígenas de América en Sonora, México, 2007* (Tlalnepantla: Casa Vieja-La Guillotina, 2013). On the Little School, see the collective volume *La Escuelita zapatista: Ensayos y testimonios* (Guadalajara: Grietas Editores, 2014). On the occasion of the thirtieth anniversary of the Zapatista uprising, a series of thirty paperback books was published, many of them related to the Zapatista journey to Europe (free access in https://alfarozapatista.jkopkutik.org/libros-de-bolsillo.

Two studies of Zapatismo are Gustavo Esteva, *Nuevas formas de la revolución: Notas para aprender de las luchas del EZLN y de la APPO* (Oaxaca: El Rebozo, 2014); also see his many other works, including a contribution to the Colloquium in Memory of Andrés Aubry mentioned above and in the volume mentioned above about the Little School, and Carlos Aguirre Rojas, *Mandar obedeciendo: Las lecciones políticas del neozapatismo mexicano* (Mexico City: Contrahistorias, 2007). There are also collective volumes, including Shannan Mattiace, Rosalva Aida Hernández, and Jan Rus, eds., *Mayan Lives, Mayan Utopias: The Indigenous Peoples of Chiapas and the Zapatista Rebellion* (Lanham, MD:

Rowman & Littlefield, 2003); Maya Lorena Pérez Ruiz, ed., *Tejiendo historias: Tierra, género y poder en Chiapas* (Mexico City: INAH, 2004); John Holloway, Fernando Matamoros, and Sergio Tischler, eds., *Zapatismo: Reflexión teórica y subjetividades emergentes* (Buenos Aires: Herramienta, 2008); and Kristine Vanden Berghe, Anne Huffschmid, and Robin Lefere, eds., *El EZLN y sus intérpretes: Resonancias del zapatismo en la academia y en la literatura* (Mexico City: UACM, 2011).

Various academics have voiced positions highly critical of Zapatismo, and I have debated with some of them. See Pedro Pitarch, "Los zapatistas y el arte de la ventriloquia," *Istor* 17 (2004). I responded in Jérôme Baschet, "Los zapatistas: ¿'Ventriloquia india' o interacciones creativas?," *Istor* 22 (2005). In Jérôme Baschet, "Punto de vista e investigación: El caso del zapatismo," *Desacatos* 33 (2010): 189–201, www.ciesas.edu.mx/desacatos/ini.html, I discuss the positions and analysis of Marco Estrada Saavedra and Juan Pedro Viqueira, eds., *Los indígenas de Chiapas y la rebelión zapatista: Microhistorias políticas* (Mexico City: Colegio de México, 2010) and Marco Estrada Saavedra, *La comunidad armada rebelde y el EZLN: Un estudio histórico y sociológico sobre las bases de apoyo zapatistas en las cañadas tojolabales de la selva lacandona, 1930–2005* (Mexico City: Colegio de México, 2007).

Among recent English-language publications, see Dylan Fitzwater, *Autonomy is in Our Hearts* (Oakland: PM Press, 2019) and Massimiliano Tomba, "1994: Zapatistas and the Dispossessed of History," in *Insurgent Universality. An Alternative Legacy to Modernity* (Oxford: Oxford University Press, 2019), 186–222.

References relevant to each chapter

Historical Prologue

On the history of Chiapas, and especially the *longue durée* of the domination suffered by Indigenous peoples, first and foremost see Andrés Aubry, *Chiapas a contrapelo: Una agenda de trabajo para su historia en perspectiva sistémica* (San Cristóbal de Las Casas: CIDECI-Contrahistorias, 2005). Also see Andrés Aubry, *Saberes en el camino: Compilación de artículos, 1984–2007* (San Cristóbal de Las Casas: Cideci-Universidad de la Tierra, 2017) and from Antonio García de León, *Resistencia y utopía* (Mexico City: Era, 1985) as well as *Fronteras interiores: Chiapas, una modernidad particular* (Mexico City: Océano, 2002). Other histories include Jan de Vos, *Vivir en frontera: La experiencia de los indios de Chiapas* (Mexico City: CIESAS, 1997) and *Una tierra para sembrar sueños: Historia reciente de la Selva Lacandona, 1950–2000* (Mexico City: FCE-CIESAS, 2002). Also see Juan Pedro Viqueira y Mario Humberto Ruz, eds., *Chiapas: Los rumbos de otra historia* (Mexico City: UNAM-CIESAS, 1995).

For *campesino* struggles and the immediate antecedents of Zapatismo, see Xóchitl Leyva Solano and Gabriel Ascencio Franco, *Lacandonia al filo del agua* (Mexico City: FCE, 1996) and Neil Harvey, *The Chiapas Rebellion: The Struggle for Land and Democracy* (Durham: Duke University Press, 1998). Harvey indicates that, between 1960 and 1993, the number of *ejidos* in Chiapas increased from 948 to 2,072, and their surface area rose from 20 to 50 percent of the total land.

On the history of the EZLN, consult Le Bot and Marcos, *El sueño Zapatista* and Muñoz Ramirez, *The Fire and The Word*. Carlos Tello Díaz, *La rebelión de las Cañadas* (Mexico City: Cal y Arena, 2000) is a study based on documents from state "intelligence," and it is therefore of dubious credibility.

The impact of Zapatismo in the years following the uprising is addressed by Adolfo Gilly, *Chiapas: La razón ardiente* (Mexico City: Era, 1996) and Carlos Montemayor, *Chiapas: La rebelión indígena de México* (Mexico City: Joaquín Mortiz, 1997).

On the San Andrés Accords, see Luís Hernández Navarro and Raúl Vera Herrera, eds., *Acuerdos de San Andrés* (Mexico City: Era, 1998).

On paramilitarization and the massacre at Acteal, see Andrés Aubry and Angélica Inda, *Los llamados de la memoria* (Tuxtla Gutiérrez: Conaculta, 2003) and Rosalva Aida Hernández Castillo, ed., *The Other Word: Women and Violence in Chiapas before and after Acteal* (International Work Group for Indigenous Affairs, 2001).

On The March of the Color of the Earth, see Paulina Fernández Christlieb and Carlos Sirvent, eds., *La marcha del EZLN al Distrito Federal* (Mexico City: UNAM-Gernika, 2001).

Chapter 1: "Autonomy is the People's Life Itself"
On autonomy, see all the textbooks from the Zapatista Little School cited above, Subcomandante Moisés's explanations in *Critical Thought*, as well as "Apuntes de las bases de apoyo del EZLN para su participación en la compartición," *Rebeldía Zapatista* 3 (September 2014): 15–26.

Studies of autonomy include Paulina Fernández Christlieb, *Justicia Autónoma Zapatista: Zona Selva Tzeltal* (Mexico City: Ediciones autónom@s, 2014); Mariana Mora, *Kuxlejal Politics: Indigenous Autonomy, Race and Decolonizing Research in Zapatista Communities* (Austin: University of Texas Press, 2017); Bruno Baronnet, Mariana Mora, and Richard Stahler-Sholk, eds., *Luchas "muy otras": Zapatismo y autonomía en las comunidades indígenas de Chiapas* (Mexico City: UAM, 2011); and Alejandro Cerda García, *Imaginando zapatismo: Multiculturalidad y autonomía indígena en Chiapas desde un municipio autónomo* (Mexico City: Porrúa, 2011).

On recuperated land, you can find more data in Mariana Mora, "A Brief Overview of the First Years of the Zapatista Autonomous Municipalities," in *Kuxlejal Politics*. An estimated 40,000 hectares [nearly 100,000 acres] of land was recuperated by the EZLN after January 1, 1994. See Daniel Villafuerte et. al., *La tierra en Chiapas: Viejos problemas nuevos* (Mexico City: Plaza y Valdés, 1999).

On Indigenous conceptions of community, see works on *comunalidad*, especially in Oaxaca. In particular, see Floriberto Díaz, *Escrito: Comunalidad, energía viva del pensamiento mixe* (Mexico City: UNAM: 2007) and Benjamín Maldonado Alvarado, *La comunalidad como una perspectiva antropológica india* (Tlatelolco: La Social, 2015).

On the importance of the *fiesta* and ritual in autonomy, see Rocío Noemí Martínez González, "La fiesta como memoria en la reconfiguración de territorios y del imaginario colectivo en el *K'in Tajimol*. Un carnaval maya-tsotsil, Municipio autónomo de Polhó, Chiapas," *Alter-Nativa* 9 (2018): 1–23, https://revistas.unc.edu.ar/index.php/alter-nativa/article/view/40946.

On autonomous education, see Bruno Baronnet, *Autonomía y educación indígena: Las escuelas zapatistas de la Selva Lacandona en Chiapas, Mexico* (Quito: Abya-Yala, 2012). He estimates that in 2008 there were a total of five hundred autonomous schools attended by 16,000 students and taught by 1,300 education promoters. See also Horacio Gómez Lara, *Indígenas, mexicanos y rebeldes: Procesos educativos y resignificación de identidades en Los Altos de Chiapas* (Mexico City: Juan Pablos-UNICACH, 2011) and Raúl Gutiérrez Narváez, "Dos proyecto de sociedad en Los Altos de Chiapas. Escuelas secundarias oficial y autónoma entre los tzotziles de San Andrés," in *Luchas "muy otras,"* 237–66.

On autonomous health, see Alejandro Cerda Garcia, *Imaginando zapatismo: Multiculturalidad y autonomía indígena en Chiapas desde un municipio autónomo* (Mexico City: Universidad Autónoma Metropolitana, 2011).

On the struggle of Zapatista women, see Guiomar Rovira, *Women of Maize: Indigenous Women and the Zapatista Rebellion* (London: Latin American Bureau, 2000); Sylvia Marcos, *Cruzando fronteras: mujeres indígenas y feminismos abajo y a la izquierda* (Santiago de Chile: Quimantu, 2017) and *Una poética de la insurgencia zapatista* (Madrid: Akal, 2023). See also Márgara Millán, *Des-ordenando el género / ¿Des-centrando la nación?: El zapatismo de las mujeres indígenas y sus consecuencias* (Mexico City: UNAM, 2014); Hilary Klein, *Compañeras: Zapatista Women's Stories* (New York: Seven Stories Press, 2015); and Rosaluz Pérez Espinosa, *Experiencia de la participación política de las mujeres zapatistas y transformación de la comunidad* (doctoral thesis) (Paris-San Cristóbal de Las Casas, EHESS-CESMECA, 2021) and "Las mujeres hicieron posible el EZLN," *Revista de la Universidad de México*, 903–4 (2023), 31–35.

On migration, see Alejandra Aquino Moreschi, *De las luchas indias al sueño americano: Experiencias migratorias de jóvenes zapotecos y tojolabales en Estados Unidos* (Mexico City: Publicaciones de la Casa Chata, 2012).

In previous works I discuss aspects of autonomy in greater detail, such as Jérôme Baschet *Adiós al capitalismo: Autonomía, sociedad del bien vivir, y multiplicidad de los mundos* (Buenos Aires: Futuro Anterior-NED, 2014) and Jérôme Baschet, "La Escuelita zapatista y el contagio de la autonomía," in *La Escuelita zapatista: Ensayos y testimonios* (Guadalajara: Grietas, 2014), 175–218.

Chapter 2: "We Can Govern Ourselves"

On the debate about power provoked by John Holloway, *Change the World without Taking Power: The Meaning of Revolution Today* (London: Pluto, 2002), see the articles published in issues 12, 14, and 16 of the journal *Chiapas*, in particular Atilio Borón, "La selva y la polis: Interrogantes en torno a la teoría política del zapatismo," *Chiapas* 12 (2001) and Sergio Rodríguez Lascano, "Sobre Marcos, John Holloway, Atilio Borón, y el poder: ¿Puede ser verde la teoría? Sí, siempre y cuando la vida no sea gris," *Rebeldía* 8 (2003), 9–17. See also Sergio Rodríguez Lascano,"Nueve tesis y una premonición sobre la otra política zapatista," *BiodiversidadLA*, https://www.biodiversidadla.org/Documentos/Nueve-tesis-y-una-premonicion-sobre-la-otra-politica-zapatista. See also John Holloway, *In, Against, and Beyond Capitalism: The San Francisco Lectures* (Oakland: PM Press, 2016).

On the crisis of classical revolutionary politics, see Sergio Tischler, "La crisis del sujeto leninista y la circunstancia zapatista," *Chiapas* 12 (2001), 129–46, later re-edited in *Revolución y destotalización* (Guadalajara: Grietas, 2013), 95–122. See also Sergio Tischler, *What is to be Done? Leninism, Anti-Leninist Marxism, and the Question of Revolution Today* (London: Pluto Press, 2002).

On the stages of neoliberalism, see Ernst Lohoff and Norbert Trenkle, *La grande dévalorisation: Pourquoi la spéculation et la dette de l'État ne sont pas les causes de la crise* (Paris: Post-Éditions, 2014).

On the historical connection between the state and the nation, see Eric Hobsbaum, *Nations and Nationalisms since 1780* (Cambridge: Cambridge University Press, 1992) and Michael Löwy, *Fatherland or Mother Earth: Essays on the National Question* (London: Pluto, 1998). Also see my comments in Jérôme Baschet, "¿Los zapatistas contra el Imperio?" *Chiapas* 13 (2002), 159–76.

On dignity, see John Holloway, "Dignity's revolt," in *Zapatista! Reinventing Revolution in Mexico*, ed. John Holloway and Eloina Pelaez (London: Pluto, 1998). An exploration of similar concepts in Indigenous cultures is Juan López Intzín, "'Ich'el-ta-muk': La trama en la construcción del lekil-kuxlejal, Hacia una hermeneusis intercultural o visibilización de saberes desde la matricialidad del sentipensar-sentisaber tzeltal" in *Prácticas otras de conocimiento(s). Entre crisis, entre guerras*, ed. Xóchitl Leyva Solano (Buenos Aires: CLACSO, 2018), 181–98. *Ich'el-ta-muk* means respect and recognition of the greatness (*grandeza*) of the other and, furthermore, it is premised on justice and equality for all. Therefore, when everyone enjoys *ich'el-ta-muk*, respect, and equality, it makes for a life that is dignified and full, which is what is meant by *lekil kuxlejal*.

On the art of listening, see Carlos Lenkersdorf, *Aprender a escuchar* (Mexico: Plaza y Valdés, 2008).

I analyze the notion of autonomy as a politics without the state in greater detail in my book *Podemos gobernarnos nosotros mismos: La autonomía, una política sin el Estado* (San Cristóbal de Las Casas: Cideci-Unitierra, 2017), radiozapatista.org/?p=25912.

On the opposition between the state and democracy, see Miguel Abensour, *Democracy Against the State* (Cambridge: Polity Press, 2011). On the notion of destitution, see Giorgio Agamben, *The Use of Bodies* (Palo Alto: Stanford University Press, 2016).

Chapter 3: *"For humanity and against capitalism!"*

On the international dimension of Zapatismo and its connections with the anti-globalization movement, see Guiomar Rovira, *Zapatistas sin fronteras: Las redes de solidaridad con Chiapas y el altermundismo* (Mexico City: Era, 2009) and "From Local to Global: The Multiscalar Dimension of the Zapatista Rebellion and the Transnational Networks of Social Mobilizations," in *Performing Citizenship: Social Movements across the Globe,* ed. Inbal Ofer and Tamar Groves (New York: Routledge, 2015).

On the concept of total war, see Eric Alliez and Maurizio Lazzarato, *Wars and Capital* (New York: Semiotext(e), 2018), in particular "Total Wars," 165–222.

On the storm, see the analysis by John Holloway, *La tormenta: Crisis, deuda, revolución y esperanza, una respuesta al desafío zapatista* (Puebla: Benemérita Universidad Autónoma de Puebla, 2013).

In *La grande devaluación,* Lohoff and Trenkle analyze financialized capitalism, an "inverted capitalism" in which real production is at the service of producing financial commodities. According to them, financial capital produces real profits, profits that are not created through the exploitation of labor and the production of value, but that are rather an anticipation of the future production of value. Therefore, if the creation of fictitious capital is to continue, it is necessary to maintain confidence in the real economy.

For discussion of the capitalist Hydra's mother head, see Anselm Jappe, *En busca de las raíces del mal: Consideraciones sobre las categorías fundamentales del capitalismo* (San Cristóbal de Las Casas: Cideci-Unitierra, 2015). In particular, see "Tesis sobre las raíces del mal," 131–40, as well as Anselm Jappe, *The Writing on the Wall: On the Decomposition of Capitalism and Its Critics* (London: Collective Ink, 2017). Also see Moishe Postone, *Time, Labor and Social Domination: A Reinterpretation of Marx's Critical Theory* (Cambridge: Cambridge University Press, 1993). Postone considers that, for Marx, capitalism is not defined by private property of the means of production, but rather by the value form of wealth and the preeminence of abstract work over concrete work.

On the notion of a crack, see the previous elaboration of John Holloway, *Crack Capitalism* (London: Pluto, 2010).

On the debate over the Anthropocene and Capitalocene, see Christophe Bonneuil and Jean-Baptiste Fressoz, *The Shock of the Anthropocene: The Earth, History and Us* (New York: Verso, 2013); and Jason Moore, "The Capitalocene, Part I: On the Nature and Origins of Our Ecological Crisis," *The Journal of Peasant Studies* 44, no. 3 (2017): 594–630, as well as *Capitalism in the Web of Life: Ecology and the Accumulation of Capital* (New York: Verso, 2015).

Chapter 4: "We Want a World Where Many Worlds Fit"

Positions distinct from mine, to which I refer in this chapter, can be found in the works mentioned above by Pitarch, "Los zapatistas y ventriloquia," Estrada Saavedra, *La comunidad armada rebelde*, and Estrada Saavedra and Viqueira, *Los indígenas de Chiapas*.

Some elements of Indigenous conceptions of Indigeneity can be found in Marshall Sahlins, *Islands of History* (Chicago: University of Chicago Press, 1985). In Hawai'i, a foreigner who resides in a community for a long time and learns proper behavior becomes a "child of the land" (*kama'āina*), a term that designates the Indigenous people, but not exclusively. In Chiapas, the expression the Indigenous use to refer to themselves—*bats'il winik* or *tojol winik* ("true man")—does not seem to imply an essence acquired at birth but rather something that one learns to be and that can also be lost, a way of behaving proper to community life. See Carlos Lenkersdorf, *Los hombres verdaderos: Voces y testimonios tojolabajes* (Mexico City: Siglo XXI, 1996), 98–105.

On the logic of nonidentity, see Holloway, *Crack Capitalism*, especially 109–13 and 212–26.

For the critique of the abstract universalism of the Enlightenment, see Theodor Adorno and Max Horkheimer, *Dialectic of the Enlightenment* (New York: Herder and Herder, 1972). Lukacs mentions that the "great danger to every humanism" lies in exalting a notion of "man-in-himself, of man absolutized abstractly." See Georg Lukacs, *History and Class Consciousness: Studies in Marxist Dialectics*, trans. Rodney Livingstone (Cambridge: MIT Press, 1972).

On notions of pluriversalism and pluniversalism, see Baschet, *Adios al capitalismo*, 122–23.

Giorgio Agamben proposes the notions of "inessential community" and being "without the condition of for belonging" in *The Coming Community* (Minneapolis: University of Minnesota Press, 1993). For Agamben, "Whatever singularity . . . that rejects all identity and every condition of belonging, is the principal enemy of the State," 87.

On the notion of *humanitas,* see Pierre Vesperini, "Le sens d'*humanitas* à Rome," *MEFRA* 127 (2015), https://journals.openedition.org/mefra/2768.

For a critical analysis of postmodernity, see Frederic Jameson, *Postmodernism, or The Cultural Logic of Late Capitalism* (Durham: Duke University Press, 1992) and Perry Anderson, *The Origins of Postmodernity* (London: Verso, 1998).

Lukács highlights the impossibility of realizing the promises of individualism within the conditions created by capitalist reification, writing "The bourgeoisie endowed the individual with an unprecedented importance, but at the same time that same individuality was annihilated by the economic conditions to which it was subjected, by the reification created by commodity production." *History and Class Consciousness*, 62.

On the relational conception of the person, see Baschet, *Adiós al capitalismo*, 102–04 and 132–33. This is something that was common to the great majority of the peoples of the world, until modernity broke with it. According to Marshall Sahlins, to recognize the interpersonal character of the self allows us to understand that we are "members of one another." See *The Western Illusion of Human Nature: With Reflections on the Long History of Hierarchy, Equality and the Sublimation of Anarchy in the West, and . . . Conceptions of the Human Condition* (Baltimore: Paradigm, 2008). See also Lenkersdorf, *Aprender a escuchar*, to whom I owe the notion of a "we self."

On the conceptions of the Mayan peoples of Chiapas and the community created among human and non-human beings who all have *ch'ulel*, see Juan López Intzin, "Yo'taninel bajtik, re-ch'ulel-izarnos y revivir lo sagrado desde nuestra propia humanidad como matriz del fin de la Jow-hidra capitalista," in *El pensamiento crítico frente a la Hidra capitalista* Vol 3, 262–76. Also see Lenkersdorf, *Los hombres verdaderos*, 106–19. On conceptions of the person in Cancúc, see Pedro Pitarch, *Ch'ulel: una etnografía de las almas tzeltales* (Mexico City: FCE, 1996).

The separation between man and nature should be understood as an anthropological aberration that has been asserted in Europe since the seventeeth century. See Philippe Descola, *Beyond Nature and Culture*, trans. Janet Lloyd (Chicago: University of Chicago Press, 2013). Descartes's words can be found in *Discourse on Method*.

For a critique of the sciences that is not postmodern, see Pierre Bourdieu, *Science of Science, and Reflexivity* (Chicago: University of Chicago Press, 2004). Also see Isabelle Stengers, *Another Science is Possible: A Manifesto for Slow Science* (Cambridge: Polity Press, 2018). In Boaventura de Sousa Santos, *Epistemologies of the South: Justice against Epistemicide* (New York: Routledge, 2014), the author considers that to articulate scientific and vernacular knowledge is to create an "ecology of knowledges."

Speaking of decolonial thought, I refer in particular to the work of Walter Mignolo, *The Idea of Latin America* (Hoboken: Wiley, 2005).

I refer as well to the work of Frantz Fanon, especially, *Black Skins, White Masks* (London: Pluto, 1986), 226, 230, in which he rejects being reduced to

Black identity and refuses to be "sealed away in the materialized Tower of the Past," to not be "a slave of the slavery that dehumanized my ancestors." He also affirms, "For us, the man who adores the Negro is as 'sick' as the man who abominates him. Conversely, the black man who wants to turn his race white is as miserable as he who preaches hatred for the whites" (10–11).

Chapter 5: "Our Struggle is for History and against Oblivion"

Some points addressed here are analyzed in greater detail in Colectivo Neosaurios, "La Rebelión de la historia," *Chiapas* 9 (2000), 7–33; Jérôme Baschet, "(Re)discutir sobre la historia," *Chiapas* 10 (2000): 7–40; Jérôme Baschet, "La historia frente al presente perpetuo: Algunas observaciones sobre la relación pasado/futuro," *Relaciones* 24 (2003): 213–39; and Jérôme Baschet, "La rebelión de la memoria: Temporalidad e historia en el movimiento zapatista," *Tramas* 38 (2012): 207–35.

An analysis of the stories of Old Antonio, and especially of the Indigenous conception of time expressed in them, can be found in Carla Valdespino Vargas, *De noches, dioses y creaciones: Un acercamiento a Relatos de el Viejo Antonio del Subcomandante Insurgente Marcos* (Toluca: UAEM, 2009).

The Zapatista analysis of the perpetual present converges with the readings that, historiographically, propose the emergence of a new configuration of historical times called "presentism." See François Hartog, *Regimes of Historicity: Presentism and Experiences of Time,* trans. Saskia Brown (New York: Columbia University Press, 2015). I also refer to my book Jérôme Baschet, *Défaire la tyrannie du présent: Temporalités émergentes et futurs inédits* (Paris: La Découverte, 2018) and to Jérôme Baschet, "Reopening the Future: Emerging Worlds and Novel Historical Futures," *History and Theory* 61/2 (June 2022): 183–208; http://doi.org/10.1111/hith.12263. See also Reinhart Koselleck, *Futures Past: On the Semantics of Historical Time* (New York: Columbia University Press, 2004). I must specify that there is a duality in Christian conceptions of time. While "the here and now" is marked by a respect for the past and its repetition, the afterlife is dominated by a linear history in expectation of the future Great Event, the end times and final judgment. Modernity's understanding of history appears to be but a secularized version of this.

The Zapatista alliance between past and future can be compared to what Löwy and Sayre have called "revolutionary romanticism," that is, a position that does not seek to go back to the past, but rather uses nostalgia for the past to project itself towards a utopian future, in a movement that is not "a return to the past but a turn through the past." See Michael Löwy and Robert Sayre, *Romanticism against the Tide of Modernity* (Durham: Duke University Press, 2002). The work of Ernst Bloch, *The Principle of Hope* (Cambridge: MIT Press, 1995) is particularly clear on this, as he calls for searching for "a future in the past" and breaking down "the barriers established between the future and the past."

I also refer to Ernst Bloch's analysis of anticipation and the desire for what is not yet. My proposal here is different from Holloway in "Dignity's Revolt," where he says revolution should be understood as "a movement from, not a movement toward." For him, just as with Walter Benjamin's messianic time, the revolution must be understood entirely in an "absolute present." See Holloway, *In, Against, and Beyond Capitalism.*

Sergio Tischler proposes a constellation formed by the thought of Walter Benjamin and the Zapatistas. See Tischler, *Tiempo y emancipación: Mijail Bajtin y Walter Benjamin en la Selva Lacandona* (Guatemala City: F&G, 2008). Also see Sergio Tischler, "La memoria ve hacia adelante: A propósito de Walter Benjamin y las nuevas rebeldías sociales," *Constelaciones: Revista de Teoria Critica* 2 (2010). On the difference between the "modern line" and the "trajectory line" (*línea-trayecto*) of traditional societies, see Tim Ingold, *Lines: A Brief History* (New York: Routledge, 2007).

On the genesis of the modern concept of revolution, see Reinhart Koselleck, *Futures Past*, "Historical Criteria of the Modern Conception of Revolution."

Notes

Preface to the English Edition

Translators' Note

1. I am very grateful to the AK Press team for taking this initiative, and for all their care in carrying it to fruition. Thanks as well to Raúl Zibechi for taking part in this process. I want to express my gratitude to the Traductores Rebeldes Autónomos Cronopios, who took on the arduous task of translation. Your enthusiasm continues to move me.
2. Subcomandante Insurgente Moisés, "Ninth Part: The new structure of Zapatista Autonomy," *Enlace Zapatista*, November 13, 2023, https://enlacezapatista.ezln.org .mx/2023/11/13/ninth-part-the-new-structure-of-zapastista-autonomy.
3. Further details can be found in the prologue and in the postscript at the end of the first chapter.
4. Captain Marcos, "Twentieth and Last Part: The Common and Non-Property," *Enlace Zapatista*, December 22, 2023, https://enlacezapatista.ezln.org.mx/ 2023/12/22/twentieth-and-last-part-the-common-and-non-property.
5. The Captain, "Tenth Part: Regarding pyramids and their uses and customary regimes," *Enlace Zapatista*, November 15, 2023, https://enlacezapatista.ezln.org. mx/2023/11/15/tenth-part-regarding-pyramids-and-their-uses-and-customary-regimes.
6. The Captain, "Tenth Part."
1. Paulina Fernandez Christlieb, *Justicia Autónoma Zapatista* (Mexico City: Ediciones autónom@s, 2014).

Introduction

1. Immanuel Wallerstein, "The Zapatistas: The Second Stage. Commentary No. 165," *Fernand Braudel Center*, July 15, 2005, https://conifer.rhizome.org/binglibraries/ fernand-braudel-center-for-the-study-of-economies-historical-systems-and-

civilizations-2/list/fbc/b1/20200514022418/http://www2.binghamton.edu/fbc/archive/165en.htm.

2. For example EZLN, *Critical Thought in the Face of the Capitalist Hydra I* (Durham, NC: PaperBoat Press, 2016), 240.

3. EZLN, *Critical Thought*, 171.

4. Translators' Note: This was a series of three sessions in 2013 during which a total of 4,500 students spent a week living with a Zapatista family and learning about their autonomous projects by participating in collective work and studying texts compiled by the Zapatistas for the occasion (see ausm.community/escuelita). Each student was assigned their own "teacher" (*maestro* or *Votán*), a Zapatista support base member who would be their guide, mentor, and translator for the week.

5. In this regard, I point out that in this book the footnotes mainly contain references to the texts and documents of the EZLN. Except in the case of a direct citation, references to other thoughts and other authors can be found in the bibliographic notes on pages 225–36.

6. Translators' note: "Marcos," by his own account a "hologram," was laid to rest in 2014, and reincarnated as Subcomandante Galeano. See Subcomandante Insurgente Galeano, "Between Light and Shadow," *Enlace Zapatista*, May 25, 2014, https://enlacezapatista.ezln.org.mx/2014/05/27/between-light-and-shadow.

7. Subcomandante Marcos, "Convocatoria al Encuentro Intercontinental," communique, May 1995, in *Documentos y Comunicados 3, 2 de octubre de 1995/24 de enero de 1997*, First edition (1997; First reprint, Mexico City: Ediciones Era, 1998), 258.

8. Yvon Le Bot and Subcomandante Marcos, *El Sueño Zapatista* (Mexico: Plaza y Janés, 1997), 306–7.

9. Subcomandante Marcos, "The World: Seven Thoughts in May 2003," trans. Irlandesa, *El Kilombo*, May 2003, https://elkilombo.org/documents/seventhoughts marcos.html.

10. Subcomandante Marcos, "The World."

11. EZLN, *Critical Thought*, 5, 181.

12. Subcomandante Marcos, "Seven Thoughts."

13. *Primer Coloquio Internacional in Memoriam Andrés Aubry. "Planeta tierra, movimientos antisistémicos"* (San Cristóbal de Las Casas: Cideci-Universidad de la Tierra, 2009), 23, 322.

14. Subcomandante Insurgente Marcos, *El Viejo Antonio*, 3rd Ed., (Mexico City: Ediciones Eón, 2010).

Historical Prologue

1. Many of the references relevant to this prologue can be found in the bibliographic notes at the end of the book.

2. Translators' note: *Finca* is usually translated as plantation or (racialized) estate. Lack of access to land forced Indigenous *campesinos* into a form of indentured

servitude, often maintained through intergenerational debt and payment in scrip only redeemable at the *finca* owner's store. Mariana Mora describes conditions on the fincas as conditions of "racialized exploitation, sexual violence and near slavery." See Mariana Mora, *Kuxlejal Politics Indigenous Autonomy, Race, and Decolonizing Research in Zapatista Communities* (Austin: University of Texas Press, 2017), 78, especially chapter 3. Paulina Fernández summarizes the power relations of life on the *fincas*, "Since their labor power is the only thing the peons, their wives, and children have, the landowner considers himself the owner of their life as well, and he forces his peons to understand this in every moment of every day." Paulina Fernández Christlieb, *Justicia Autónoma Zapatista, Zona Tzeltal* (Mexico City: Estampa/Ediciones Autónom@s, 2014), 50.

3. Intervention by Sebastián Gómez, October 15, 1974, cited in Antonio García de León, "La vuelta del Katún (Chiapas: a veinte años del Primer Congreso Indígena)," *Chiapas* 1 (1995): 131–32, https://revistachiapas.org/No1/ch1leon.html.

4. Andrés Aubry and Angélica Inda, *Los llamados de la memoria: Chiapas, 1995–2001* (Tuxtla-Gutiérrez: Conaculta, 2003), Part 4.

5. Xóchitl Leyva and Gabriel Ascencio, *Lacandonia al filo del agua* (Mexico City: FCE, 1996), 159.

6. Testimony of Macario, from the autonomous municipality 17th of November in the zone of Morelia, cited in "Social Memories of Struggle and Racialized (E)states" in Mora, *Kuxlejal Politics*, 71.

7. Major Moisés, who in those years was a member of the *Union de Uniones*, recounts the betrayal of Orive, his expulsion, and the restructuring of the organization by the Indigenous themselves. Yvon Le Bot and Subcomandante Marcos, *El Sueño Zapatista* (Mexico: Plaza y Janés, 1997), 167–71.

8. Le Bot and Marcos, *El Sueño*, 146–47.

9. Laura Castellanos, *México Armado: 1943–1981* (Mexico City: Ediciones Era, 2007).

10. The proportion of mestizos and Indigenous, as well as the gender composition [five men and one woman] can be found in the account of Subcomandante Marcos, "Fire and Word," November 10, 2003, in *¡Ya Basta!: Ten Years of the Zapatista Uprising*, ed. Žiga Vodovnik (Oakland: AK Press, 2004), 629–42.

11. Subcomandante Marcos, "Fire and Word."

12. Translators' note: "Support bases" refers to the civilian communities that the Zapatista army recruits from and relies on for material support. "EZLN" refers to the armed organization led by the Comandantes, and "Zapatistas" either refers to the military plus support bases, or other times only to the support bases. As they have developed their autonomous project, the Zapatistas have increasingly built a horizontal system of self-government within the support bases that is independent of the EZLN and its vertical military structure.

13. The process of clandestine recruitment has been described by various local authorities of the EZLN in the video offered as material for the second grade of the

Zapatista Little School in 2014. See also the account of then Major Moisés in Le Bot and Marcos, *El Sueño zapatista*, 171–72, as well as that of the teacher Galeano in his notebook in EZLN, *Critical Thought in the Face of the Capitalist Hydra I* (Durham, NC: Paperboat Press, 2016), 52–53.

14. Le Bot and Marcos, *El Sueño*, 177–81.

15. Le Bot and Marcos, *El Sueño*, 182.

16. Le Bot and Marcos, *El Sueño*, 148–51.

17. Interview with Tessa Brisac and Carmen Castillo (October 24, 1994) in *Discusión Sobre La Historia* (Mexico City: Taurus, 1995), 131–42. In a sharper formulation: "We underwent a process of re-education, of remodeling. As if they had disarmed us … and put us back together again, but in another form." Le Bot and Marcos, *Sueño Zapatista*, 151. Also: "The contact with the communities implied a process of re-education that was stronger and more terrible than the kind of electroshock treatment customary in psychiatric clinics." "Plática del SCI Marcos y el Tte. Coronel I. Moisés con los miembros de la Caravana que llegaron al Caracol de La Garrucha," *Enlace Zapatista*, August 2, 2008, enlacezapatista.ezln.org.mx/2008/08/02/platica-del-sci-marcos-y-el-tte-coronel-i-moises-con-los-miembros-de-la-caravana-que-llegaron-al-caracol-de-la-garrucha.

18. Le Bot and Marcos, *El Sueño*.

19. Translators' note: Che Guevara and the Cuban revolutionaries popularized the assertion that a small *foco* of guerrilla fighters based in the countryside could overthrow a dictatorship. See Che Guevara, *Guerrilla Warfare* (Melbourne: Centro de Estudios Che Guevara, 2006) and Regis Debray, *Strategy for Revolution* (New York: Monthly Review Press, 1970).

20. "Plática del SCI Marcos y el Tte. Coronel I. Moisés."

21. "Plática del SCI Marcos y el Tte. Coronel I. Moisés."

22. The expression "Indianization of the EZLN" is used in Le Bot and Marcos, *El Sueño zapatista*, 150.

23. Translators' note: The Mexican Coffee Institute (INMECAFE in Spanish) was formed in 1973 to provide technical assistance and credit to coffee producers. President Salinas de Gortari dissolved it in 1989, at the behest of structural adjustment policies required by international financial institutions.

24. Le Bot and Marcos, *El Sueño*, 190–91.

25. Le Bot and Marcos, *El Sueño*, 194–96.

26. Detailed indications about the positions and the movements of the regiments of the EZLN can be found in Subcomandante Marcos, "Fire and Word," 629–42.

27. Translators' note: The Feast of Saint Sylvester is a Catholic celebration held on New Year's Eve.

28. EZLN, "Declaration from the Lacandon Jungle," January 1, 1994, in Subcomandante Marcos, *Our Word Is our Weapon: Selected Writings*, ed. Juana Ponce de León (New York: Seven Stories Press, 2001), 13–15.

29. Translators' note: This is in reference to "Ya basta!," an evocative call from the EZLN's "First Declaration of the Lacandon Jungle" that then became the principle slogan of their uprising.

30. EZLN, "Declaration from the Lacandon Jungle."

31. EZLN, "El Despertador Mexicano," December 1993 in *Documentos y Comunicados 1, 1 de enero de 1994/8 de agosto de 1994*, First edition (1994; Sixth reprint, Mexico City: Ediciones Era, 2003), 36–48.

32. Communiqué on the anniversary of the formation of the EZLN, November 17, 1994, DC 2, 132. The other facts mentioned in this paragraph can be found in *Sueño Zapatista*, 214–20, 226–27.

33. EZLN, *Critical Thought*, 52–55.

34. Le Bot and Marcos, *El Sueño*, 225.

35. In this regard, see Subcomandante Insurgente Marcos, "Fire and Word," 629–42.

36. Subcomandante Marcos, "Intervención del Subcomandante Marcos en la Mesa 1 del Encuentro Intercontinental," July 30, 1996 in EZLN, *Documentos y Comunicados 3, 2 de octubre de 1995/24 de enero de 1997*, First edition (1997; First reprint, Mexico City: Ediciones Era, 1998), 322. (Translators' note: the term "civil Zapatismo" invokes or interpellates a new political actor, "civil society.")

37. EZLN, *Documentos y Comunicados 1*, 82–83, 94–95.

38. Translators' note: This was the Zapatistas' name for their meeting spaces with civil society, harkening to the city in central Mexico where a famous convention was held in 1914. The Convention touched off the high point of the Mexican Revolution, as Pancho Villa's forces broke with the centrist Carranza and entered into an alliance with Emiliano Zapata's Southern Liberation Army.

39. EZLN, *Documentos y Comunicados 2, 15 de agosto de 1994/29 de septiembre de 1995*, First edition (1995; Third reprint, Mexico City: Ediciones Era, 2001), 169–82.

40. EZLN, *Documentos y Comunicados 2*, 234.

41. Translators' note: The Zapatistas' several *consultas* were referenda in which they asked their supporters, both in Mexico, and internationally, to weigh in on strategic questions that confronted them. These referenda involved considerable effort in Mexico where Zapatista men and women organized the voting in every state in the country. Internationally, these referenda happened according to local practices and capacities.

42. EZLN, "Palabras en el aniversario de la formación del EZLN," November 17, 1994, in *Documentos y comunicados 2*, 136.

43. Regarding the formation of paramilitary groups and their modus operandi, see Aubry and Inda, *Los Llamados*, chaps. 14–20.

44. Subcomandante Insurgente Marcos, "To the FZLN Founding Conference," *The Struggle Site*, September 13, 1997, https://www.struggle.ws/mexico/ezln/1997/ccri_to_fzln_conf_se97.html.

45. Subcomandante Insurgente Marcos, "The Zapatistas and Newton's Apple," *The*

Struggle Site, May 10, 1999, https://www.struggle.ws/mexico/ezln/1999/marcos_
newton_may99.html.

46. Subcomandante Insurgente Marcos, "To Senor Ernesto Zedillo Ponce de Leon,"
The Struggle Site, November 2000, https://www.struggle.ws/mexico/ezln/2000/
marcos_zedillo_nov.html.

47. Translators' note: *Indigenismo* was a political project pursued by the PRI in wake
of the Mexican Revolution. It was an attempt to address the so-called Indian Problem through assimilation, to be pursued through educational policy that valorized
Indigenous cultures as relics of the past and distributed resources to Indigenous
communities in exchange for political loyalty.

48. "A Time to Ask, a Time to Demand and a Time to Act," in Gloria Muñoz Ramírez,
The Fire and the Word: A History of the Zapatista Movement, trans. Laura Carlsen
and Alejandro Reyes Arias (San Francisco: City Lights Books, 2008), 283.

49. Muñoz Ramírez, *The Fire and the Word*, 283.

50. Comandante Brus Li, "Palabras en la movilización del 1 de enero de 2003," en
Rebeldía 3, 2003, https://enlacezapatista.ezln.org.mx/2003/01/01/comandante
-brus-li-palabras-para-los-pueblos-indigenas.

51. Translators' note: We have translated *junta* as "council" to avoid the strong associations in English with military rule, and the imperialist associations, in the US, of
Latin American governments with military strongmen. The Royal Spanish Academy
lists as one of the eight meanings of *junta*: "a group of individuals named to direct the
affairs of a collectivity;" and suggests as synonyms, "committee," "assembly," "collectivity," and "commission." We have followed other translations in choosing "council."

52. EZLN, "Sixth Declaration of the Selva Lacandona," *Enlace Zapatista*, June 30, 2005,
https://enlacezapatista.ezln.org.mx/2005/06/30/sixth-declaration-of-the-selva
-lacandona.

53. Subcomandante Marcos, "Chiapas: The Thirteenth Stele, Part III- A name: Each
Caracol Now Had a Name Assigned." *The Struggle Site*, July 2003, https://struggle
.ws/mexico/ezln/2003/marcos/caracolJULY.html.

54. EZLN, "Sixth Declaration."

55. *Primer Coloquio Internacional in Memoriam Andrés Aubry "Planeta tierra, movimientos antisistémicos* (San Cristóbal de Las Casas: Cideci-Universidad de la Tierra,
2009), 181.

56. Subcomandante Marcos, "Them and Us. III. - The Overseers," *Enlace Zapatista*,
January 25, 2013, https://enlacezapatista.ezln.org.mx/2013/01/25/them-and-us-iii
-the-overseers. Translators' note: Calling the forty thousand Zapatistas who
marched that day "bosses" (*jefas y jefes*) is a bit of Zapatista humor, indicating that
the people are in charge, and the government obeys.

57. Subcomandante Insurgente Marcos, "Them and Us. v. The Sixth," *Enlace Zapatista*,
January 27, 2013, https://enlacezapatista.ezln.org.mx/2013/01/27/them-and-us-v
-the-sixth.

58. Translators' note: "Comparte" is the imperative form of the verb *compartir*, to share. So "CompArte for Humanity" literally means "Share Art for Humanity"!

59. Subcomandante Galeano, "Between Light and Shadow," *Enlace Zapatista*, May 24, 2014, https://enlacezapatista.ezln.org.mx/2014/05/27/between-light-and-shadow.

60. Galeano, "Between Light and Shadow."

61. CNI and EZLN, "May the Earth Tremble at Its Core," *Enlace Zapatista*, October 18, 2016, https://enlacezapatista.ezln.org.mx/2016/10/18/may-the-earth-tremble -at-its-core.

62. This final section was written in January 2024 for the present English edition.

63. Jérôme Baschet, "Amarga celebración: los 25 años de la experiencia zapatista," *Radio zapatista*, January 10, 2019, https://radiozapatista.org/?p=30068.

64. EZLN, "Words of the EZLN's CCRI-CG to the Zapatista Peoples on the 25th Anniversary of the Beginning of the War against Oblivion," *Enlace Zapatista*, December 31, 2018, https://enlacezapatista.ezln.org.mx/2019/01/09/words-of-the -ezlns-ccri-cg-to-the-zapatista-peoples-on-the-25th-anniversary-of-the-beginning -of-the-war-against-oblivion.

65. On intense urbanization in the Yucatán, see the documentary *Mayapolis*. Renaud Lariagon, *Mayapolis: Tourisme et expansion urbaine dans la Péninsule du Yucatan*, October 14, 2023, YouTube video, https://www.youtube.com/ watch?v=rs_VQkb-DS4. On the risks of the Mayan Train, see the reporting by the *New York Times*. Maria Abi-Habib, "Over Caves and Over Budget, Mexico's Train Project Barrels Toward Disaster," *New York Times*, August 28, 2022, https://www.nytimes.com/2022/08/28/world/americas/maya-train-mexico -amlo.html.

66. EZLN, "And, We Broke the Siege," *Enlace Zapatista*, August 17, 2019, https:// enlacezapatista.ezln.org.mx/2019/08/20/communique-from-the-ezln-ccri-cg -and-we-broke-the-siege.

67. EZLN, "EZLN Closes Caracoles Due to Coronavirus and Calls on People not to Abandon Current Struggles," *Enlace Zapatista*, March 16, 2020, https://enlace zapatista.ezln.org.mx/2020/03/17/ezln-closes-caracoles-due-to-coronavirus-and -calls-on-people-not-to-abandon-current-struggles.

68. Subcomandante Insurgente Moisés, "Part Six: A Mountain on the High Seas," *Enlace Zapatista*, October 5, 2020, https://enlacezapatista.ezln.org.mx/2020/10/07/ part-six-a-mountain-on-the-high-seas; Comandante Don Pablo Contreras y Subcomandante Insurgente Moisés, "Part One: A Declaration . . . for Life," *Enlace Zapatista*, January 1, 2021, https://enlacezapatista.ezln.org.mx/2021/01/01/part -one-a-declaration-for-life.

69. Sup Galeano, "421st Squadron," *Enlace Zapatista*, April 17, 2021, https://enlace zapatista.ezln.org.mx/2021/04/20/421st-squadron.

70. Subcomandante Insurgente Moisés, "Part Six."

71. Moisés, "Part Six."

72. Subcomandante Insurgente Moisés, Sup Galeano, and the Sixth Commission of the EZLN, "After the Battle, No Landscape Will Remain (On the Russian Army's Invasion of Ukraine)," *Enlace Zapatista*, March 2, 2022, https://enlacezapatista.ezln.org.mx/2022/03/07/after-the-battle-no-landscape-will-remain/; EZLN, "Alto a las Guerras: Ecos del Domingo 13," *Enlace Zapatista*, March 14, 2022, https://enlacezapatista.ezln.org.mx/2022/03/14/alto-a-las-guerras-ecos-del-domingo-13.

73. This is a "tax" that organized crime extorts from shops and business owners.

74. CCRI-CG del EZLN, "Chiapas on the Verge of Civil War," *Enlace Zapatista*, September 19, 2021, https://enlacezapatista.ezln.org.mx/2021/09/20/chiapas-on-the-verge-of-civil-war.

75. This expression is found in the ninth part of the communiqué, detailing the new structure of autonomy. See Subcomandante Moisés, "Ninth Part: The New Structure of Zapatista Autonomy," *Enlace Zapatista*, November 12, 2023, https://enlacezapatista.ezln.org.mx/2023/11/13/ninth-part-the-new-structure-of-zapastista-autonomy.

76. EZLN, "First Part: The Motives of the Wolf," *Enlace Zapatista*, October 22, 2023, https://enlacezapatista.ezln.org.mx/2023/10/23/first-part-the-motives-of-the-wolf.

77. Capitán Insurgente Marcos, "Second Part: Do Dead People Sneeze?" *Enlace Zapatista*, October 29, 2023, https://enlacezapatista.ezln.org.mx/2023/10/30/second-part-do-dead-people-sneeze.

78. Capitán Insurgente Marcos, "Third Part: Dení," *Enlace Zapatista*, November 2, 2023, https://enlacezapatista.ezln.org.mx/2023/11/03/third-part-deni.

79. At the same time, they confirmed that the autonomous spaces known as the Caracoles will remain.

80. Subcomandante Moisés, "Tenth Part: Regarding Pyramids and Their Uses and Customary Regimes," *Enlace Zapatista*, November 14, 2023, https://enlacezapatista.ezln.org.mx/2023/11/15/tenth-part-regarding-pyramids-and-their-uses-and-customary-regimes.

81. Subcomandante Moisés, "Ninth Part."

82. Subcomandante Moisés, "Ninth Part."

Chapter 1: "Autonomy Is the People's Life Itself"

1. First level textbooks for the course *Freedom According to the Zapatistas*. The four textbooks are: *Autonomous Government I, Autonomous Government II, Autonomous Resistance*, and *Participation of Women in Autonomous Government* (https://centro.community/escuelita/ and https://radiozapatista.org/?page_id=20294).

2. I would like to highlight the importance given to the arts and sciences, as shown by the Zapatista involvement in the "CompArte" (*sharing / with art*) and "ConSciencia" (*conscience / with science*) conferences. In August 2018, Subcomandante Galeano declared the following: "Our [own path] is based in some of the roots of

the originary (or Indigenous) communities: the collective, mutual support and solidarity, care for the earth, the cultivation of the arts and sciences, and constant vigilance against the accumulation of wealth. These roots, along with the arts and sciences, are our guide." Subcomandante Insurgente Moisés and SupGaleano, "300, Part II: A Continent as a Backyard, a Country as a Cemetery, Pensamiento Único as a Government Program, and a Small, Very Small, Ever So Small Rebellion," *Enlace Zapatista*, August 25, 2018, https://enlacezapatista.ezln.org.mx/2018/08/25/300 -part-ii-a-continent-as-a-backyard-a-country-as-a-cemetery-pensamiento-unico -as-a-government-program-and-a-small-very-small-ever-so-small-rebellion-sub comandante-insurgente-moises-supgalea.

Translators' note: Both *ejidos* and communal land are forms of collective or social land tenure, particular to Mexico. They are often indistinguishable in practice. *Ejidos* were collectively owned, but individually titled. Until the Reform of 1992, while it could be inherited, *ejido* land could not be bought or sold. Communal land is not individually titled, even though it is farmed individually, and *comuneros* cannot sell their lands, unless by agreement of the assembly, they convert to *ejidos*. A *cargo* is a traditional honorific responsibility assumed for a designated period in Indigenous and other Mexican rural communities. It entails a certain set of tasks that the person charged with it must carry out for the collective benefit. *Cargo*—literally, a burden—suggests that those who take them on are understood to do so as a service to the community.

3.   The relationship between community and territory is so close that, in Tsotsil (as well as other Mayan languages in Chiapas), the same word *jlumaltik*, designates the territory and the community that lives on it.

4.   Subcomandante Insurgente Marcos, "Entre el árbol y el bosque. Palabras del EZLN en la mesa redonda 'Frente al despojo capitalista,'" *Enlace Zapatista*, July 17, 2007, https://enlacezapatista.ezln.org.mx/2007/07/18/mesa-redonda-frente- al-despojo-capitalista-la-defensa-de-la-tierra-y-el-territorio-17-de-julio-de-2007. In the words of the Zapatista support bases: "All human beings should care for, respect, love, and defend the principal basis of the life of all living beings—Mother Earth. Because in it, we obtain all that we need for life, and from it we receive all our means of living. Mother Earth is the entire planet: the mountains, the valleys, the canyons, the lagoons, the rivers, the sea, the air, the plants, the animals. "Apunt- es de las bases de apoyo del EZLN para su participación en la compartición," *Re- beldía Zapatista*, September 3, 2014, 15.

5.   Congreso Nacional Indígena, Espejos, accessed January 9, 2024, https://www .congresonacionalindigena.org/espejos. The National Indigenous Congress and the EZLN have identified twenty-nine *espejos* (mirrors) throughout Mexico of In- digenous territories attacked by productive or infrastructural megaprojects.

6.   Alongside cultivation for self-subsistence are small parcels where families grow organic coffee that is mostly marketed through Zapatista cooperatives and inter-

national solidarity networks. The profits from the sale of the coffee allow them to buy needed products that the communities do not produce, such as cooking oil and sugar.

7. The extent of recuperated lands varies greatly across the different Zapatista zones. There is a great deal in Morelia, but almost none in Oventic in the Highlands.

8. *Autonomous Resistance: First-Grade Textbook for the Course "Freedom According to the Zapatistas,"* (material from the Zapatista Little School, 2013), https://ausm .community/wp-content/uploads/2014/09/EZLN-Autonomous-Resistance .pdf, 7–9, 77.

9. EZLN, *Critical Thought in the Face of the Capitalist Hydra I* (Durham, NC: Paperboat Press, 2016), 62–64.

10. *Autonomous Government II: First-Grade Textbook for the Course "Freedom According to the Zapatistas,"* 14, 20, 38–39. See also the presentation about autonomous health in the video "El pilar de la autonomía y la vida de los partidistas," given by the Tercios Compas del Caracol II, November 2018. Tercios Compas, "El pilar de la autonomía y la vida de los partidistas," *Vimeo*, 2018, https://vimeo.com/652507938.

11. *Autonomous Government II*, 4–5, 16–19, 29–30, 38–39; *Autonomous Government I: First-Grade Textbook for the Course "Freedom According to the Zapatistas"* (material from the Zapatista Little School, 2013), https://ausm.community/wp-content/uploads/2014/09/EZLN-Autonomous-Government-I.pdf, 26.

12. "We are teaching our promoter how to go about educating. Without someone to guide them, there is no education. We are showing them where to walk." Family elder, La Garrucha zone, 2007, cited in Bruno Baronnet, *Autonomía y educación indígena: Las escuelas zapatistas de la Selva Lacandona en Chiapas*, México (Quito: Abya-Yala editores, 2012), 128.

13. "The education promoters are simple: It is not that they are teachers, they are young adults who know how to read and write and help with that." *Autonomous Government II*, 38.

14. "Our education comes from our word. It is our knowledge because it always comes from the community, because we promoters are in partnership with the children we support. Each shares with the others what they know, working to learn together, step by step, always as equals." Educational promoter, La Garrucha zone, quoted in Baronnet, *Autonomía y educación indígena*, 122.

15. "While teaching natural sciences, we should . . . incorporate the scientific knowledge with that of our Indigenous peoples, as well as the empirical knowledge of the students." Cited in Raúl Gutiérrez Narváez, "Dos proyectos de sociedad en Los Altos de Chiapas. Escuelas secundarias oficial y autónoma entre los tsotsiles de San Andrés" in *Luchas Muy Otras: Zapatismo y Autonomía en las Comunidades Indígenas de Chiapas*, ed. Bruno Baronnet, Mariana Mora Bayo, and Richard Stahler-Sholk (Mexico City: Universidad Autónoma Metropolitana, 2011), 257, https://www

.casadelibrosabiertos.uam.mx/contenido/contenido/Libroelectronico/luchas_muy_otras.pdf.

16. Comments regarding the administration of Autonomous Municipality Francisco Villa, La Garrucha zone, in Paulina Fernández Christlieb, *Justicia Autónoma Zapatista: Zona Selva Tzeltal* (Mexico City: Ediciones autónom@s, 2014), 341–44.

17. Press release, June 9, 1995, cited in Guiomar Rovira, *Women of Maize: Indigenous women and the Zapatista rebellion*, trans. Anna Keave (London: Latin America Bureau, 2000).

18. Subcomandante Marcos, "¡Insurgentas! (La Mar en marzo)," March 8, 2000, in EZLN, *Documentos y Comunicados 4, 14 de febrero de 1997/2 de diciembre de 2000*, First edition (Mexico City: Ediciones Era, 2003), 418.

19. EZLN, *Critical Thought*, 107.

20. *Participation of Women in Autonomous Government. First-Grade Textbook for the Course "Freedom According to the Zapatistas"* (material from the Zapatista Little School, 2013), https://ausm.community/wp-content/uploads/2014/09/EZLN-Participation-of-Women-in-Autonomous-Government.pdf, 24, 53–58, 71–72.

21. *Participation of Women*, 12.

22. *Participation of Women*, 11.

23. María, of Marez Francisco Villa, Caracol III, quoted in *Participation of Women*, 41.

24. Yolanda, of Marez Magdalena de la Paz, Caracol II, quoted in *Participation of Women*, 25.

25. Ana, of Marez El Trabajo, Caracol V, quoted in *Participation of Women*, 71–72.

26. Colectivo de promotorxs de educación (Oventik), *La Libertad*, CompArte, 2018, https://radiozapatista.org/wp-content/uploads/2018/08/IMG_3360_1024x683.jpg.

27. EZLN, *Critical Thought*, 108.

28. *Participation of Women*, 18.

29. EZLN, *Documentos y Comunicados 5: La Marcha del Color de la Tierra, 2 de diciembre de 2000/4 de abril de 2001*, First edition (Mexico City: Ediciones Era, 2003), 305.

30. For example: "Then neoliberal globalization wants to destroy the nations of the world so that only one nation or country remains, the country of money, of capital." EZLN, "Sixth Declaration from the Lacandon Jungle," *Enlace Zapatista*, June 30, 2005, https://enlacezapatista.ezln.org.mx/2005/06/30/sixth-declaration-of-the-selva-lacandona.

31. Quoted in Jérôme Baschet, "La Escuelita zapatista y el contagio de la autonomía" in Baschet, *La Escuelita Zapatista* (Guadalajara: Grietas Editores, 2014), 175–218.

32. EZLN, *Critical Thought*, 78.

33. EZLN, *Critical Thought*, 79–80. Subcomandante Moisés explains how this also takes place among those who train the education and health promoters, saying

that they do not receive a wage or any other kind of monetary support, but their communities support them by tending to their *milpas*, coffee crops, and animals.

34. *Autonomous Resistance,* 7–8, 54. For example, collective work at a regional level (in this case, the organization of a warehouse so that the communities' grocery stores can stock up) makes it possible to support the health promoters at the Hospital San José del Río, at the Caracol de La Realidad. Collective work is not only working the fields and tending the animals: it can mean a corner or grocery store, handicraft production, transportation, and even tourism, as in the case of the swimming spots at Morelia.

35. Christlieb, *Justicia Autónoma,* 114.

36. Christlieb, *Justicia Autónoma,* 211.

37. While he underscores their limited use of money, Subcomandante Moisés explains that these needs led them to create "Zapatista banks." These are solidarity funds used to make loans with very low interest rates, particularly to support those with serious illnesses. EZLN, *Critical Thought,* 82–83.

38. The "struggle that the people make" is "to build their good life." "Apuntes de bases de apoyo del EZLN para su participación en la compartición," *Rebeldía zapatista* 3, September 2014, 23.

39. The description of the levels of autonomous government is mostly based on what I learned at the Little School and on the information compiled in the Little School's four textbooks. I also draw on Subcomandante Moisés's explanations in *Critical Thought.* EZLN, *Critical Thought,* 115–55.

40. See the wide-ranging investigation of Paulina Fernández Christlieb, *Justicia Autónoma,* which I rely on for the examples mentioned and the quotations from the autonomous authorities of the zone of La Garrucha.

41. *Autonomous Government II,* 6–9. Translators' note: An *albañil* is a builder or construction worker, usually one with many skills.

42. Christlieb, *Justicia Autónoma,* 134.

43. *Autonomous Government I,* 3.

44. Teacher Fidel, personal communication during the author's participation in the Little School, Cideci-Unitierra, August 2013.

45. *Autonomous Government I,* 20, 39.

46. Teacher Marisol, personal communication during the author's participation in the Little School, Cideci-Unitierra, August 2013.

47. "There are things which were done with the people's participation and can now be done without consulting the people. . . . If the people are not consulted, that's when we get nonconformity, and then the people get demoralized." *Autonomous Government I,* 51–52.

48. The portrait of "Compa Jolil," president of an autonomous municipality, is exemplary of the modesty with which a *cargo* is carried out. Although the *cargos* do have prestige, this does not mean that the person who assumes one is more important

than the rest. Paulina Fernández, "Compa Jolil, or the motivations of the autonomous Zapatista authorities," *Second international seminar of reflection and analysis,
Planet Earth: Anti-systemic movements* (Cideci-Unitierra, January 1, 2012), https://
radiozapatista.org/?p=4996&lang=en.

49. Subcomandante Insurgente Marcos, "Tercer Viento: Un digno y rabioso color de
la tierra. Tercer mesa del 3 de Enero," *Enlace Zapatista*, January 4, 2009, https://
enlacezapatista.ezln.org.mx/2009/01/04/tercer-viento-un-digno-y-rabioso-color
-de-la-tierra-tercer-mesa-del-3-de-enero.

50. Teacher Fidel, personal communication during the author's participation in the
Little School, Cideci-Unitierra, August 2013.

51. Teacher Jacobo, personal communication during the author's participation in the
Little School, Cideci-Unitierra, August 2013.

52. This alludes to the distinction proposed by John Holloway between "power-over"
and "power-to" (which is discussed below, in the first section of chapter 2).

53. Teacher Jacobo, personal communication during the author's participation in the
Little School, Cideci-Unitierra, August 2013.

54. In precisely this way Jacques Rancière defines democracy as "the power peculiar to
those who have no more entitlements to govern than to submit." Jacques Rancière,
Hatred of Democracy (New York: Verso, 2014).

55. *Autonomous Resistance*, 37–38.

56. Christlieb, *Justicia autónoma*, 326–45.

57. Zapatista support bases designate exhaustion as one of the principal difficulties
they experience (for example, see Christlieb, *Justicia autónoma*, 339).

58. Comandante David, "Discurso del Comandante David en el aniversario del 1 de
enero de 1994 (1 de enero de 2009)," *Enlace Zapatista*, enlacezapatista.ezln.org
.mx/2009/01/02/acto-de-conmemoracion-al-15-aniversario-del-levantamiento
-armado-oventic-1-de-enero-de-2009. See also *Autonomous Resistance*, 38–39.

59. Christlieb, *Justicia autónoma*, 315–18.

60. Author's note (January 2024): In the years since this book was first written in 2018,
and especially since the Covid-19 pandemic, the temptation to migrate to the United States and stay for a few years has once again spread widely among the Indigenous youth of Chiapas, and even among Zapatistas.

61. The young Zapatista Selena expressed a critical attitude toward migration during
the seminar "Critical Thought in the Face of the Capitalist Hydra." She compares
non-Zapatista youth, whom she qualifies as "poor-poor" with the Zapatistas:
"They are poor like us, but they are also poor thinkers because they leave their
communities and when they come back, they bring bad ideas with them, other
ways of living. . . . On the other hand, we Zapatistas are poor but rich in thinking.
Why? Because even though we have shoes and clothes and cellphones, we don't
change our thinking or our way of life, because it doesn't matter to us as Zapatista youth how we are dressed or what kinds of things we have. What's important

to us is that the work we do is for the good of the community." EZLN, *Critical Thought*, 104.

62. *Autonomous Government I*, 51–52.

63. *Autonomous Government I*, 31–33.

64. In regard to the formation of autonomous municipalities, "The Thirteenth Stele" explains that they would be "detached" from the political-military structure of the EZLN. The same logic was repeated on a larger scale with the creation of the Good Government Councils. "The Thirteenth Stele. Part Five: A History," *The Struggle Site*, July 2003, https://struggle.ws/mexico/ezln/2003/marcos/history JULY.html.

65. Subcomandante Marcos, "Reading a video, part 2: Two flaws," *Alainet*, August 21, 2004, https://www.alainet.org/es/node/110505.

66. *Autonomous Government I*, 15. "Two decades ago the EZLN was the organization, referent, and the leadership of the Indigenous communities. Today it is they who lead us, and we who obey. Before, we directed and organized them; now our work is to see how we can support their decisions. Before we were out in front, marking the way toward destiny. Today we are behind our *pueblos*, often running to catch up with them." Subcomandante Galeano, "Lessons on Geography and Globalized Calendars," April 14, 2017, *Enlace Zapatista*, https://enlacezapatista.ezln.org .mx/2017/05/08/lessons-on-geography-and-globalized-calendars.

67. Subcomandante Marcos said of the growth of the EZLN in the eighties: "The military structure of the EZLN somewhat 'contaminated' a tradition of democracy and self-government. One way to say it is that the EZLN was an anti-democratic element within a relation of direct community democracy," "The Thirteenth Stele."

68. Concerning the relation between the civil and the military, the Sixth Declaration recognizes: "They say it's easy, but in practice it's difficult because it takes many years, first preparing for war, then the war itself, and the political-military becomes a habit." EZLN, "Sixth Declaration."

69. "Apuntes de las bases de apoyo del EZLN para su participación en la compartición," *Rebeldía zapatista* 3 (September 2014): 21. The document clarifies: "These six points [mentioned in the quote] are meant to do away with individual leadership at all levels. In this way we are re-organizing and re-educating ourselves . . . all the time, every day, and at all hours."

70. "Resistance is what allows us to build autonomy. If there is no resistance, we can't keep building autonomy." An explanation by my *votán* in the Little School. Personal communication during the author's participation in the Little School, Cideci-Unitierra, August 2013.

71. Drafts of *Civil War in France*, quoted by Teodor Shanin in *Late Marx and the Russian Road* (New York: Monthly Review Press, 1983), 89.

72. "We have our small slice of freedom." Subcomandante Insurgente Moisés, "The Capitalist World is a Walled Plantation," April 12, 2017, *Enlace Zapatista*, https://enlace

zapatista.ezln.org.mx/2017/04/26/the-capitalist-world-is-a-walled-plantation
-subcomandante-insurgente-moises.

73. Subcomandante Moisés, personal communication during the author's participation in the Little School, Cideci-Unitierra, August 2013.

74. In the words of one of the Zapatista support bases: "It is our path; they are our steps. We have conquered our liberty, and no one has given it to us. We don't owe it to anyone. It is our history that we make each day, every hour, everywhere." ("Apuntes de las bases de apoyo del EZLN para su participación en la compartición," *Rebeldía zapatista* 3 [September 2014]: 26).

    In the homage to Professor Galeano (May 2014), Subcomandante Marcos affirmed that "there are thousands of compañeros and compañeras like him in the Indigenous Zapatista communities, with the same determination, the same commitment, the same clarity, and one single destination: freedom." "Between Light and Shadow," *Enlace Zapatista*, May 24, 2014, https://enlacezapatista.ezln.org.mx/2014/05/27/between-light-and-shadow.

75. The first expression was used by the support bases in the autonomous municipality of November 17, in the region of Morelia: "Autonomy is for life, it is about the possibility of a new life," cited in Mariana Mora, *Kuxlejal Politics: Indigenous Autonomy, Race, and Decolonizing Research in Zapatista Communities* (Austin: University of Texas Press, 2017), 18. The second seems to be more common throughout Zapatista communities and was used in the play *La muerte y la vida*, performed by support bases in the La Realidad region in the 2018 CompArte Festival (Caracol of Morelia, August 9).

76. This section was written in January 2024 for the English edition.

77. Subcomandante Insurgente Moisés, "Ninth Part: The new structure of Zapatista Autonomy," *Enlace Zapatista*, November 13, 2023, https://enlacezapatista.ezln.org.mx/2023/11/13/ninth-part-the-new-structure-of-zapastista-autonomy.

78. It is necessary to distinguish between "regions" and "zones." Regions, consisting of various communities, existed before, but only as an organizational level in the EZLN's military structure, and not as a unit within the structures of civilian autonomy. The zones are much bigger entities that—prior to this new stage—joined together various municipalities (while the municipality grouped together various "regions").

79. The Captain, "Tenth Part: Regarding pyramids and their uses and customary regimes," *Enlace Zapatista*, November 15, 2023, https://enlacezapatista.ezln.org.mx/2023/11/15/tenth-part-regarding-pyramids-and-their-uses-and-customary-regimes.

80. The Captain, "Twentieth and Last Part: The Common and Non-Property," *Enlace Zapatista*, December 22, 2023, https://enlacezapatista.ezln.org.mx/2023/12/22/twentieth-and-last-part-the-common-and-non-property.

81. The Captain, "Twentieth and Last Part."

Chapter 2: "We Can Govern Ourselves"

1. Subcomandante Marcos, "Carta de Marcos a Gaspar Morquecho," February 2, 1994 in EZLN, *Documentos y Comunicados 1, 1 de enero de 1994/8 de agosto de 1994*, First edition (1994; Sixth reprint, Mexico City: Ediciones Era, 2003), 125.

2. Subcomandante Marcos, "Encuentro Internacional por la Humanidad y Contra el Neoliberalismo," May 1996, in EZLN, *Documentos y Comunicados 3, 2 de octubre de 1995/24 de enero de 1997*, First edition (1997; First reprint, Mexico City: Ediciones Era, 1998), 258.

3. Subcomandante Marcos, "First Declaration of La Realidad for Humanity and against Neoliberalism," January 1996, *The Struggle Site*, https://www.struggle.ws/mexico/ezln/ccri_1st_dec_real.html.

4. Subcomandante Marcos, "A la sociedad civil," August 30, 1996, in EZLN, *Documentos y Comunicados 3*, 371.

5. EZLN, "Fourth Declaration of the Lacandon Jungle" in Subcomandante Insurgente Marcos, *¡Ya Basta!: Ten Years of the Zapatista Uprising*, ed. Žiga Vodovnik (Oakland: AK Press, 2004), 667. Translators' note: The FZLN was an initiative of the EZLN in 1997 to create a civil society organization adhering to the same ideology as the Zapatista army. It dissolved in 2005 with the "Sixth Declaration of the Lacandon Jungle" and the preparations for the Other Campaign.

6. For example: "the EZLN does not struggle in order to take Power," Subcomandante Galeano and Subcomandante Moisés, "A story to try to understand," *Enlace Zapatista*, November 26, 2016, https://enlacezapatista.ezln.org.mx/2016/11/26/a-story-to-try-to-understand. Translators' note: For Baschet's use of the notion of the "Zapatista word," see Introduction.

7. Subcomandante Marcos, "Entrevista al Subcomandante Marcos por Julio Scherer," March 10, 2001, in EZLN, *Documentos y Comunicados 5: La Marcha del Color de la Tierra, 2 de diciembre de 2000/4 de abril de 2001*, First edition (Mexico City: Ediciones Era, 2003), 351–52. Translators' note: Scherer is the founder of Proceso, Mexico's premier magazine for investigative reporting.

8. Translators' note: This is when Villa and Zapata's armies forced Carranza out of Mexico City, marking the high point of the Mexican Revolution. They briefly occupied the capital before choosing to leave it and fight from their respective territories. The episode at the foot of the presidential chair has become symbolic of the political ideologies and dilemmas of the revolutionaries, since both men were reluctant to sit in the chair. Villa suggested taking turns, while Zapata refused to sit in it at all and suggested burning it instead. After retaking Mexico City, Carranza made it his power base for defeating Zapata and Villa.

9. Subcomandante Marcos, "Letter to Angel Luis Lara, alias El Ruso: sobre la inauguración del Aguascalientes en Madrid," *Enlace Zapatista*, October 12, 2002, enlacezapatista.ezln.org.mx/2002/10/12/a-angel-luis-lara-alias-el-ruso-sobre-la-inauguracion-del-aguascalientes-en-madrid.

10. "Together we know that within our rebellions is our "NO" to the politics of destruction that capitalism carries out across the world. And we know that within our resistances are the seeds of the world that we want." August 2014, https:// enlacezapatista.ezln.org.mx/2014/10/13/invitation-to-the-world-festival-of -resistances-and-rebellions-against-capitalism-where-those-above-destroy-we -below-rebuild-2. Also: "We continue to walk with two feet: rebellion and resistance, the 'no' and the 'yes,' the 'no' to the system and the 'yes' to our autonomy, which means that we have to construct our own path toward life." "300, Part II," August 2018, https://enlacezapatista.ezln.org.mx/2018/08/25/300-part-ii-a-continent-as -a-backyard-a-country-as-a-cemetery-pensamiento-unico-as-a-government -program-and-a-small-very-small-ever-so-small-rebellion-subcomandante -insurgente-moises-supgalea. Regarding the use of these notions, one can consult my contribution "Resistencia, rebelión, insurrección" in *Conceptos y fenómenos fundamentales de nuestro tiempo*, edited by Pablo González Casanova (Mexico City: UNAM, 2013), conceptos.sociales.unam.mx/conceptos_final/487trabajo.pdf.

11. *Change the World without Taking Power: The Meaning of Revolution Today* (London: Pluto Press, 2002).

12. On this debate, see the bibliographic notes at the end of the book.

13. Subcomandante Marcos, "Platica con los miembros de la caravana que llegaron a La Garrucha," *Enlace Zapatista*, August 2, 2008, enlacezapatista.ezln .org.mx/2008/08/02/platica-del-sci-marcos-y-el-tte-coronel-i-moises-con -los-miembros-de-la-caravana-que-llegaron-al-caracol-de-la-garrucha.

14. Subcomandante Marcos, "Intervención del Subcomandante Marcos en la Mesa 1 del Encuentro Intercontinental," July 30, 1996 in EZLN, *Documentos y Comunicados* 3, 323.

15. "This was, therefore, a revolution not against this or that, legitimate, constitutional, republican or imperialist form of state power. *It was a revolution against the state itself*, of this supernaturalist abortion of society, a resumption by the people for the people of its own social life." "The Character of the Commune," *The Civil War in France, First Draft*, 1871, cited by Maximilien Rubel, "Marx, theoretician of anarchism," Marxists Internet Archive, 1973, https://www.marxists.org/archive/ rubel/1973/marx-anarchism.htm (my italics).

16. Karl Marx, "The Civil War in France," Marxists Internet Archive, 2010, https:// www.marxists.org/archive/marx/works/download/pdf/civil_war_france.pdf. Translators' note: Marx's phrase here is also commonly translated as "local municipal liberty."

17. CCRI-CG del EZLN, "Otras Formas de Lucha," January 25, 1994, in EZLN, *Documentos y Comunicados 1*, 103.

18. Subcomandante Insurgente Galeano, "Between Light and Shadow," May 24, 2014, *Enlace Zapatista*, https://enlacezapatista.ezln.org.mx/2014/05/27/between-light -and-shadow.

19. Subcomandante Insurgente Marcos, "The Seven Loose Pieces of the Global Jigsaw Puzzle (Neoliberalism as a Puzzle)," June 1997, in ¡Ya Basta!: Ten Years of the Zapatista Uprising, ed. Žiga Vodovnik (Oakland: AK Press, 2004), 257–79.

20. Subcomandante Marcos. "First Declaration of La Realidad for Humanity and against Neoliberalism," January 30, 1996, The Struggle Site, https://www.struggle.ws/mexico/ezln/ccri_1st_dec_real.html.

21. Ignacio Ramonet, Marcos. La dignité rebelle: conversations avec le sous-commandant Marcos (París: Galilée, 2001), 65–66.

22. Subcomandante Marcos, "The World: Seven Thoughts in May 2003," El Kilombo, May 2003, translated by Irlandesa, https://elkilombo.org/documents/seven thoughtsmarcos.html.

23. Marcos, "Seven Thoughts."

24. Insofar as Marcos affirms that the society of power doesn't seek to constitute a world state, this is distinct from the thesis of Empire in the works of Michael Hardt and Antonio Negri. Michael Hardt and Antonio Negri, Empire (Cambridge: Harvard University Press, 2000). For them, Empire implies a new regime of sovereignty that integrates national states in a supranational structure, with the production of a sovereign supranational law, and above all with a political force that has the authority to regulate the world market, the international monetary system, and the use of military force.

25. Subcomandante Marcos, "SCI Marcos: De la Reflexión Crítica, Individu@s y Colectiv@s. Carta Segunda a Luis Villoro en el Intercambio Epistolar sobre Ética y Política," Radio Zapatista, April 12, 2011, https://radiozapatista.org/?p=2513.

26. EZLN, Critical Thought in the Face of the Capitalist Hydra I (Durham, NC: Paperboat Press, 2016), 263.

27. The role of the state in neoliberalism is not homogeneous and, in fact, we can distinguish three different stages: a) in its beginnings, above all at the beginning of the 1980s, national states (and their political classes) implemented the decisions that led to the neoliberal reconfiguration of capitalism (liberalization of financial markets; public debt, privatizations, etc.), themselves creating the conditions for the destruction of their own sovereignty; b) at the end of the 1980s and in the following decade, there was a brief "golden age" of neoliberalism during which, once the conditions had been created for growth, the state could reduce its interventions in the economy; c) the crash of 2000 and the crisis of 2007–09 proved that only states could avoid the contagion of crisis by huge programs of support to businesses and banks, reminding us that the state had always been the ultimate guarantor of the free market. This points toward a certain recuperation of state interventionism without it meaning the end of neoliberalism; it could simply be an inflexion within the neoliberal phase of capitalism.

28. It is possible to debate the relationship between the state and the nation, since if

the EZLN no longer considers the defense of the state as relevant to the anticapitalist struggle, it still maintains a positive view of the nation that it tries to rescue from its ongoing destruction (recall that the struggle for national liberation, the inheritance of anti-imperialist perspectives, is inscribed in the name of the EZLN itself). It remains to ask if such a dissociation between the state and the nation isn't in fact impossible when historically they have gone hand in hand (the construction of the nation and its imaginary being a determinant element in the imposition of state power). Or perhaps is it possible to elaborate another sense of the nation understood as the (multiple marginalized peoples—*abajos*) the marginals in all their multiplicity that doesn't necessarily translate into the state form (as Subcomandante Marcos suggested in his interview with J. Scherer). Subcomandante Marcos, "Entrevista," 371.

29.   Subcomandante Insurgente Moisés and Subcomandante Galeano, "300, Part II."

30.   See Ernst Lohoff and Norbert Trenkle, *La grande dévalorisation. Pourquoi la spéculation et la dette de l'État ne sont pas les causes de la crise* (París: Post-Éditions, 2014).

31.   It is worth sharing the following: "Because what we are fighting for is for the state to become part of the museum of the prehistory of humanity," so that in the future one could say "that monster dominated us, subordinated us, and frightened us day and night . . . until one day we decided that it was time to say enough! So we got it in order, and we disappeared it." Sergio Rodríguez Lascano, *La crisis del poder y nosotr@s* (Mexico City: Ediciones Rebeldía, 2010), 76.

32.   Subcomandante Marcos, "SCI Marcos. A Death . . . Or a Life "(Fourth Letter to Don Luis Villoro in the Exchange on Ethics and Politics), *Enlace Zapatista*, December 12, 2011, https://enlacezapatista.ezln.org.mx/2011/12/12/sci-marcos-a-deathor-a-life-fourth-letter-to-don-luis-villoro-in-the-exchange-on-ethics-and-politics.

33.   EZLN, *Critical Thought*, 164.

34.   "A Storm and a Prophecy—Chiapas: The Southeast in Two Winds" (1992) in Marcos, *Our Word Is Our Weapon*, 22–38. Also: "From above, only wars and catastrophes will come. From below, the peace with democracy, liberty, justice, and dignity will be born, and that is how we name the world which we all want." "Of bombs, firefighters and light bulbs," *The Struggle Site*, November 1998, https://www.struggle.ws/mexico/ezln/1998/ccri_bombs_cs_nov98.html, as well as "Above and Below: Masks and Silences," in ¡*Ya Basta!*, 319–41.

35.   Translators' note: The transcript is available at "Subcomandante Marcos, entrevista con Julio Scherer," *Enlace Zapatista*, March 10, 2001, https://enlacezapatista.ezln.org.mx/2001/03/10/subcamandante-marcos-entrevista-con-julio-scherer.

36.   EZLN, "Them and Us. v. the Sixth," *Enlace* Zapatista, January 27, 2013, https://enlacezapatista.ezln.org.mx/2013/01/27/them-and-us-v-the-sixth.

37. "Editorial: Más allá de la compartición," *Rebeldía zapatista* 3 (September 2014): 1–2.

38. "When you look to the left, you should not look up, but down. The above is just a capitulation with seats and governments, disguised as modern good sense." Subcomandante Marcos, "Abajo a la Izquierda," *Enlace Zapatista*, February 28, 2005, https://enlacezapatista.ezln.org.mx/2005/02/28/abajo-a-la-izquierda. The expression "the politics from above" can be found, for example, in Subcomandante Marcos, "Ellos y Nosotros, parte VII: L@s más pequeñ@s," *Enlace Zapatista*, February 21, 2013, https://enlacezapatista.ezln.org.mx/2013/02/21/them-and-us-vii-the-smallest-of-them-all.

39. Subcomandante Insurgente Marcos, "On Wars: First letter by Subcomandante Insurgente Marcos to Don Luis Villoro," *Radio Zapatista*, January–February 2011, https://radiozapatista.org/pdf/Marcos_letter.pdf.

40. Subcomandante Marcos, "Carta Segunda Sobre la Ética y Política."

41. Sup Marcos "Them and Us. VI. - the Gaze," *Enlace Zapatista*, February 9, 2013, https://enlacezapatista.ezln.org.mx/2013/02/09/them-and-us-vi-the-gaze.

42. EZLN, "Them and Us. v. the Sixth." The relationship between the above and the below is synthesized in the "Mandón," a figure of power in all its dimensions, from the most mythical to its incarnations in capital and the State. For example: "Then the first gods explained to them that the time was going to come when Mandón was going to want to dominate the entire world and enslave everything the world had, that he was going to destroy and kill. That Mandón's strength was to be great, and there would not be an equal force in the world then. The only way to resist and fight against Mandón was to be many and different, so that Mandón doesn't just grab them as one and defeat them all." "Séptimo Viento: Unos Muertos Dignos Y Rabiosos," *Enlace Zapatista*, January 6, 2009, https://enlacezapatista.ezln.org.mx/2009/01/05/sexto-viento-una-otra-digna-rabia. See also "Them and Us. VI. - The Gaze"; as well as EZLN, *Critical Thought*, 19, 236.

43. "Let's look in any corner of the planet and find ourselves, as equals, without above or below, without command or obedience, with women defying the destiny of utilitarian decoration; with young people resisting conformism and resignation; with the other loves that protest against the abnormality with which they are cataloged and classified; with the workers and peasants resisting the four sharp-toothed wheels of capitalism, and with the Indigenous people who are guardians of the land, the mother, and life." Subcomandante Marcos, "De la política, sus finales y sus principios," *Enlace* Zapatista, June 11, 2007, https://enlacezapatista.ezln.org.mx/2007/06/12/de-la-politica-sus-finales-y-sus-principios.

44. Subcomandante Marcos, "Abajo A la Izquierda."

45. Sup Marcos, "Them and Us. VII. - the Smallest of them All," *Enlace Zapatista*, February 21, 2013, https://enlacezapatista.ezln.org.mx/2013/02/21/them-and-us-vii-the-smallest-of-them-all.

46. "Below is the child, yes. Knowing how to look at him, we will be able to look into tomorrow." Subcomandante Marcos, "Palabras del Subcomandante Marcos en la UNAM," March 21, 2001, in EZLN, *Documentos y Comunicados 5*, 266.

47. Communiqué adopting the National Democratic Convention resolutions, August 18, 1994, in EZLN, *Documentos y Comunicados 2, 15 de agosto de 1994/29 de septiembre de 1995*, First edition (1995; Third reprint, Mexico City: Ediciones Era, 2001), 27. The EZLN also clarifies "its commitment not to interfere in the holding of elections within rebel territories," August 15, 1994, EZLN, *Documentos y Comunicados 2*, 25–26.

48. EZLN, *Critical Thought*, 294–97.

49. EZLN, 294–97.

50. "Carta al niño Miguel," March 6, 1994, in EZLN, *Documentos y Comunicados 1*, 191–93 (it also calls for abandoning "the love of death and the fascination with martyrdom"). "The Sixth Declaration of the Lacandon Jungle" also indicates that "the Zapatistas are soldiers in order for there to be no soldiers," EZLN, "Sixth Declaration of the Lacandon Jungle."

51. CCRI-CG del EZLN, "Opening Remarks at the First Intercontinental *Encuentro* for Humanity and against Neoliberalism," July 27, 1996, in Marcos, *Our Word Is Our Weapon*, 111.

52. EZLN, *Documentos y Comunicados 1*, 95–99, 102–04.

53. Subcomandante Marcos, "Discurso del Subcomandante Marcos ante la CND," August 8, 1994, in EZLN, *Documentos y Comunicados 1*, 305–12.

54. Subcomandante Marcos, "Entrevista," 343.

55. *Primer Coloquio Internacional in Memoriam Andrés Aubry "Planeta tierra, movimientos antisistémicos* (San Cristóbal de Las Casas: Cideci-Universidad de la Tierra, 2009), 231–32. The symposium took place in December, 2007.

56. They reiterate this connection in "300, part III," a communique from August 29, 2018. They not only assert their willingness to confront "any and every overseer," but also "those whose intentions for hegemony and imposed homogeneity lie just below their vanguardist dreams." "300, part III," *Enlace Zapatista*, August 29, 2018, https://enlacezapatista.ezln.org.mx/2018/08/29/300-part-iii-a-challenge-real-autonomy-an-answer-multiple-proposals-and-a-few-anecdotes-about-the-number-300.

57. Subcomandante Marcos, "Them and Us. v. the Sixth."

58. Marcos, "Séptimo Viento."

59. Sup Marcos, "Them and Us: I- the (Un)reasonables above," *Enlace Zapatista*, January 23, 2013, https://enlacezapatista.ezln.org.mx/2013/01/23/them-and-us-i-the-unreasonables-above.

60. Galeano, "Between light and shadow."

61. *Planeta Tierra*, 232.

62. A fuller evaluation is available in various installments of Marcos, "The Zapatistas and the Otra: The Pedestrians of History," *Anarkismo*, September 25, 2006, https://www.anarkismo.net/article/3798.

63. Translators' note: The *Sexta* refers to the loose organization of adherents to "The Sixth Declaration of the Lacandon Jungle."

64. Sup Marcos, "Them and Us. VI. - the Gaze."

65. "Them and Us, v.- the Sixth." Earlier, in the closing address of the 1996 International Encounter, they spoke about creating "an echo that turns itself into many voices, into a network of voices that, seeing Power to be deaf, decides to speak to itself, knowing itself to be one and many, finding itself in its desire to listen and be listened to, recognising itself as different in the tonalities and levels of voices forming it." ("Closing Words of the EZLN at the Intercontinental Encounter, 2nd Declaration of La Realidad," *United Diversity Library*, https://library.uniteddiversity.coop/More_Books_and_Reports/Zapatista_2nd_Declaration_LaRealidad.pdf).

66. Moises and Galeano, "300, Part III."

67. Sup Marcos, "Them and Us. VI. - The Gaze."

68. We find an example of this in 2011, during the Movement for Peace with Justice and Dignity, in the EZLN's response to Javier Sicilia's decision to dialogue with the state's Executive: "It's true that we don't yet understand why the movement has dedicated so much energy and effort to interaction with a political class that long ago lost any will to govern and is really no more than a gang of criminals. Maybe they will go about discovering it for themselves. But we don't judge and, thus, we neither condemn nor absolve. We try to understand their steps and the yearning that drives them." Subcomandante Marcos, "Perhaps ... (Third Letter to Don Luis Villoro in the interchange on Ethics and Politics)," *Radio Zapatista*, August 25, 2011, https://radiozapatista.org/?p=3963&lang=en.

69. Marcos, "Séptimo Viento."

70. Marcos, "Them and Us I."

71. CCRI-CG del EZLN, "Second Declaration of La Realidad and against Neoliberalism," August 3, 1996, in Marcos, *Our Word Is Our Weapon*, 124–26; Subcomandante Insurgente Moisés and Subcomandante Insurgente Galeano, "300 Part III."

72. "Siete pensamientos en mayo de 2003," *Rebeldía*, May 7, 2003, 5.

73. Marcos, "Fourth Letter to Don Luis Villoro."

74. Marcos, "Fourth Letter to Don Luis Villoro."

75. Le Bot and Marcos, *El Sueño Zapatista*, 146.

76. See the bibliographic notes at the end of the book.

77. "Conferencia de prensa durante los Diálogos de San Andrés," *La Jornada*, June 10, 1995, cited in John Holloway, "La revuelta de la dignidad," *Chiapas*, 5 (1997): 22–23.

78. CCRI-CG del EZLN, "Words of the EZLN in Puebla, Puebla," *The Struggle Site*, February 27, 2001, https://www.struggle.ws/mexico/ezln/2001/ccri/ccri_puebla_feb.html.

79. CCRI-CG del EZLN, "Words of the EZLN in Puebla."

80. Subcomandante Marcos, "The Story of Dreams," December 1995, in *Our Word Is Our Weapon*, 381.

81. Subcomandante Marcos, "Intervención del Subcomandante Marcos en la Mesa 1 del Encuentro Intercontinental," July 30, 1996 in EZLN, *Documentos y Comunicados 3*, 323.

82. Subcomandante Insurgente Marcos, "Tercer Viento: Un digno y rabioso color de la tierra. Tercer mesa del 3 de Enero," *Enlace Zapatista*, January 4, 2009, https://enlacezapatista.ezln.org.mx/2009/01/04/tercer-viento-un-digno-y-rabioso-color-de-la-tierra-tercer-mesa-del-3-de-enero.

83. Marcos, "Séptimo Viento."

84. *Planeta Tierra*, 21–22. The importance of partying and dancing had been highlighted for a long time: "It may seem little from a distance, but you see that recognizing the other, respecting them and listening to them, produces things as tremendously transcendental as a dance." ("Comunicado sobre las movilizaciones contra la matanza de Acteal," January 20, 1998, in EZLN, *Documentos y Comunicados 4*, 152).

85. Subcomandante Marcos, "Clausura del Encuentro Continental Americano," April 7, 1996, in EZLN, *Documentos y Comunicados 3*, 222; Le Bot and Marcos, *El Sueño Zapatista*, 302.

86. Marcos, "Tercer Viento."

87. *Planeta Tierra*, 233–39.

88. Marcos, "Clausura del Encuentro."

89. CCRI-CG del EZLN, "Demands Submitted by the Zapatistas during the Feb. '94 dialogue," *The Struggle Site*, March 1, 1994, https://www.struggle.ws/mexico/ezln/ccri_di_demand_mar94.html.

90. National Advisors of the EZLN, "The Dialogue of San Andres and the Rights of Indigenous Culture," *The Struggle Website*, February 15, 1996, https://www.struggle.ws/mexico/ezln/1996/advisors_on_SA_deal.html.

91. Teacher Elizabeth, Personal communication during the author's participation in the Little School, Cideci-Unitierra, August 2013.

92. "Palabra de la vocera Marichuy en Tehuacán, Puebla—19 de nov.," *Radio Zapatista*, November 20, 2017, https://radiozapatista.org/?p=23904.

93. Teacher Eloisa, personal communication during the author's participation in the Little School, Cideci-Unitierra, August 2013.

94. Filosofía del Derecho, 301, cited in Eric Weil, *Hegel y el Estado* (Buenos Aires: El Aleph, 1999), 115.

95. Giorgio Agamben, *Stasis: Civil War as a Political Paradigm* (Stanford, CA: Stanford University Press, 2015).

96. Agamben, *Stasis*.

97. Teacher Jacobo, personal communication during the author's participation in the Little School, Cideci-Unitierra, August 2013.

98. "We did not have a guide, we did not know how to make autonomy . . . we do not have a book to look at, to follow." *Autonomous Government I: First-Grade Textbook for the Course "Freedom According to the Zapatistas"* (material from the

Zapatista Little School, 2013), 44, https://ausm.community/wp-content/uploads /2014/09/EZLN-Autonomous-Government-I.pdf.

99. *Autonomous Government I*, 54.

100. For example, members of the Good Government Council in La Realidad divide into two groups that relieve each other every fifteen days, while in Oventik there are three groups that sit one week each. In La Realidad, at first the Council had eight members, then twelve, and later twenty-four. Initially, the Council members also served on the municipal council, but combining these two *cargos* proved to be too difficult and the roles were separated. *Autonomous Government I*, 9, 11, 25, 49.

101. For example, the system of low-interest loans accounts for situations when the debtor cannot repay the money. This manner of considering the specificity of each case, and even canceling loans whose repayment is impossible, is anything but a rigid application of the rules. *Autonomous Government II: First-Grade Textbook for the Course "Freedom According to the Zapatistas"* (material from the Zapatista Little School, 2013), https://ausm.community/wp-content/uploads/2014/09/ EZLN-Autonomous-Government-II.pdf.

102. Moisés and Galeano, "300, Part II."

103. Moisés and Galeano, "300, Part II."

104. In the opposition between *poder* and *potencia*, the Zapatista *other* politics is clearly on the side of the second. In the words of Sergio Rodríguez Lascano, the Zapatista experience seeks to generate "a dynamic force that does not accumulate power (*poder*) but rather communicates a power (*potencia*)." Sergio Rodríguez Lascano, *La crisis del poder y nosotr@s* (Mexico: Ediciones Rebeldia, 2010), 79.

105. The expression "against the state" is used here in the sense given by Pierre Clastres when he analyzes the mechanisms that existed in Amazonian societies to prevent the emergence of the state form that they did not yet know. *Society against the State: The Leader as Servant and the Humane Uses of Power Among the Indians of the Americas* (New York: Urizen Books, 1977).

106. EZLN, "May the Earth Tremble at Its Core," *Enlace Zapatista*, October 18, 2016, https://enlacezapatista.ezln.org.mx/2016/10/18/may-the-earth-tremble-at-its -core. On the notion of destitution and deficient process, see the bibliographic notes at the end of the book.

107. The mention of "power from below' (in opposition to "power from above") also appears in Subcomandante Insurgente Galeano, "Between Light and Shadow." In "Apuntes de las bases de apoyo del EZLN para su participación en la compartición," we find the expression "power of the people" used to refer to "governing ourselves in common," or, simply autonomy, i.e. in the same sense that we are proposing here ("Apuntes de las bases de apoyo del EZLN para su participación en la compartición," *Rebeldia Zapatista*, September 3, 2014, 19, 23).

Chapter 3: "For Humanity and against Capitalism!"

1. "Durito," April 10, 1994, in EZLN, *Documentos y Comunicados 1, 1 de enero de 1994/8 de agosto de 1994*, First edition (1994; Sixth reprint, Mexico City: Ediciones Era, 2003), 217–19.

2. EZLN, "Third Declaration from the Lacandon Jungle" in Subcomandante Insurgente Marcos, *¡Ya Basta!: Ten Years of the Zapatista Uprising*, ed. Žiga Vodovnik (Oakland: AK Press, 2004), 653–60; EZLN, *Documentos y Comunicados 2, 15 de agosto de 1994/29 de septiembre de 1995*, First edition (1995; Third reprint, Mexico City: Ediciones Era, 2001), 256–68.

3. Subcomandante Marcos, "The Seven Loose Pieces of the Global Jigsaw Puzzle (Neoliberalism as a Puzzle)" in Marcos, *¡Ya Basta!*, 257–79.

4. "Clausura del Encuentro Continental Americano," April 7, 1996 in EZLN, *Documentos y Comunicados 3, 2 de octubre de 1995/24 de enero de 1997*, First edition (1997; First reprint, Mexico City: Ediciones Era, 1998), 221–30.

5. *Crónicas intergalácticas. EZLN. Primer Encuentro Intercontinental por la Humanidad y contra el Neoliberalismo* (Mexico City: Planeta Tierra, 1997).

6. CCRI-CG del EZLN, "Second Declaration of La Realidad and against Neoliberalism," August 3, 1996, in Subcomandante Marcos, *Our Word is our Weapon: Selected Writings*, ed. Juana Ponce de León (New York: Seven Stories Press, 2001), 124–27.

7. Boaventura de Sousa Santos, "The World Social Forum and the Global Left," *Politics Society* 36, no. 2 (2008).

8. Before its main formulation in "The Seven Loose Pieces of the Global Jigsaw Puzzle," the term "Fourth World War" appears in "First Declaration of La Realidad for Humanity and against Neoliberalism" (January 30, 1996) and at various times during the same Intercontinental Meeting in 1996. Subcomandante Marcos, "The Seven Loose Pieces;" Subcomandante Insurgente Marcos, "First Declaration of La Realidad for Humanity and against Neoliberalism," *The Struggle Site*, https://www.struggle.ws/mexico/ezln/ccri_1st_dec_real.html). Subsequently, it appears in several documents mentioned below.

9. Subcomandante Galeano, "Trump, Ockham's Razor, Schrödinger's Cat, and the Cat-Dog," *Enlace Zapatista*, December 28, 2017, https://enlacezapatista.ezln.org.mx/2018/01/08/trump-ockhams-razor-schrodingers-cat-and-the-cat-dog.

10. "¿Cuáles son las características fundamentales de la IV Guerra Mundial? (plática en La Realidad, 20 de noviembre de 1999)," in Subcomandante Insurgente Marcos, *Escritos sobre la Guerra y la Economía Política*, ed. Sergio Rodríguez Lascano (Mexico City: Pensamiento Crítico Ediciones, 2017), 153–83; *Primer coloquio In memoriam Andrés Aubry. "Planeta Tierra: Movimientos Antisistémicos"* (San Cristóbal de Las Casas: Cideci-Universidad de la Tierra, 2009), 24.

11. "¿Cuáles son las características fundamentales," 156.

12. EZLN, *Critical Thought in the Face of the Capitalist Hydra I* (Durham, NC: Paperboat Press, 2016), 270.

13. Marcos, "The Seven Loose Pieces."

14. Subcomandante Insurgente Marcos, "On Wars: First letter by Subcomandante Insurgente Marcos to Don Luis Villoro," *Radio Zapatista*, January–February 2011, https://radiozapatista.org/pdf/Marcos_letter.pdf.

15. Marcos, "First Letter to Don Luis Villoro."

16. Marcos, "First Letter to Don Luis Villoro."

17. Marcos, "The Seven Loose Pieces," 262.

18. "¿Cuáles son las características fundamentales?," 161.

19. Marcos, "The Seven Loose Pieces"; "Nuestro siguiente programa: ¡Oximoron!," April 2000 in EZLN, *Documentos y Comunicados 4, 14 de febrero de 1997/2 de diciembre de 2000*, First edition (Mexico City: Ediciones Era, 2003), 427–44.

20. The expression "military war"—in no way a pleonasm—is from Subcomandante Galeano. "Trump, Ockham's Razor, Schrodinger's Cat, and the Cat-Dog." It had also been used in Subcomandante Insurgente Marcos, "El mundo: Siete pensamientos en mayo de 2003," *Enlace Zapatista*, May 2, 2003, https://enlacezapatista .ezln.org.mx/2003/05/02/el-mundo-siete-pensamientos-en-mayo-de-2003-mayo -del-2003.

21. EZLN, *Critical Thought*, 267.

22. EZLN, *Critical Thought*, 276.

23. "¿Cuáles son las características fundamentales," 165–66.

24. "¿Cuáles son las características fundamentales," 165–66.

25. The concept appears at the end of World War I, when it became clear that the war was carried out both in the field of industrial production (armament capacity) and on the front. "The loss of a worker can be more serious than that of a soldier," a quotation from the Italian general Giulio Douhet in 1917, cited in Alliez y Lazzarato, *Wars and Capital* (New York: Semiotext(e), 2018), 169. World War II was even more clearly a total war, because it mobilized all its forces on an unprecedented productive, scientific, social, and subjective scale. It also featured a dramatic increase in civilian deaths, particularly because entire cities were carpet-bombed. For more on this, see the bibliographic notes at the end of the book.

26. Qiao Liang and Wang Xiangsui, *Unrestricted Warfare* (Beijing: PLA Literature and Arts Publishing House, 1999, www.c4i.org/unrestricted.pdf). "Financial war is a form of non-military warfare which is just as terribly destructive as a bloody war," Liang y Xiangsui, *Unrestricted Warfare*, 51. "In future wars, there will be more hostilities like financial warfare, in which a country subjugates without spilling a drop of blood," Liang and Xiangsui, *Unrestricted Warfare*, 224. "Information warfare, financial warfare, trade warfare . . . are rendering more and more obsolete the idea of confining warfare to the military domain . . . while constricting the battlespace in the narrow sense. At the same time, we have turned the entire world into a battle field in the broad sense." Liang y Xiangsui, *Unrestricted Warfare*, 221.

27. EZLN, *Critical Thought*, 267. Later, in December 2018, Subcomandante Galeano ap-

peared to distance himself from the analysis of capitalism as war, saying "The late SupMarcos insisted that the capitalist system could not be understood without the concept of war. Supposing, of course, that it is a concept. He would say that war was the motor that permitted, first, the expansion of capitalism, and then its consolidation as a world system . . . I bring this up because, in contrast to that dead guy, in my understanding, capitalism could be studied as a crime," from "Trump, Ockham's Razor." The two readings—capitalism as war and as a crime—are also complementary. In *Critical Thought*, there are chapters titled both "The Genealogy of a Crime" and "A World War" (the latter is written by Subcomandante Marcos and Galeano).

28.   The Colloquium in Memoriam Andrés Aubry featured seven theses, two of which were about war. One was that "The capitalist system cannot be understood without the concept of war. Its survival and growth fundamentally depend on war and everything that goes along with it." Second was that "The production of new commodities and opening of new markets are now pursued by conquering and reconquering territories and social spaces that were of no prior interest to capital. Ancestral knowledge and genetic code, as well as natural resources such as water, forests, and air are now commodities on the open market (or markets yet to be created). Whether they like it or not, those who find themselves within the spaces and territories of these markets are enemies of capital," *Primer Coloquio*, 32.

29.   *Primer Coloquio*, 32; EZLN, *Critical Thought*, 268. Also: "The system's ship floats adrift, the tagline on its hull a declaration of principles, a program, and a plan of action: '*Bellum Semper. Universum Bellum. Universum Exitium.*' 'War forever. World war. Universal destruction,'" EZLN, *Critical Thought*, 255–56.

30.   Marcos, "First Letter to Don Luis Villoro."

31.   EZLN, *Critical Thought*, 181.

32.   EZLN, *Critical Thought*, 180.

33.   EZLN, *Critical Thought*, 277–78.

34.   EZLN, *Critical Thought*, 301.

35.   EZLN, *Critical Thought*, 180.

36.   EZLN, *Critical Thought*, 243.

37.   EZLN, *Critical Thought*, 278–80, 328–29.

38.   "These same rulers found in the many-headed hydra an antithetical symbol of disorder and resistance, a powerful threat to the building of state, empire, and capitalism." Peter Linebaugh and Marcus Rediker, *The Many-Headed Hydra: Sailors, Slaves, Commoners, and the Hidden History of the Revolutionary Atlantic* (Boston: Beacon Press, 2000), 2.

39.   EZLN, *Critical Thought*, 179.

40.   EZLN, *Critical Thought*, 180.

41.   Comandante Zebedeo, "Palabras a los pueblos del mundo," *Enlace Zapatista*, August 9, 2003, https://enlacezapatista.ezln.org.mx/2003/08/09/comandante-zebedeo-palabras-a-los-pueblos-del-mundo.

42. EZLN, *Critical Thought*, 179.
43. EZLN, *Critical Thought*, 302.
44. EZLN, *Critical Thought*, 243. In trying to understand the capitalist system and its genealogy, Subcomandante Galeano mentions several times the usefulness of Marx's work (which he feminizes here): "You could of course tell me that Karla Marx didn't even manage to glimpse the complex shapes that currently make up the Hydra (the capitalist system). But what we see is that some of the fundamental concepts that s/he used to destroy the political economy of that time not only remain solid, but have been confirmed by the present." EZLN, *Critical Thought*, 244–45.
45. EZLN, *Critical Thought*, 301, 305.
46. EZLN, *Critical Thought*, 302.
47. EZLN, *Critical Thought*, 179.
48. EZLN, *Critical Thought*, 180–81.
49. EZLN, *Critical Thought*, 181.
50. EZLN, *Critical Thought*, 301.
51. EZLN, *Critical Thought*, 18–19.
52. EZLN, *Critical Thought*, 4.
53. EZLN, *Critical Thought*, 252–53.
54. *Primer Coloquio*, 32.
55. In August 2018, they once again rejected the idea of a terminal crisis, writing "Is this the terminal crisis of capitalism? Not by a long shot. The system has demonstrated that it is capable of overcoming its own contradictions, and even functioning with and within them." And they also emphasize that this crisis "calls into question our continued existence on the planet." Subcomandante Marcos and Subcomandante Galeano, "300, Part I: A Plantation, a World, a War, Slim Chances," *Enlace Zapatista*, https://enlacezapatista.ezln.org.mx/2018/08/22/300-part-i-a-plantation-a-world-a-war-slim-chances-subcomandante-insurgente-moises-supgaleano.
56. EZLN, *Critical Thought*, 182.
57. EZLN, *Critical Thought*, 182–83.
58. EZLN, *Critical Thought*, 272.
59. Translators' note: This is a play on words, as the Spanish *seminario* is like *semillero* or seedbed. In this sense, the seminar was a space for cultivating ideas.
60. EZLN, *Critical Thought*, 273–76.
61. EZLN, *Critical Thought*, 255. They also say that a potential mother head would be "the social relations of production, where some have capital and others have only their capacity to work," EZLN, *Critical Thought*, 179.
62. *Primer Coloquio*, 32
63. See the bibliographic notes at the end of the book. When Marx writes that "the capital-relation can be nothing other than the process which divorces the worker from the ownership of the conditions of his own labor," we should understand this

separation as his most general description of the capitalist relations of production. Such a separation is maintained when the means of production are state property. Karl Marx, *Capital: A Critique of Political Economy,* vol. 1 (London: Penguin Books, 1976), 874.

64. EZLN, *Critical Thought,* 168.
65. EZLN, *Critical Thought,* 168.
66. EZLN, *Critical Thought,* 170.
67. EZLN, *Critical Thought,* 168.
68. EZLN, *Critical Thought,* 170.
69. EZLN, *Critical Thought,* 171.
70. EZLN, *Critical Thought,* 279.
71. *Planeta Tierra,* 33.
72. EZLN, *Critical Thought,* 255.
73. Ignacio Ramonet and Subcomandante Marcos, *La dignité rebelle* (París: Galilée, 2001).
74. See the bibliographic notes at the end of the book.
75. Jason Moore, *Capitalism in the Web of Life: Ecology and the Accumulation of Capital* (London: Verso, 2015).
76. "A la Señora Sociedad Civil," May 18, 1996, in EZLN, *Documentos y Comunicados 3,* 246–47; "A la Sociedad Civil," August 30, 1996, in EZLN, *Documentos y Comunicados 3,* 370–73; "Civil Society that so Perturbs" in Marcos, *Our Word Is Our Weapon,* 128–32.
77. "Los Arroyos Cuando Bajan," May 28, 1994, in EZLN, *Documentos y Comunicados 1,* 243. Translators' note: CU is the Ciudad Universitaria, campus of the National Autonomous University of Mexico; Sedena is the Secretary of National Defense; CNTE is the National Education Workers' Coordination; CTM is the Confederation of Mexican Workers; and the Zócalo is Mexico City's central plaza.
78. CCRI-CG del EZLN, "Opening Remarks at the First Intercontinental *Encuentro* for Humanity and against Neoliberalism," July 27, 1996, in Marcos, *Our Word Is Our Weapon,* 112.
79. EZLN, *Critical Thought,* 268.
80. "El Despertador Mexicano," December 1993 in EZLN, *Documentos y Comunicados I,* 36. Translators' note: *El Despertador Mexicano* (the Mexican alarm clock) was the EZLN's internal newspaper prior to the January 1, 1994, uprising.
81. EZLN, *Critical Thought,* 266.
82. EZLN, "Sixth Declaration of the Selva Lacandona," *Enlace Zapatista,* June 2005, https://enlacezapatista.ezln.org.mx/sdsl-en.
83. Subcomandante Marcos, "De la Política, Sus Fines, y Sus Principios," *Enlace Zapatista,* June 12, 2007, https://enlacezapatista.ezln.org.mx/2007/06/12/de-la-politica-sus-finales-y-sus-principios. The phrase is also mentioned in the organization of the tables of the World Festival of Dignified Rage in Mexico City (December 2008).

84. David Harvey, *The New Imperialism* (Oxford: Oxford University Press, 2003).

85. Subcomandante Marcos, "De la Política."

86. Subcomandante Marcos, "Them and Us. V. The Six," *Enlace Zapatista*, January 27, 2013, https://enlacezapatista.ezln.org.mx/2013/01/27/them-and-us-v-the-sixth.

87. Subcomandante Marcos, "Mensaje del Subcomandante Marcos en el Instituto Politécnico Nacional," March 16, 2001, in *Documentos y Comunicados 5: La Marcha del Color de la Tierra, 2 de diciembre de 2000/4 de abril de 2001*, First edition (Mexico City: Ediciones Era, 2003), 238–39.

88. If we choose not to include it under this expanded notion of dispossession, the ecocide mentioned here could very well be the fifth wheel of capitalism.

89. A broad conception of the proletariat allows it to be defined as "the vast mass of workers who have lost all power over the use of their own lives." Guy Debord, *The Society of the Spectacle*, trans. Donald Nicholson-Smith (New York: Zone Books, 1994), 84.

90. Marxism has a long tradition of identifying the antagonism between capitalism and humanity. The young Marx described political economy as a consistent realization of the negation of man. Karl Marx, *Manuscripts of 1844*, trans. Martin Milligan (New York: Dover Publications, 2007). He stated that in the capitalist world man is "lost to himself," creating the conditions "to revolt against that inhumanity." Karl Marx and Frederick Engels, *The Holy Family Or Critique of Critical Critique*, trans. by Richard Dixon (Moscow: Foreign Languages Publishing House, 1956), 52. Later, Georg Lukács denounced "how capitalism violates and destroys everything human" and "the dehumanized and dehumanizing function of the commodity relation." Georg Lukács, *History and Class Consciousness*, trans. Rodney Livingstone (London: Merlin Press, 1971), 190, 92. For him, the reifications produced by capitalist social relations "strip man of his human essence" in such a way that "the more culture and civilization . . . take possession of him, the less able he is to be a human being." Lukács, *History*, 136.

Chapter 4: "We Want a World Where Many Worlds Fit"

1. See the bibliographic notes at the end of the book. Translators' note: "Support bases" refers to the civilian communities that the Zapatista army recruits from and relies on for material support. "EZLN" refers to the armed organization led by the Comandantes, and "Zapatistas" either refers to the military plus support bases, or other times only to the support bases. As they have developed their autonomous project, the Zapatistas have increasingly built a horizontal system of self-government within the support bases that is independent of the EZLN and its vertical military structure.

2. Carlos Salinas de Gortari, *México: Un paso difícil a la modernidad* (Mexico City: Plaza & Janés, 2000).

3. EZLN, "Declaration from the Lacandon Jungle" in Subcomandante Marcos, *Our*

Word is our Weapon: Selected Writings, ed. Juana Ponce de León (New York: Seven Stories Press, 2001), 13–15.

4. EZLN, *Documentos y Comunicados 1, 1 de enero de 1994/8 de agosto de 1994*, First edition (1994; Sixth reprint, Mexico City: Ediciones Era, 2003), 73–74.

5. General Command, Clandestine Indigenous Revolutionary Committee [CCRI-CG, as it will be referred to in all subsequent citations], "Letter to the Guerrero Council of 500 Years of Indigenous Resistance," *LANIC*, February 1, 1994, http://lanic.utexas.edu/project/Zapatistas/chapter04.html.

6. CCRI-CG of the EZLN, "Demands Submitted by the Zapatistas during the Feb. '94 dialogue," *The Struggle Site*, March 1, 1994, https://www.struggle.ws/mexico/ezln/ccri_di_demand_mar94.html.

7. Yvon Le Bot and Subcomandante Marcos, *El Sueño Zapatista* (Mexico: Plaza y Janés, 1997), 202–03. A few pages earlier, he speaks of an Indigenous war, not of a single ethnic group (*etnia*) but of the four principal ethnic groups of the state; at the same time, he says "It is a war for national demands, not only Indigenous, but national," Le Bot and Marcos, *El Sueño*, 196.

8. "The Indigenous question will not have a solution if there is not a RADICAL transformation of the national pact. The only means of incorporating the Indigenous of the nation with justice and dignity is to recognize the characteristics of their own social, cultural, and political organization. Autonomy is not separation; it is integration of the most humble and forgotten minorities of contemporary Mexico. . . . Today we repeat: OUR STRUGGLE IS NATIONAL." EZLN, "Third Declaration from the Lacandon Jungle," January 1, 1995, in Subcomandante Insurgente Marcos, *¡Ya Basta!: Ten Years of the Zapatista Uprising*, ed. Žiga Vodovnik (Oakland: AK Press, 2004), 657.

9. Subcomandante Marcos, "Seven questions for whom it may concern," *Campus Activism*, January 24, 1997, http://www.campusactivism.org/akreider/ezln/seven.txt.

10. "We Are Here. We Have Arrived. Speech by Subcomandante Marcos, EZLN. March 11, 2001," trans. Justin Podur, *In These Times*, https://inthesetimes.com/issue/25/10/marcos2510.html.

11. In the understanding of the Indigenous of Chiapas (and probably in that of many Indigenous peoples of the world), belonging to your people isn't an essence that is acquired by birth, but is something that comes to be, that develops by learning little by little to incorporate a way of living that is appropriate. See the bibliographic notes at the end of the book for more on this.

12. CCRI-CG del EZLN, "Letter to the Guerrero Council."

13. CCRI-CG del EZLN, "Five Hundred Years of Indigenous Resistance" in Marcos, *Our Word Is Our Weapon*, 40.

14. Translators' note: In Mexico the holiday is called Día de la Raza, literally "Day of the Mestizo Race."

15. Marcos, *Our Word Is Our Weapon*, 93.
16. Marcos, "Speech in the Zócalo of Mexico City."
17. CCRI-CG del EZLN, "Words of the EZLN in Puebla, Puebla," *The Struggle Site*, February 27, 2001, https://www.struggle.ws/mexico/ezln/2001/ccri/ccri_puebla_feb.html.
18. CCRI-CG del EZLN, "503 Years Later, the Persecution Continues," *The Struggle Site*, October 12, 1995, https://www.struggle.ws/mexico/ezln/ccri_503_years_oct95.html.
19. This refutes the argument that connecting Indigeneity and dignity implies that Indigenous peoples share an essential dignity greater than that of non-Indigenous peoples.
20. The encounter is recounted by Mariana Mora Bayo, "Decolonizing Politics: Zapatista Indigenous Autonomy in an Era of Neoliberal Governance and Low Intensity Warfare," PhD diss., University of Texas, 2008, 267–70.
21. Bruno Baronnet, *Autonomía y Educación Indígena: Las Escuelas Zapatistas de la Selva Lacandona en Chiapas, México* (Quito: Abya-Yala editores, 2012), 278–99. Baronnet has provided a summary of the book in English in "Rebel Youth and Zapatista Autonomous Education," *Latin American Perspectives* 35, no. 4 (2008): 112–24.
22. Baronnet, *Autonomía y Educación Indigena*, 280.
23. Baronnet, *Autonomía y Educacion Indigena*, 281.
24. Dialogue between knowledges is not easy, especially when it requires reconciling the distinct perspectives of science and the Mayan cosmovision: "When studying each theme we should always ask: What did our ancestors the Mayas know about this and what do we know? What did our elder mothers and fathers know? How did the ancestors handle them and how do we handle these issues today? After we will ask about the same themes: What does modern science, developed over more than 500 years, know and do thanks to its exploitation of humanity and the planet?," cited by Raúl Gutiérrez Narváez, "Dos proyectos de sociedad en Los Altos de Chiapas. Escuelas secundarias oficial y autónoma entre los tzotziles de San Andrés," in *Luchas Muy Otras: Zapatismo y Autonomía en las Comunidades Indígenas de Chiapas*, ed. Bruno Baronnet, Mariana Mora Bayo, and Richard Stahler-Sholk (Mexico City: Universidad Autónoma Metropolitana, 2011), https://www.casadelibrosabiertos.uam.mx/contenido/contenido/Libroelectronico/luchas_muy_otras.pdf, 257.
25. You can find a Zapatista explanation of interculturality (without using this word) in Subcomandante Marcos's remarks at the encounter "Paths of Dignity: Indigenous Rights, Memory, and Cultural Heritage" at the Escuela Nacional de Antropología y Historia on March 12, 2001. "I know that it might be disconcerting to some that, in speaking of culture from the Indigenous point of view, I appeal to other voices, Borges and Coleridge in this case, but that is how I remind myself, and remind you, that culture is a bridge for everyone, above cal-

endars and borders, and, as such, must be defended. And so we say, and say to ourselves, 'No to cultural hegemony,' 'No to cultural homogeneity,' and 'No to any form of hegemony and homogeneity.'" Subcomandante Marcos, "Paths of Dignity: Indigenous Rights, Memory, and Cultural Heritage," *The Struggle Site*, March 12, 2001, https://www.struggle.ws/mexico/ezln/2001/march/marcos_paths_mar12.html.

26. Subcomandante Insurgente Marcos, "On Wars: First letter by Subcomandante Insurgente Marcos to Don Luis Villoro," *Radio Zapatista*, January–February 2011, https://radiozapatista.org/pdf/Marcos_letter.pdf.

27. Marcos, "First Letter to Don Luis Villoro."

28. Marcos, "First Letter to Don Luis Villoro."

29. National Indigenous Congress, "Second Declaration of the CNI-EZLN Exchange on the Dispossession of our Peoples." *Enlace Zapatista*, September 1, 2014, https://enlacezapatista.ezln.org.mx/2014/09/01/2nd-declaration-of-the-cni-ezln-exchange-on-the-dispossession-of-our-peoples.

30. Subcomandante Marcos, "Opening Remarks at the First Intercontinental *Encuentro* for Humanity and against Neoliberalism," July 27, 1996, in *Our Word Is Our Weapon*, 112.

31. Subcomandante Marcos, "La Historia de los Espejos," *Enlace Zapatista*, June 1995, https://enlacezapatista.ezln.org.mx/1995/06/09/la-historia-de-los-espejos-durito-iv-el-neoliberalismo-y-el-sistema-de-partido-de-estado-durito-v.

32. Subcomandante Marcos, "Instrucciones Para Leer la Invitación-Convocatoria al Encuentro Intercontinental por la Humanidad y contra el Neoliberalismo," *Enlace Zapatista*, May 1996, https://enlacezapatista.ezln.org.mx/1996/06/09/invitacion-al-encuentro-intercontinental-por-la-humanidad-y-contra-el-neoliberalismo.

33. Subcomandante Insurgente Marcos, "'Búsqueda," *Enlace Zapatista*, March 31, 2001, https://enlacezapatista.ezln.org.mx/2001/03/31/en-juchitan-subcomandante-marcos-la-historia-de-la-busqueda.

34. Marcos, "L@s Otr@s que Somos," *Enlace Zapatista*, June 2, 2006, https://enlacezapatista.ezln.org.mx/2006/06/02/el-delegado-zero-en-la-enah-2-de-junio.

35. Moreover, we should avoid essentializing non-identity thinking, as to strengthen its opposition to identity-based thinking rather than weaken it.

36. "We have decided that Marcos today ceases to exist. He will go hand in hand with Shadow the Warrior and the Little Light so that he doesn't get lost on the way. Don Durito will go with him, Old Antonio also." Subcomandante Galeano, "Between Light and Shadow," *Enlace Zapatista*, May 24, 2014, https://enlacezapatista.ezln.org.mx/2014/05/27/between-light-and-shadow.

37. Subcomandante Marcos, "Rewind 3," *Enlace Zapatista*, November 17, 2013, https://enlacezapatista.ezln.org.mx/2013/11/19/rewind-3-2.

38. "The territory for our work is now clearly delimited: the planet called 'Earth,' located in what is called the solar system." Subcomandante Insurgente Marcos, "Them

and Us. v. The Sixth," *Enlace Zapatista*, January 27, 2013, https://enlacezapatista .ezln.org.mx/2013/01/27/them-and-us-v-the-sixth.

39. Translators' note: "Planetary" is opposed to "global."

40. Subcomandante Marcos, "Nuestro siguiente programa: ¡Oximoron!," *Enlace Zapatista*, April 2000, https://enlacezapatista.ezln.org.mx/2000/04/01/oximoron -la-derecha-intelectual-y-el-fascismo-liberal.

41. Subcomandante Insurgente Moisés and Subcomandante Insurgente Galeano, "The walls above, the cracks below (and to the left)," *Enlace Zapatista*, February 2017, https://enlacezapatista.ezln.org.mx/2017/02/16/the-walls-above-the -cracks-below-and-to-the-left.

42. Subcomandante Insurgente Marcos, "First Declaration of La Realidad for Humanity and against Neoliberalism," *The Struggle Site*, January 30, 1996, https://www .struggle.ws/mexico/ezln/ccri_1st_dec_real.html.

43. "¡Insurgentas! (La Mar en marzo)," *Enlace Zapatista*, March 8, 2000, https:// enlacezapatista.ezln.org.mx/2000/03/08/insurgentas-la-mar-en-marzo-carta-6-e -la-historia-del-aire-de-la-noche.

44. See the bibliographic notes at the end of the book.

45. Translators' note: The Spanish *caracol* refers to both the conch shell and its spiral shape. The Zapatistas gave it a third meaning, naming their autonomous self-government centers Caracoles.

46. Subcomandante Marcos, *Chiapas: The Thirteenth Stele*, "Part One: A Conch," *The Struggle Site*, July 2003, https://struggle.ws/mexico/ezln/2003/marcos/resistance 13.html.

47. Marcos, *The Thirteenth Stele*, "Part One: A Conch."

48. Subcomandante Marcos expressed it in the following way: "Marxism left many gaps . . . and one of the most serious is the Indigenous question." Le Bot and Marcos, *El Sueño Zapatista*, 127–28.

49. See the bibliographic notes at the end of the book.

50. According to Wallerstein, historically existing universalism is in fact "European universalism," while the project of "universal universalism" has until today hardly been sketched. Immanuel Wallerstein, *European Universalism, the Rhetoric of Power* (New York: New Press, 2006).

51. Zapatista writings seldom use the words "universal," "universalism," or "universality." Their uses are generally negative, as in the case of "Universal Destruction," the motto of the capitalist ship. EZLN, *Critical Thought*, 190–96.

52. Marcos, "Opening Remarks" in *Our Word Is Our Weapon*, 114. The expression was used on other occasions, for example when speaking about the diversity of the rebellions that might join without subordination: "We are all the same because we are different." "Them and Us IV–the pains of those below," January 27, 2013, https://enlacezapatista.ezln.org.mx/2013/01/27/them-and-us-part-iv-the-pains -of-those-below.

53. "The world we want is one in which many worlds fit." "Fourth Declaration from the Lacandon Jungle," January 1, 1996 in Marcos, *¡Ya Basta!*, 669.

54. It is worth noting that at the moment of affirming the planetary as the terrain of struggle, for the customary "From the mountains of the Mexican Southeast," Subcomandante Marcos substitutes "From any corner of any world." "Them and Us: Four New Essays by Subcomandante Marcos," *ROAR Magazine*, January 25, 2103, https://roarmag.org/essays/them-and-us-subcomandante-marcos.

55. Subcomandante Galeano, "The Last Honeybun in the Mountains of Southeastern Mexico," *Enlace Zapatista*, August 9, 2018, https://enlacezapatista.ezln.org.mx/2018/09/09/the-last-honeybun-in-the-mountains-of-southeastern-mexico.

56. CCRI-CG del EZLN, "Words of the EZLN in Puebla," *The Struggle Site*, February 27, 2001, https://www.struggle.ws/mexico/ezln/2001/ccri/ccri_puebla_feb.html.

57. For example: "Because the world is not the property of any flag. It belongs to all of us (*todas, todos, todoas*)." CNI, CIG, and EZLN, "Joint Communique from the CNI, CIG, and EZLN Rejecting the NAIM (New International Airport of Mexico) and Voicing Support for and Solidarity with Migrant Populations," *Enlace Zapatista*, October 26, 2018, https://enlacezapatista.ezln.org.mx/2018/10/27/joint-communique-from-the-cni-cig-and-ezln-rejecting-the-naim-new-international-airport-of-mexico-and-voicing-support-for-and-solidarity-with-migrant-populations. Translators' note: In a gendered language, the Spanish *todos* means "all men" and *todas* is "all women." In addressing their audience, the Zapatistas use the neologism *todoas* to also interpolate all nonbinary people.

58. Words in the framework of the San Andres Dialogues, *La Jornada*, August 10, 1996, p. 9. See the bibliographic notes at the end of the book.

59. See the bibliographic notes at the end of the book.

60. See the bibliographic notes at the end of the book.

61. Subcomandante Marcos, "Intervención en la Mesa 1 del Primer Encuentro Intercontinental por la Humanidad y contra el Neoliberalismo," *Biblat*, July 30, 1996, https://biblat.unam.mx/hevila/ContrahistoriasLaotramiradadeClio/2013/no20/2.pdf.

62. "The sense of community that is palpable in the Indigenous communities isn't exclusive to them. It also appears in other sectors of those below and is most developed among those who struggle and resist." Subcomandante Insurgente Marcos, "Tercer Viento: Un digno y rabioso color de la tierra, Tercer mesa del 3 de Enero," *Enlace Zapatista*, January 4, 2009, https://enlacezapatista.ezln.org.mx/2009/01/04/tercer-viento-un-digno-y-rabioso-color-de-la-tierra-tercer-mesa-del-3-de-enero.

63. Subcomandante Marcos, "Marcos Reports Back in Oventik," *The Struggle Site*, April 1, 2001, https://www.struggle.ws/mexico/ezln/2001/march/report_back_marcos_apr1.html. Translators' note: In each of these sentences, Marcos is using

tú, the singular version of "you," and not *ustedes,* the plural version ("you all") that one would expect him to use when addressing a group.

64. See the examples mentioned in chapter 2.
65. John Womack, Jr., *Zapata and the Mexican Revolution* (New York: Vintage, 1970).
66. Subcomandante Marcos, "To Alvaro Cepeda Neri of *La Jornada,*" January 26, 1994, in Ben Clarke and Clifton Ross, ed., *Voice of Fire: Communiques and Interviews from the Zapatista National Liberation Army* (Berkeley, CA: New Earth Publications, 1994), 60–63.
67. Subcomandante Galeano, "The EZLN's Sixth Commission at the close of 'Con-sciences for Humanity': 'From the Diaries of the Cat-Dog,'" *Enlace Zapatista,* January 22, 2018, https://enlacezapatista.ezln.org.mx/2018/01/22/the-ezlns-sixth-commission-at-the-close-of-consciences-for-humanity-from-the-diaries-of-the-cat-dog-supgaleano.
68. Subcomandante Marcos, "Second Declaration of La Realidad and against Neoliberalism," August 3, 1996, in Marcos, *Our Word Is Our Weapon,* 119.
69. EZLN, "Words of the EZLN at UNAM," *The Struggle Site,* March 21, 2001, https://www.struggle.ws/mexico/ezln/2001/march/unam_mar21.html.
70. Subcomandante Marcos, "Seven Thoughts in May 2003," *El Kilombo,* May 2003, https://elkilombo.org/documents/seventhoughtsmarcos.html.
71. EZLN, "Words of the EZLN at UNAM."
72. Subcomandante Marcos, "The Long Journey from Despair to Hope," *Genius,* September 22, 1994, https://genius.com/Subcomandante-marcos-the-long-journey-from-despair-to-hope-annotated.
73. Subcomandante Marcos, "Always and Never against Sometimes," September 12, 1998 in *¡Ya Basta!,* 348–49.
74. Subcomandante Marcos, "Of Critical Reflection, Individuals and Collectives. Second Letter to Luis Villoro of the Epistolary Exchange on Ethics and Politics," April 2, 2011, http://enlacezapatista.ezln.org.mx/2011/04/11/sci-marcos-de-la-reflexion-critica-individus-y-colectivs-carta-segunda-a-luis-villoro-en-el-intercambio-espistolar-sobre-etica-y-politica.
75. See the bibliographic notes at the end of the book.
76. EZLN, *Critical Thought,* 60. See also the text of Subcomandante Marcos, "Entre el árbol y el bosque" as well as "Apuntes de las bases de apoyo del EZLN para su participación en la compartición." "Entre el árbol y el bosque. Palabras del EZLN en la mesa redonda 'Frente al despojo capitalista,'" *Enlace Zapatista,* July 17, 2007, https://enlacezapatista.ezln.org.mx/2007/07/18/mesa-redonda-frente-al-despojo-capitalista-la-defensa-de-la-tierra-y-el-territorio-17-de-julio-de-2007; "Apuntes de las bases de apoyo del EZLN para su participación en la compartición." *Rebeldía Zapatista,* 3, September 2014, 15. See the following quote as well from Don Durito of the Lacandona: "The Indigenous see the earth as mother; they see the capitalist as one who doesn't have a mother," *Primer Coloquio Internacional in Memoriam An-*

drés Aubry "Planeta tierra, movimientos antisistémicos (San Cristóbal de Las Casas: Cideci-Universidad de la Tierra, 2009), 177.

77. *Participation of Women in Autonomous Government. First-Grade Textbook for the Course "Freedom According to the Zapatistas"* (material from the Zapatista Little School, 2013), https://ausm.community/wp-content/uploads/2014/09/EZLN-Participation-of-Women-in-Autonomous-Government.pdf, 18.

78. Gerardo (Delegate of the Junta de Buen Gobierno), "Cultural Politics" in *Autonomous Resistance: First-Grade Textbook for the Course "Freedom According to the Zapatistas"* (material from the Zapatista Little School, 2013), https://ausm.community/wp-content/uploads/2014/09/EZLN-Autonomous-Resistance.pdf, 79.

79. See the bibliographic notes at the end of the book.

80. Among their explanations for convoking the event we find: "Third: That the sciences and the arts rescue the best of humanity. Fourth: That the sciences and the arts now represent the only serious opportunity for the construction of a more just and rational world." Subcomandante Marcos, "Zapatista Convocation for 2016 Activities," *Enlace Zapatista,* February 2016, https://enlacezapatista.ezln.org.mx/2016/03/01/zapatista-convocation-for-2016-activities.

81. Subcomandante Galeano explicitly critiques postmodernism in various speeches. For example: "But if someone comes who says they are going to tell us that science needs to do postmodern philosophy and take the existential variables of each person into account, well, the assembly is going to listen to you, but they aren't going to tell you to go ahead. They are going to propose that you infiltrate Skynet and convince Artificial Intelligence to accept your scientific proposal." "What's Next? II. The Urgent and the Important," *Enlace Zapatista*, January 3, 2017, https://enlacezapatista.ezln.org.mx/2017/02/22/whats-next-ii-the-urgent-and-the-important.

82. See the bibliographic notes at the end of the book.

83. Subcomandante Galeano, "The Flower is to Blame," *Enlace Zapatista*, December 27, 2016, https://enlacezapatista.ezln.org.mx/2017/01/16/the-flower-is-to-blame.

84. Personal notes, Cideci-Unitierra, January 4, 2017.

85. In this sense, Zapatista word-thought is like that of Frantz Fanon (but not to the ways postcolonial thinkers have made use of his thought). See the bibliographic notes at the end of the book for more on this.

Chapter 5: "Our Struggle is For History and against Oblivion"

1. As opposed to "Power's men in gray, who plotted to sell dignity and forget history." CCRI-CG del EZLN, "Civil Society That So Perturbs" (September 19, 1996) in Subcomandante Marcos, *Our Word is our Weapon: Selected Writings*, ed. Juana Ponce de León (New York: Seven Stories Press, 2001), 128.

2. "Comunicado para el segundo aniversario del levantamiento," December 22, 1995, in EZLN, *Documentos y Comunicados 3, 2 de octubre de 1995/24 de enero de 1997,* First edition (1997; First reprint, Mexico City: Ediciones Era, 1998), 63. Also: "We

fight against this loss of memory, against death and for life. We fight the fear of a death because we have ceased to exist in memory." EZLN, "Fourth Declaration from the Lacandon Jungle (January 1, 1996)," in Subcomandante Insurgente Marcos, *¡Ya Basta!: Ten Years of the Zapatista Uprising*, ed. Žiga Vodovnik (Oakland: AK Press, 2004), 661–62.

3. "Mensaje de los Comandantes del EZLN a los Cinturones de Paz en San Andrés," July 12, 1996 in EZLN, *Documentos y Comunicados 3*, 305.

4. "Shared history, what else is a nation?" *De bombas, bomberos y bombillas*, November 1998, in EZLN, *Documentos y Comunicados 4, 14 de febrero de 1997/2 de diciembre de 2000*, First edition (Mexico City: Ediciones Era, 2003), 258.

5. Yvon Le Bot and Subcomandante Marcos, *El Sueño Zapatista* (Mexico: Plaza y Janés, 1997), 336.

6. Le Bot and Marcos, *El Sueño*, 160–61, 172.

7. "In 1992, when the 500-year anniversary of the Discovery of America was celebrated, we failed to perceive a very important issue for Indigenous communities, the nature of the Conquest, what the 'Discovery of America' really meant." LeBot and Marcos, *El Sueño*, 189–90.

8. The communiqués privilege post-Independence history, while colonial history is barely present. They mention the conquest of Chetumal, the failure to honor the New Laws by Felipe II, and quote the 1528 Anonymous Manuscript of Tlatelolco. EZLN, *Documentos y Comunicados 2, 15 de agosto de 1994/29 de septiembre de 1995*, First edition (1995; Third reprint, Mexico City: Ediciones Era, 2001), 202; EZLN, *Documentos y Comunicados 3*, 445; EZLN, *Documentos y Comunicados 4*, 180.

9. CCRI-CG del EZLN, "503 Years Later, the Persecution Continues," *The Struggle Site*, October 12, 1995, https://www.struggle.ws/mexico/ezln/ccri_503_years_oct95.html.

10. For example: "Before those who today feast on our blood and turn it into their wealth were even a dream in the dark void of time, our ancestors—that is to say, us—already governed ourselves with reason and justice, and our world was not worse than this one in which they now force us to die." CCRI-CG del EZLN, "Mensaje Con Motivo de 2 de Octubre," October 2, 1994, in EZLN, *Documentos y Comunicados 2*, 85.

11. There are only two brief mentions of the history of Chiapas: the first (1992) refers to the Act of Annexation to Mexico in 1824 and the second (1994) mentions the death of the Chiapaneca people in the Sumidero Canyon. "Chiapas: el Sureste En Dos Vientos, una Tormenta Y una Profecía," in EZLN, *Documentos y Comunicados 1, 1 de enero de 1994/8 de agosto de 1994*, First edition (1994; Sixth reprint, Mexico City: Ediciones Era, 2003), 62; EZLN, *Documentos y Comunicados 1*, 115).

12. CCRI-CG del EZLN, "Words of the EZLN in the Zócalo of Mexico City," *The Struggle Site*, March 11, 2001, https://www.struggle.ws/mexico/ezln/2001/march/zocalo_mar11.html.

13. EZLN, "Fifth Declaration from the Lacandon Jungle," July 19, 1998 in Subcomandante Insurgente Marcos, *¡Ya Basta!*, 678.

14. CCRI-CG del EZLN, "Words of the EZLN in Milpa Alta, D.F." *The Struggle Site*, March 9, 2001, https://www.struggle.ws/mexico/ezln/2001/march/milpa_alta_mar9.html.

15. Subcomandante Insurgente Marcos, "Inauguración del Encuentro Continental Americano in EZLN," April 6, 1996, in *Documentos y Comunicados 3*, 205–13; Subcomandante Insurgente Marcos, "Homenaje a Miguel Enríquez Espinosa," *Enlace Zapatista*, October 9, 2004, https://enlacezapatista.ezln.org.mx/2004/10/09/octubre-se-llama-miguel.

16. See the texts cited in the Introduction and in chapter 4 of this book.

17. CCRI-CG del EZLN, "503 Years Later"; CCRI-CG del EZLN, "Comunicado Sobre el Festejo de Independencia," September 15, 1994 in EZLN, *Documentos y Comunicados 2*, 44.

18. Subcomandante Marcos, "The Tale of the Little Newspaper Vendor," *The Struggle Site*, September 3, 1997, https://www.struggle.ws/mexico/ezln/1997/marcos_news_vendor_sep.html; Subcomandante Marcos, "Letter to 'Commander in Chief Zapata,'" *The Struggle Site*, April 10, 1997, https://www.struggle.ws/mexico/ezln/1997/marcos_to_zapata_apr.html.

19. Subcomandante Marcos, "Donde Durito Nombra a Marcos su Escudero," April 4, 1995 in EZLN, *Documentos y Comunicados 2*, 298.

20. "As in 1919, we Zapatistas must pay in blood for our cry of Land and Freedom! As in 1919, the supreme government kills us to quell our rebellion." CCRI-CG del EZLN, "A Las Bases del EZLN," April 10, 1994 in EZLN, *Documentos y Comunicados 1*, 213.

21. EZLN, *Documentos y Comunicados 5: La Marcha del Color de la Tierra, 2 de diciembre de 2000/4 de abril de 2001*, First edition (Mexico City: Ediciones Era, 2003), 90–103.

22. Translators' note: The Plan de Ayala was written in 1911 and stated the core demands animating the Liberation Army of the South during the Mexican Revolution. It set the stage for today's Zapatistas by radically upending property relations, dispossessing the *hacienda* (or *finca*) owning class, and putting this land under collective control. Indeed, the EZLN's 1993 Revolutionary Agrarian Law closely resembles the Plan of Ayala. Under the plan, the Indigenous and peasant communities of Morelos lived within a commune that resembles today's Zapatista communities in Chiapas. Furthermore, the Plan of Ayala was a key precedent to the revolutionary Constitution of 1917 that established the collective landholding category of the *ejido*.

23. CCRI-CG del EZLN, "Words of the EZLN in Xochimilco, D.F.," *The Struggle Site*, March 10, 2001, https://www.struggle.ws/mexico/ezln/2001/march/xochimilco_mar10.html.

24. Subcomandante Marcos, "Marcos on May Day and Tupac Amaru," *The Struggle Site*, April 25, 1997, https://www.struggle.ws/mexico/ezln/marcos_tupac_amaru .html; Subcomandante Marcos, "Bernal Busca la Gobernatura de Tamaulipas," September 7, 1996, in EZLN, *Documentos y Comunicados 3*, 378.

25. EZLN, *La Palabra de los Armados de Verdad y Fuego* (Mexico City: Fuenteovejuna, 1994–1995), 1:131. 2:226–27, 244–45.

26. Cited in Enrique Florescano, *Memoria Mexicana*, Second Edition (Mexico City: FCE, 1994), 142.

27. According to Subcomandante Marcos, the Indigenous people "have a very curious sense of time. One doesn't know what time period they are talking about: They could be telling you a story that happened a week ago, or 500 years ago, or when the world began." Interview by Tessa Brisac and Carmen Castillo, October 24, 1994, in Adolfo Gilly, Subcomandante Marcos, and Carlo Ginsburg, *Discusión Sobre la Historia* (Mexico City: Taurus, 1995), 133–34.

28. CCRI-CG del EZLN, "Votán-Zapata or Five Hundred Years of History," April 10, 1994, in Marcos, *Our Word Is Our Weapon*, 20.

29. Subcomandante Marcos, "Carta de Marcos a Remitentes que aún no Obtienen Respuesta," December 13, 1994 in EZLN, *Documentos y Comunicados 2*, 160–62; Gilly, Marcos, and Ginsburg, *Discusión Sobre la Historia*, 134.

30. CCRI-CG del EZLN, "Votán," 20.

31. For example, Subcomandante Marcos, "Ski Masks and Other Masks" (January 20, 1994) in Ben Clarke and Clifton Ross, ed., *Voice of Fire*, 57.

32. Le Bot and Marcos, *El Sueño*, 311, 369; Subcomandante Marcos, "Carta de Marcos: La Muerte nos Visita," February 20, 1995 in EZLN, *Documentos y Comunicados 2*, 234.

33. Marcos, "Inauguración del Encuentro Intercontinental," 205–13.

34. CCRI-CG del EZLN, "Words of the EZLN in Cuautla, Morelos," *The Struggle Site*, March 7, 2001, https://www.struggle.ws/mexico/ezln/2001/march/cuautla _mar7.html.

35. CCRI-CG del EZLN, "503 Years Later." "Our fight is for a roof over our heads that has dignity, and the bad government destroys our homes and our history," EZLN, "Fourth Declaration," 661.

36. "We looked inside ourselves, and we looked at our history: We saw our eldest fathers suffer and struggle, we saw our grandfathers struggle, we saw our fathers with fury in their hands . . . and the dead, our dead, saw that we were renewed, and they called to us again, to dignity and to the struggle." "Five Hundred Years of Indigenous Resistance" (February 1, 1994) in Marcos, *Our Word Is Our Weapon*, 41. Elsewhere, we read, "The mountain told us to take up arms so we would have a voice. . . . It told us to protect our past so we would have a future. In the mountains, the dead live: our dead." "Opening Remarks at the First Intercontinental *Encuentro* for Humanity and against Neoliberalism," July 27, 1996, in *Our Word Is Our Weapon*, 110.

37. In the collective interviews conducted by Paulina Fernández Christlieb, the *finca*

and the burden of grievances that it represents are an indispensable referent for understanding the construction of autonomy. Paulina Fernández Christlieb, *Justicia Autónoma Zapatista: Zona Selva Tzeltal* (Mexico City, Ediciones autónom@s, 2014), chapter 1. See also how then-Major Moisés (now Comandante Moisés) refers to the suffering of his parents in the *fincas*. Le Bot and Marcos, *El Sueño*, 165–67.

38. "La Mesa de San Andrés. Entre los Olvidos de Arriba y la Memoria de Abajo," *Enlace Zapatista*, February 27, 1998, https://enlacezapatista.ezln.org.mx/1998/02/27/la-mesa-de-san-andres-entre-los-olvidos-de-arriba-y-la-memoria-de-abajo.

39. EZLN, *Documentos y Comunicados 4*, 182.

40. "Comunicado del Subcomandante Marcos a la Digna Argentina," March 24, 2001 in EZLN, *Documentos y Comunicados 5*, 286–87.

41. Translators' note: *Coleto* is a term used to refer to the mestizo inhabitants of San Cristobal de las Casas. It is said to derive from the *coleta* or ponytail worn by the Spanish conquerors, and signals an identification with them. Sometimes *ladino* is also used in the region.

42. "Durito y una de estatuas y pájaros," *Rebeldia*, May 7, 2003, 1–2.

43. "Durito y una de estatuas y pájaros," 1–2.

44. "Palabras del Subcomandante Marcos en Chinameca, Morelos," March 8, 2001 in EZLN, *Documentos y Comunicados 5*, 205–06.

45. In addition to previously cited communiqués, see "Votán Zapata" in *Our Word Is Our Weapon*, 19–21; "Emiliano died, but not his struggle nor his thinking," *The Struggle Site*, April 10, 1995, https://www.struggle.ws/mexico/ezln/ccri_zapata_apr95.html; EZLN, *Documentos y Comunicados 3*, 230–33.

46. "Palabras del Comandante Mister en Chinameca," March 8, 2001, in EZLN, *Documentos y Comunicados 5*, 207.

47. See the note in the reissue of Andrés Aubry's book, *San Cristóbal de Las Casas: Su historia urbana, demográfica y monumental, 1528–1990* (1991, Reedición San Cristóbal de Las Casas: Batsil K'op, 2017).

48. Subcomandante Marcos, "Letter to John Berger," May 12, 1995, in Marcos, *Our Word Is Our Weapon*, 262.

49. EZLN, "Fourth Declaration," 660–62.

50. Subcomandante Marcos, "The Table at San Andrés," March 1998 in *¡Ya Basta!*, 284.

51. Marcos, "Table at San Andrés," 284.

52. "In the new 'world history,' the present defeats the past and takes hold of the future. Today is the new tyrant, and one must swear allegiance and obedience to it." Subcomandante Marcos, "An inverted periscope or memory, a buried key," February 24, 1998, in *¡Ya Basta!*, 315.

53. Subcomandante Marcos, "Closing Words to the National Indigenous Forum (excerpt)," January 9, 1996, in *Our Word Is Our Weapon*, 94.

54. Subcomandante Marcos, "Encuentro Intercontinental Por La Humanidad y Contra el Neoliberalismo," May 1996 in EZLN, *Documentos y Comunicados 3*, 257. Also:

"Power says to itself: 'I exist because I am necessary, I am necessary because I exist, therefore: I exist and I am necessary.'" Subcomandante Marcos, "La historia de los espejos," June 1995 in EZLN, *Documentos y Comunicados 2*, 373.

55. Subcomandante Marcos, "Propone a Berlín Como Sede del 'Intergaláctico' Europeo," January 30, 1996, in EZLN, *Documentos y Comunicados 3*, 129–31. A counterproposal follows: "Why not begin again there, with Power's symbol of the end of History and the eternity of its mandate?"

56. Subcomandante Marcos y el EZLN, *La rebelión de la memoria* (San Cristóbal de las Casas: CIDECI-Unitierra, 2010), 277.

57. "Just as Alice discovers that—to reach the Red Queen—she must walk backward, we must turn to the past in order to advance and improve ourselves. In the past we can find paths to the future," January 30, 1996. *Documentos y Comunicados 3*, 129–31. "We are the stubborn history that repeats itself so as not to repeat once again, looking back to be able to walk forward." EZLN, *Documentos y Comunicados 3*, 255. Durito similarly states: "Crabs are sailors, beetles' relatives, those wise ones who know that the best way to advance is backward," July 5, 1996. EZLN, *Documentos y Comunicados 3*, 298.

58. Subcomandante Marcos, "Clausura del Foro Para la Reforma del Estado," July 6, 1996 in EZLN, *Documentos y Comunicados 3*, 301.

59. Marcos, "Closing Words," 94.

60. CCRI-CG del EZLN, "503 years later."

61. Marcos, "Encuentro Intercontinental," 257.

62. Marcos, "Encuentro Intercontinental," 257.

63. Translators' note: Vicente Fox, president of Mexico, 2000 to 2006.

64. Subcomandante Marcos, "Paths of Dignity: Indigenous Rights, Memory, and Cultural Heritage," *The Struggle Site*, March 12, 2001, https://www.struggle.ws/mexico/ezln/2001/march/marcos_paths_mar12.html.

65. "They offered us a nicer corner in the museum of history," March 17, 1995. EZLN, *Documentos y Comunicados 2*, 285. On the contrary, we find the following: "Return to the past? Little by little the possibility of a plural future appears, of looking around and recognizing the communities' traditional ways and customs (*usos y costumbres*), their capacity for novelty. They are living beings, not the fossils that the propaganda of global power would like them to be," May 1996. EZLN, *Documentos y Comunicados 3*, 263.

66. See bibliographic notes at the end of the book.

67. See bibliographic notes at the end of the book.

68. CCRI-CG del EZLN, "503 Years Later."

69. These quotes are directly from Walter Benjamin's "Theses on the Philosophy of History," read by Galeano. See EZLN, *Critical Thought in the Face of the Capitalist Hydra I* (Durham, NC: Paperboat Press, 2016), 14, 239.

70. See bibliographic notes at the end of the book.

71. EZLN, *Critical Thought*, 276.

72. EZLN, *Critical Thought*, 276. Also: "But this 'modernization' or 'progress' has no other objective than to maintain above those who are above in the only way it is possible for them to be there, that is, on the backs of those below." "Them and Us. V. the Sixth," *Enlace Zapatista*, January 27, 2013, https://enlacezapatista.ezln.org .mx/2013/01/27/them-and-us-v-the-sixth.

73. EZLN, *Critical Thought*, 170.

74. Subcomandante Marcos and Subcomandante Galeano, "300, part I: A Plantation, a World, a War, Slim Chances," *Enlace Zapatista*, August 2018, https://enlacezapatista .ezln.org.mx/2018/08/22/300-part-i-a-plantation-a-world-a-war-slim-chances -subcomandante-insurgente-moises-supgaleano. When the notion of Progress becomes difficult to sustain, substitute words emerge, such as development, modernization, or civilization. In the same document, we read: "That is how so-called 'civilization' is founded: what the originary peoples need is to 'get out of poverty,' that is, they need a wage. . . . To 'civilize' an originary community is to convert its population into a salaried work force, that is, with purchasing power." Subcomandante Marcos and Subcomandante Galeano, "300, Part I."

75. First draft of the letter to Vera Zasulich (February–March 1881), quoted in Teodor Shanin, *The Late Marx and the Russian Road: Marx and the Peripheries of Capitalism* (New York: Monthly Review Press, 1983), 106.

76. Subcomandante Moisés and Subcomandante Galeano, "The walls above, the cracks below (and to the left)," *Enlace Zapatista*, February 2017, https:// enlacezapatista.ezln.org.mx/2017/02/16/the-walls-above-the-cracks-below-and -to-the-left.

77. Subcomandante Galeano, "Prelude: Timepieces, the Apocalypse and the Hour of the Small," *Enlace Zapatista*, April 12, 2017, https://enlacezapatista.ezln.org.mx/ 2017/04/24/prelude-timepieces-the-apocalypse-and-the-hour-of-the-smallsub comandante-insurgente-galeano. During the Dialogues, Comandante David commented, "We—as Indigenous people—have rhythms, ways of understanding, of reaching decisions, of making agreements. And when we explained this to [the government negotiators], they treated it like a joke. They said, 'We don't understand why you say that, because we see that you wear Japanese watches. So how is it that you say you have an Indigenous clock when your watch is from Japan?,'" *La Jornada*, May 17, 1995. Comandante Tacho later said, "They didn't learn. They see us backwards. We use time and not the clock." *La Jornada*, May 18, 1995.

78. Explanatory text accompanying the painting *La Libertad*. Colectivo de promotorxs de educación (Oventik), *La Libertad*, CompArte 2018, https://radiozapatista .org/wp-content/uploads/2018/08/IMG_3360_1024x683.jpg. Elsewhere we read: "The warrior must seek the rhythm, that is, accompaniment between the parts of the whole. This is distinct from speed, which ends up leaving out what is important as it attends to what is urgent." "Dos políticas y una ética," *Enlace Zapa-*

tista, June 2007, https://enlacezapatista.ezln.org.mx/2007/06/09/conferencia -etica-y-politica-en-el-auditorio-che-guevara-8-de-junio.

79.   Galeano, "Prelude."

80.   Walter Benjamin, "Thesis on the Concept of History," in Michael Löwy, *Fire Alarm: Reading Walter Benjamin's "On the Concept of History"* (London-New York: Verso, 2005), 92.

81.   Benjamin, "Thesis," XV; Marcos, "Paths of Dignity."

82.   We should note that, in each of these relationships, that which is transformed ends up being the most important aspect, going so far as to change the meaning of what is reclaimed.

83.   We find this early on, in Old Antonio's story "The History of Questions," found in the postscript to a December 1994 communiqué. It reads: "Since then, the gods walk with questions. . . . So that is how the true men and women learned that questions help to walk, to not just stand still. Since then, the true men and women walk by asking, and to arrive they say good-bye, and to leave they say hello." Speaking directly to Subcomandante Marcos, Old Antonio concludes by saying, "You've learned now that in order to know and walk, you have to ask questions." Subcomandante Marcos, "The Story of the Questions" in *Our Word Is Our Weapon*, 415.

84.   For example, EZLN, *Critical Thought*, 14, 29, 109. The phrase first appeared in 2005, anticipating the release of the "Sixth Declaration of the Lacandon Jungle": "Six months ago, we started with this business of 'what's missing is yet to come.'" Subcomandante Insurgente Marcos, "Carta a la sociedad civil nacional e internacional," *Enlace Zapatista*, June 21, 2006, enlacezapatista.ezln.org.mx/2005/06/21/ carta-a-la-sociedad-civil-nacional-e-internacional. A few months later, they write that "what's missing is yet to come" synthesizes the "Zapatista gaze," which is aware of "what is left to do, what's inconclusive—this is our inheritance." *Rebeldía* 37, November 2005, 3.

85.   The Zapatista struggle is seen as a way to "challenge the laws of probability." Subcomandante Moisés and Subcomandante Galeano, "300, Part III: A Challenge, Real Autonomy, an Answer, Multiple Proposals, and a Few Anecdotes about the Number 300," *Enlace Zapatista*, August 29, 2018, https://enlacezapatista.ezln .org.mx/2018/08/29/300-part-iii-a-challenge-real-autonomy-an-answer-multiple -proposals-and-a-few-anecdotes-about-the-number-300.

86.   "Going over and over" is one way of putting this idea that the straightest path is not necessarily the best one. The Subcomandantes write that the "Zapatista method of turning an idea over and over" is a way that—through questioning and the "comings and goings of the word, of listening ears"—an idea does (or does not) grow into a collective proposal. Subcomandante Moisés and Subcomandante Galeano, "A History to Try to Understand," *Enlace Zapatista*, November 17, 2016, https:// enlacezapatista.ezln.org.mx/2016/11/26/a-story-to-try-to-understand.

Final Thoughts

1.   Translators' Note: See the discussion of proportionality in chapter 2.

Index

Marx, Karl, 83, 93, 209, 264n44, 264–65n63, 266n90; *Communist Manifesto*, 113; on revolution, 253n15

"Mayan Train" project, 43–44, 45

mediation, 70–71

memory, 197–202 passim

Mexican Constitution, 26, 32–36 passim, 56, 103, 200

Mexican Revolution, 194–95, 200, 241n38, 252n8; Plan de Ayala, 195, 275n22

migration, 79, 249–50nn60–61

milpas, 55, 56, 67, 184

mining, resistance to, 44, 56

Mister, Comandante, 200

Moctezuma Barragán, Esteban, 31

modernity, 177–78, 184, 210, 211, 214, 235

Moisés, Subcomandante, 41–44 passim, 50–51, 67, 85, 100, 128, 209; on critical thought, 135–36; on *El Despertador Mexicano*, 192; on Keynesianism, 98; as Major Moisés, 29; on Mother Earth, 183; replacement of Marcos, 41, 107, 157; "small slice of freedom," 83, 220; on voting, 104

money, 66–67, 141, 202, 203; loans, 248n37, 260n101

Mora, Mariana, 239n2

morality, 112–13

Mother Earth. *See* Earth

N

NAFTA (North American Free Trade Movement), 28, 56

National Indigenous Congress

(CNI), 32, 35, 38, 42, 56, 124, 157, 158; Second Assembly, 34

National Indigenous Forum, 32, 159

nationalism, Zapatista. *See* Zapatista nationalism

National Liberation Forces (FLN), 24, 27

nature, 146, 183, 184–85; human separation from, 175, 178

North American Free Trade Movement. *See* NAFTA (North American Free Trade Movement)

O

Ocosingo, 27, 29, 31, 48, 201

organized crime, 49, 130

Orive, Adolfo, 23

Other Campaign, 37–40 passim, 108, 111, 167

Oventik, 33, 178–79; CELMRAZ, 169; Good Government Council, 201, 260n100; secondary school, 58, 163

P

Party of the Democratic Revolution (PRD), 35, 38

Pedro, Subcomandante, 28

Peña Nieto, Enrique, 38

People's Front in Defense of Land, 38, 48

Plan de Ayala, 195, 275n22

"planetary community," 176–77

PRD. *See* Party of the Democratic Revolution (PRD)

PRI. *See* Revolutionary Institutional Party (PRI)

Progress, 191, 204–16 passim, 279n74
Proletarian Line, 23

R
racism, 160, 171
rage, dignified. *See* "dignified rage"
Ramona, Comandanta, 61, 62
Rancière, Jacques, 249n54
reparation and restitution, 71
revolution, 91, 93, 94, 216; Marx
    on, 253n15. *See also* Mexican
    Revolution
Revolutionary Institutional Party
    (PRI), 14, 24, 30, 34, 103;
    Indigenismo, 242
Rincón, Robledo, 30–31
Rodríguez Lascano, Sergio, 255n31,
    260n104
Ruiz, Samuel, 21, 22, 23, 30
Ruíz Massieu, José, 30
Russian Revolution, 93

S
Salinas de Gortari, Carlos, 25, 26,
    29, 56, 156, 199, 200; as Mac-
    beth, 203; Mexican Coffee
    Institute, 240n23
San Andrés Accords on Indigenous
    Rights and Culture, 32–35
    passim, 53, 62, 103, 113, 118,
    158, 219; government non-
    compliance, 202; women's
    participation, 62
San Cristóbal de las Casas, 27, 28,
    33, 36; Cathedral Dialogues,
    1994, 30, 62, 103, 157; March
    of 10,000, 26–27, 157; statue
    toppling, 27, 157, 192, 199

science, 185–87, 246–47n15, 273n80
"Second Declaration of the Lacan-
    don Jungle," 30
self-government, 82–84 passim.
    See also Good Government
    Councils
Setzer, Elmar, 27
"Seven Loose Pieces of the Global
    Jigsaw Puzzle" (Marcos), 126,
    132
Sexta, 40, 106, 108, 110, 111
"Sixth Declaration of the Lacandon
    Jungle," 17, 36–40 passim, 81,
    105, 109–10, 127, 148–49, 167;
    on civil-military relationship,
    250n68; "from below and for
    below," 99, 102; on soldiers,
    257n50
skin color, 160, 161
Squadron 421, 46–48
state, 92–99 passim, 117–20 passim,
    124, 254–55nn27–28, 255n31,
    260n105
State Council of Indigenous
    and Peasant Organizations
    (CEIOC), 30, 33
statues, 199–200; toppling of, 27,
    157, 192, 199
storm metaphor, 138–39, 142, 144,
    145, 153

T
Tacho, Comandante, 113, 279n77
"Them and Us," 40, 99–100, 101, 106,
    109, 150
theology of liberation. *See* libera-
    tion theology
"Third Declaration of the Lacandon
    Jungle," 126, 267n8

AK PRESS is small, in terms of staff and resources, but we also manage to be one of the world's most productive anarchist publishing houses. We publish close to twenty books every year, and distribute thousands of other titles published by like-minded independent presses and projects from around the globe. We're entirely worker run and democratically managed. We operate without a corporate structure—no boss, no managers, no bullshit.

The **FRIENDS OF AK PRESS** program is a way you can directly contribute to the continued existence of AK Press, and ensure that we're able to keep publishing books like this one! Friends pay $25 a month directly into our publishing account ($30 for Canada, $35 for international), and receive a copy of every book AK Press publishes for the duration of their membership! Friends also receive a discount on anything they order from our website or buy at a table: 50% on AK titles, and 30% on everything else. We have a Friends of AK ebook program as well: $15 a month gets you an electronic copy of every book we publish for the duration of your membership. *You can even sponsor a very discounted membership for someone in prison.*

Email **friendsofak@akpress.org** for more info, or visit the website: **https://www.akpress.org/friends.html**.

There are always great book projects in the works—so sign up now to become a Friend of AK Press, and let the presses roll!